"Sam Keen breathes pure life into the spiritual void we all may feel at times. He rekindles awareness of the presence of the divine in ordinary life, and guides the reader to an on-going exploration of personal psychological and spiritual attitudes. His hymns and philosophical groundnotes contain the power to help heal the split—that 'nameless separation'—that divides us from our world and from ourselves."

—Clarissa Pinkola Estes, Ph.D., author of *The Gift of Story* and *Women Who Run With the Wolves*

"Sam Keen was my teacher in years past and continues to be now. He is one of the wisest men living today. This book touches my own deepest personal needs and has opened up some valid new choices for me."

—John Bradshaw, author of *Homecoming, Creating Love,* and *Family Secrets*

"Sam Keen has become a trustworthy guide and mentor to those of us who refuse to settle for either the tired clichés of religion as usual or the hollow promise of a totally secular way of life. In the great tradition of Maimonides' *Guide to the Perplexed* he accompanies the reader on an absorbing odyssey toward a form of spirituality that is livable within the stresses of everyday life, and he does so with generosity, humor, and the experiences of a life lived rather than observed. No one can read this absorbing book without being reassured and strengthened by it."

—Harvey Cox, Thomas Professor of Divinity, Harvard University

"Sam Keen is one of our liveliest minds. It's a joy to go with him as a guide to the byways of the soul in the search for greater meaning in life."

—Daniel Goleman, author of *The Meditative Mind*

"Keen asks the hardest of questions . . . Where is the spirit world? How do we get there? And why is it following me? He supplies us with a map to the invisible dimension of the sacred that lies within each of us."

—Mickey Hart, author of *Planet Drum*

"Sam Keen does it again. With brilliance, wit, and courage he addresses the demanding questions of our time for meaning and direction: for spirituality. His discoveries like his queries are strong, sometimes blunt, but we are gratified by the deeps he explores and the light he brings. In discussing the intimate personal and spiritual concerns we all have, Keen is refreshingly pragmatic in a field where other writers are too often exotic and esoteric. He teaches us not to be afraid of mystery nor of ourselves — indeed is there a difference? — for this we are thankful. This book needs to be read now!

> — Matthew Fox, internationally known lecturer and author on social justice and spirituality, and author of *The Reinvention of Work: A New Vision of Livelihood for Our Time*

"Sam's done it now — put it all together. With the deepest soul I've known in this lifetime, Keen has now blended the courageous cool of a superb mind with the belly fire of a strong man. He's giving us his magnum opus, the book he's been living toward through 30 years of love and laughter."

> — T. George Harris

"I sometimes wonder where the real philosophers have gone. One can be found on a horse ranch in the Sonoma Valley. Sam Keen has written a tough-minded, perceptive and sensitive book about one of the great questions of our times, the need for spiritual fulfillment in our lives. And yet, *Hymns to an Unknown God* is not another plea for uncritical or unthinking acceptance of the usual mainstream religions. He sharply distinguishes between religion and spirituality and urges us to discover our own spirituality in a deeply personal way. More profound and more moving than *Fire in the Belly*, Keen is the new public philosopher that many people have been looking for."

> — Robert Solomon, Quincy Lee Centennial Professor of Philosophy, University of Texas

BOOKS BY SAM KEEN

To Love and Be Loved

Hymns to an Unknown God

Inward Bound

Fire in the Belly

Your Mythic Journey
(with Anne Valley-Fox)

The Passionate Life

To a Dancing God

Faces of the Enemy

SAM
KEEN

Hymns to an Unknown God

AWAKENING THE SPIRIT IN EVERYDAY LIFE

BANTAM BOOKS

New York   Toronto   London   Sydney   Auckland

This edition contains the complete text
of the original hardcover edition.
NOT ONE WORD HAS BEEN OMITTED.

HYMNS TO AN UNKNOWN GOD
A Bantam Book
PUBLISHING HISTORY

Bantam hardcover edition published August 1994
Bantam trade paperback edition/October 1995

ISBN 0-553-37517-2

Published simultaneously in the United States and Canada

*Bantam Books are published by Bantam Books, a division of Random House, Inc. Its
trademark, consisting of the words "Bantam Books" and the portrayal of a rooster,
is Registered in U.S. Patent and Trademark Office and in other countries. Marca
Registrada. Bantam Books, 1540 Broadway, New York, New York 10036.*

PRINTED IN THE UNITED STATES OF AMERICA

BVG 10 9 8 7 6 5

Special thanks to:

Laurance Rockefeller,
for magnanimous support
of the spiritual renaissance.

Leslie Meredith,
an editor in the grand tradition.

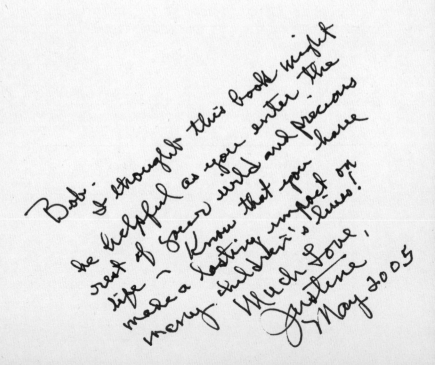

Bob — I thought this book might
be helpful as you enter the
rest of your wild and precious
life — Know that you have
made a lasting impact on
many children's lives!
Much love,
Justine
May 2005

"For sixty years I have been forgetful,
every minute, but not for a second
has this flowing toward me stopped or slowed.
I deserve nothing. Today I recognize
that I am the guest the mystics talk about.
I play this living music for my Host.
Everything today is for the Host."

NICHOLSON, MATHNAWI, BOOK I 2084

"My life has been one long song,
a hymn to an unknown God."

SAM KEEN

Contents

CHAPTER 4

Approaches to an Unknown God

CHAPTER 5

In the Presence of the Holy

CHAPTER 6

The Path Through the Mindscape

CHAPTER 7

Graceful Sensuality: Embodying the Spirit

CHAPTER 8

Carnal Knowledge: Sex and Spirit

CHAPTER 9

Inspired Earth and Animal Spirits

CHAPTER 10

The Public Spirit: Creating a Compassionate Community

CHAPTER 11

Death: The Final Question

CHAPTER 12

Consecrating Our Days:
A Sampler of Rituals for Living

The Yearning

"Any journalist worth his or her salt knows the real story today is to define what it means to be spiritual. This is the biggest story — not only of the decade but of the century."

BILL MOYERS

Spirit: "the animating or vital principle; that which gives life to the physical organism in contrast to its purely material elements; the breath of life."

WEBSTER'S DICTIONARY

Spirit.
Breath.
The animating principle.
The prime mover.

Breathing out. Breathing in.
Expiration. Inspiration.
Dying and borning again.

In every cycle of breath, between the emptying and the inflowing, there is a moment of absolute calm, an instant when history comes to an end. Then, the yearning begins, the divine discontent, the lungs praying to be filled, the body longing to be animated by spirit.

To catch the invisible wind, to map the itinerary of spirit, study the outlines of longing. Just as an echo in a cave brings news of unfathomable depths, in our yearning is our nostalgia for the future. In the emptiness between breaths, we hear a whispered promise of fulfillment, we sense the redolence of a rose now only in the bud.

Breathe through us, breath of God, fill us with life anew.

VOICES OF YEARNING

"As the hart panteth after the water brooks,
so panteth my soul after thee, O God."

PSALM 42

What does the concept of spirit mean to us today? Do most of us even have a sense of it anymore? And of those of us who still believe in a place for the spirit, a place called soul, a god, how many have a daily experience of it? Is it possible in this chaotic day and age to have a sense of the sacred in everyday life, or do we have to check our spirits and our god at the workplace door?

What might it mean to live in a spiritual manner in these traumatic times? Today, the reality of the spiritual dimension is most obvious by its absence. We yearn for something that will give a sense of meaning and purpose to our daily lives, something more engaging than paying lip service to the idea of God or attending worship on the weekend. We are haunted by a vacuum. Our hearts are shaped by something that hasn't happened to us — yet. Multitudes of modern seekers are full of emptiness, aching to be soulful, longing for a spark of inspiration that will ignite a passion that will lift them beyond the pettiness of getting and spending, that will animate their minds, their bodies, their spirits. We are hungry to recover the sense of the sacred that is currently painfully missing from our love affairs, families, jobs, and politics.

No week passes when some friend or stranger does not speak to me about the yearning.

One night not long ago, after too much wine (in vino veritas), an old friend — fortysomething, brilliant, sophisticated, successful in her career as an event promoter, exhausted after a year of sixty-hour weeks — poured out her heart to me: "None of it means anything anymore.

Nothing I do. All I want is to have a few animals, grow a garden, and pray. I am from the death-of-God generation. I always despised religion. My father worked on the atomic bomb, and I always prided myself on my scientific intelligence. I don't even have any image of God. But I can't manage my life anymore without prayer."

Another friend, a recently "discovered" artist in his early sixties, confided: "After weathering several midlife crises, I am finally comfortable with myself, have a good marriage, and have gotten my children launched and out of the nest. In the last years I have become moderately famous and financially successful beyond my wildest expectations. I have bought everything I ever wanted — an elegant house, a fine car, adventurous vacations in exotic parts of the world. I have given to the charities of my choice and been generous to my family and friends. As far as I can tell, I don't have any unmet needs or unfulfilled desires. But I yearn for some kind of fulfillment I can't even imagine or name, except to call it spiritual."

A new acquaintance, a Los Angeles real estate developer just turned fifty, a multimillionaire with a taste for fast cars and Italian fashions who is at once tough-minded and generous, told me over dinner in a fine restaurant: "I've always enjoyed making money, and I've been good at it. I like the good things money can buy — a Maserati and a world-class house. Money has always taken care of me. But it isn't enough anymore. There is a void that money doesn't fill. I need to change my life."

In what was to have been a casual phone conversation, a San Francisco lawyer I have known for years — forty-nine, quicksilver, handsome, master of puns and wit, sharp dresser, twenty-four years on alcohol and drugs, seven years sober — began to talk about life rather than law: "It all began when a friend said, 'You can't keep doing all this shit, or you're going to kill yourself. Why don't you come to an AA meeting with me?' By then, I was feeling desperate. I hated myself and was filled with enormous anxiety, fear, and pain, but I couldn't imagine anything that would make me feel okay. One day I was driving down the road, and I started to cry, and I didn't want anyone to see me so I put on my sunglasses. Then I started to howl, and I had to roll up the windows so people on the freeway couldn't hear me. So I went to the meeting.

"The first thing that struck me was the faces. There were smiles. And they welcomed me. I could see that no matter what problems these people had — and they had lots of them — they didn't have my problem anymore. They weren't isolated, lonely, or hopeless. Their faces kindled my yearning for peace and a sense of well-being. Somehow, they made me realize that it was possible that somewhere down the road I could feel I was okay, that I could be connected with other people instead of being shut up in my own squirrel cage with my fear.

"Today, more than seven years later, a young man came into my office, and he was filled with hatred because a woman had falsely accused him of sexually abusing her child. After I explained that there was no legal case against him, I told him he should pray for her because otherwise he would never be able to understand her, forgive her, or get rid of pain he carried around. It reminded me of the first time I prayed. My wife had done something that hurt me, and for once I was innocent of the charge. So I had spent much of the day eaten up by anger, filled with resentment, and plotting revenge. My pain was so immense, I knew I had to find some way to get rid of it. I had a copy of the AA prayer, so I sat in my car in the parking lot and read it. 'God, I offer myself up to thee . . . relieve me of the bondage to myself so I can do thy will.' It embarrassed me. I had always denied the existence of God, of any power greater than myself. But nevertheless, I read it again and again, and before long I began to feel relief. Instead of being caught up in my pain, I began to understand why my wife had lashed out at me and I found I could forgive her. Since then I pray, because it makes me taller, stretches me toward what is here. I don't pray to some superpower to make things better. But I open myself to the power that infuses and informs all life and pray to be relieved of the bondage to myself."

A couple of years ago, I received a letter from a woman I admire, an adventurous seeker, mother of three, and ex-wife of a famous doctor. She explained to me why she has become a devotee of Indian guru Bhagwan X. "The hunger that led me to Bhagwan was the great unanswered question of the twentieth century: 'To what may we surrender?' "

I replied to her letter: "You have the right question, but the wrong answer."

The spiritual craving of our time is triggered by the perennial human need to connect with something that transcends the fragile self, to surrender to something larger and more lasting than our brief moment in history.

These voices are a small part of a chorus of longing of a new community of seekers who are setting out on a quest. Perhaps you are one of those who are alive with longing that cannot be satisfied by traditional religious answers. While orthodox believers seek to follow in the footsteps of Jesus, Moses, or Mohammed, untold numbers of spiritual seekers have begun to explore uncharted paths. Many people who a decade ago would have been embarrassed to acknowledge their longings for transcendence are speaking openly about inner journeys and vision quests. Spirituality is in. Millions who have become disillusioned with a secular view of life but are unmoved by established religion in any of its institutional forms are setting out on a quest for something — some missing value, some absent purpose, some new meaning, some presence of the sacred.

Here are some of the features of the changing spiritual landscape, the renaissance of our time:

We are experiencing a rise of spiritual individualism and uncorseted religious experimentation. The new quest is for "a road less traveled" (five hundred weeks and counting on *The New York Times* bestseller list). Gallup reports that by the end of the 1970s, "a surprising number of Americans were developing an interest in the inner or spiritual life. A projected 6 million persons were involved in transcendental meditation, 5 million in Yoga, 3 million in the charismatic movement, and 2 million in Eastern religions. . . . Noncredal and nonauthoritarian Religious Science, Unity, and New Thought churches are growing rapidly." The trends that are shaping religion as we move toward the turn of the century are "an intensive spiritual search and a continuing desire for inward and spiritual growth, coupled in some measure with a rejection of the authority of the churches."[1]

Many people are exploring the relevance of American Indian religion and practices — vision quests, the ceremonial use of peyote, and the like.

There is a growing interest in myth and ritual. Carl Jung has been rediscovered. The books and PBS documentaries of Joseph Campbell have achieved unprecedented success. A dozen or more related magazines, such as *Parabola* and *Gnosis*, have sprouted up in the last decade.

East has met West. Zen, Tibetan Buddhism, and dozens of assorted Indian gurus have introduced many Westerners to meditation and spiritual disciplines — aikido, kung fu, and jujitsu academies teaching the martial arts are found in every major city.

Alcoholics Anonymous and similar twelve-step programs are replacing addiction with dependence on "a Higher Power."

Therapists are exploring the common boundary between spirituality and psychotherapy, and the American Psychiatric Association has included a new diagnostic category, "Religious or Spiritual Problem," in the fourth edition of its standard *Diagnostic and Statistical Manual*.

A feminist spirituality has rediscovered the Goddess and introduced feminine metaphors for the holy into the language and liturgies of every major denomination.

There is growing pressure to introduce "the fourth R," religion, into the public school curriculum.

Medical pioneers are showing that love and spirituality play an important role in healing.

The ecological movement has gone beyond the notion of a sustainable economy and limits of growth to embrace a spiritual commitment to reverence for life. Within the Roman Catholic Church, creation spirituality is capturing the imagination of many. Thomas Berry suggests that we put the Bible on the shelf for twenty years and learn to read the natural world as scripture. There is a growing awareness that the ecological perspective is, in essence, a theological revolution based on a sense of the sacredness of all life.

Fortune 500 executives are telling us that work should provide opportunities for personal and spiritual growth as well as financial rewards.

Systems theory has emerged as the dominant trend in most disciplines, from psychology to computer science, replacing the old
method of piecemeal analysis, in which we broke everything down
into its component parts. The tendency in recent thought is to stress
synthesis, networks, interaction, process. The old notion that the
whole is the sum of the parts has been replaced by the idea that
the parts can only be understood as functions of the dynamics of the
whole. The nineteenth-century vision of lonely billiard-ball atoms
accidently colliding with each other to form the varieties of life has
been replaced by a vision of a universe made up of an intricate web
of relationships, a net of jewels.

The old warfare between science and religion has ended, and a new
romance has begun. A marriage is in the making between physics
and mysticism. Quantum physics has demonstrated the limit of the
old time-bound, space-bound Newtonian materialistic universe of
isolated atoms. Paul Davies, professor of mathematical physics at the
University of Adelaide, concludes: "Through conscious beings the
universe has generated self-awareness. This can be no trivial detail,
no minor by-product of mindless, purposeless forces. We are truly
meant to be here."[2]

Perhaps your success or failure in love or work has left you with an
urgent need to find some greater meaning and purpose in your life.
Perhaps a near encounter with disease or death has eaten away at your
old certainties and filled you with doubts. Perhaps your despair at the
madness of modernity has created a hunger for hope, a need for a new
vision of the sacred.

The crisis and quest I describe and map in *Hymns to an Unknown God* is both cultural and personal, both modern and perennial.
The search to determine whether there is any reality that answers to
the names of spirit, soul, or God can only be a passionate existential
journey to discover the deepest meaning of being a person. In this
sense, every woman and man in every age faces a crisis, a time of
reckoning when she or he is challenged to explore and define the self,
to find a vision and a set of values that give meaning to daily life. To
help you in your self-examination, Chapters 1 through 6 provide

detailed ways and questions for dissecting your life and the sources of
your happiness and unhappiness, and a blueprint for sacralizing your
life. The following four chapters show you ways in which you can
integrate your new views of self and spirit in your sexual and love
relationships, in your work, in your ways of being in the environment,
and in creating a new kind of compassionate community. The final
chapter suggests more than fifteen rituals for consecrating everyday
life.

Just as there is no universal diet that is healthy for all persons, just as
Jack Sprat could eat no fat and his wife could eat no lean, no single
spiritual diet will be nourishing for everyone. The ways we metabolize
meaning are as profoundly different as the ways we metabolize food.
Some thrive on a diet of elaborate symbols and will be nourished by a
high church liturgy, an intricate Tibetan tanka, or a Jungian mandala.
Others are allergic to excessive theological ritual and will do much
better with Quaker silence or Zen meditation.

Probably, at this moment when gender roles are being redefined, the
spiritual fare necessary to nourish women and men is different. More
coffee for women, more chamomile tea for men. As a general rule,
women need to explore the spiritual dimensions of aggression and men
to practice the discipline of yielding, caretaking, and wondering. As I
tried to demonstrate in *Fire in the Belly*, most characteristics and roles
by which we have traditionally defined men and women, masculine
and feminine, are artificial. The segregation of the virtues along gender
lines — men are rational, aggressive, warlike; women are emotional,
intuitive, receptive, nurturing — is integral to the ways in which our
personalities and egos are formed, informed, and misinformed by our
culture. Spirit, our capacity to transcend our familiar and cultural
conditioning, has no gender, no nationality, no class, no color, no race.

The first part of the spiritual journey should properly be called
psychological rather than spiritual because it involves peeling away the
myths and illusions that have misinformed us. Then we may begin to
understand that we become soulful human beings only in the process
of transcending the predicates — nationality, race, gender, class,
color — that previously seemed to define our identity. During the psychological phase of the journey, men and women follow opposite and
complementary paths to recover what was denied in their adolescent

sundering into gender. Once men and women become conscious of the gifts and wounds of gender and incorporate the history of the alienation between the sexes into their autobiographies, they embark on that common journey that I trace throughout this book. If *Fire in the Belly* is an exploration of the unique experience that colors men's (and women's) experience, *Hymns to an Unknown God* is a map of the path we travel together, when the questions of masculinity and femininity, male and female roles, have been left far behind.

The search for spirit, for God, is ultimately the quest to know ourselves in our heights and depths. It is the task of Everyman and -woman and of every heroic journey to go beyond our certitudes and doubts, beyond our sure knowledge and understanding, in the direction of an ever-unfolding truth. It was, is, and always will be the greatest human adventure. Please join me on this journey that promises to lead us in the direction of that Unknown God to whom we may surrender and so be filled with a sense of the sacredness of our days.

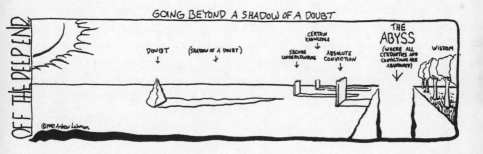

CHAPTER 1

Dying Gods and
the Awakening Spirit

"We are living, we are dwelling
In a grand and awful time,
In an age on ages telling
To be living is sublime.
Hark! the waking up of nations,
Hosts advancing to the fray.
Hark! what soundeth is creation's
Groaning for the latter day."

> *The Hymnbook* of the Presbyterian
> Church, no. 356

"America's Deepening Crisis of Spirit. Social, intellectual leaders find a loss of faith, abundance of cynicism in the heart of the country."

> *San Francisco Examiner*, July 8, 1990

THE CRISIS OF SPIRIT

At dusk on a bleak November day in 1957, I sat in a classic old lecture hall at Harvard and listened to Paul Tillich, possibly the greatest Protestant theologian of our century. It was a time of cultural optimism, of growing religious and political liberalism. I was newly married

and well on my way to fulfilling my version of the American dream —
being a professor in a small college, living with my family on a quiet,
elm-lined street. The future seemed bright. Sweet reason and its technological consort were to be the gods of the brave new age. Multinational
corporations were erasing the boundaries between nations. Although
the unofficial religion of America was anti-Communism, the cold war
was only medium cool. The great theologians of the era — Paul Tillich,
Reinhold Niebuhr, and Karl Barth — all warned against nationalism
and fundamentalism. Christians were beginning to enter into dialogue
with Hindus and Buddhists. On this particular day, Tillich was lectur-
ing to us about the importance of understanding that all religious
statements were symbolic. They are linguistic lace, allowing only a hint
of the fabric of the mystery of being. No religion possesses any literal
truth, he said, and warned us against the idolatry of religion. He advised
us to look for the presence of the sacred in the everyday secular world.

As darkness fell, someone stood up in class and said, "Dr. Tillich, in
three minutes the Russian sputnik satellite will come into view in the
skies over Cambridge." We all filed out onto the steps, craned our necks
upward, and waited for the appearance of the new star. In awe, we
watched this new angel of light come into view and silently traverse the
dome of heaven, announcing the coming of the Space Age. When we
returned to the lecture hall, Tillich spoke about the "greatness of man"
in whose hands had been placed the charge and the capacity to have
dominion over the earth. That evening, we all felt the potential grandeur of the future. In retrospect, in the middle of this seeming epiphany of coming glory I recognize that there was a minor omen we failed
to heed. No sooner had Tillich uttered the phrase "the grandeur of
man" than a baby who had been sleeping in a bassinet beside his
mother began to cry. Our attention switched immediately from the star
to the child, and Tillich finished his sentence with the phrase "and the
smallness of man."

Yesterday's tomorrows have turned out differently from what we
imagined. Medieval forms of fundamentalism, theocracy, holy wars,
and the politics of fanaticism are back in fashion, tearing nations into
warring tribes and filling the byways with hordes of refugees. We are
bombarded with stories of violence, division, fracture, betrayal, and
scandal. Our cities are filled with huddled masses of the homeless and

wandering gangs of hopeless young barbarians. The economy stagnates while the stock market soars. World population expands faster than it can be thinned by famine, plague, or war. Unnumbered species disappear before the relentless assault of humankind. Holes in the ozone and AIDS suggest that nature is reacting against us. Everywhere governments and civic institutions are impotent to manage runaway change. Meanwhile, multitudes of the affluent spend their leisure time in malls trying to find stylish luxuries to consume that will ultimately be banished to already overflowing landfills.

Once we expected that, as Dietrich Bonhoeffer said, "Man had come of age," but we appear to have regressed into childishness. Where we once imagined a new world order, there now is chaos; where we once imagined tolerance, there is now fanaticism; where we once imagined a hopeful application of technology, there is now pollution; where we once imagined a leisure revolution, there is now a frenzy of stressed-out workers. Our predictions were no more accurate than the psychics who forecast the future in the pages of *The National Enquirer*.

And my own personal tomorrows? They also turned out differently from what I had imagined. No quiet streets, secure job, or unbroken covenants of faith lay in my future. Instead were divorce and remarriage, a thermonuclear family, a career as an intellectual gypsy, the loss of many beliefs, and a long journey into the unknown country that lies to the east of Eden.

Ever since the 1950s, many of us in the Western world seem to have been in an extended spiritual crisis. The great religious myths of the past are losing their power to inform our lives with meaning, purpose, and hope. We are privileged and condemned to live on the cusp between epochs reminiscent of the time when humankind switched from hunting and gathering to agriculture or passed from agriculture to industrial economy. Old values, visions, worldviews, and ways of organizing social, economic, and political life are transmuting.

In the twilight between the death of the old gods and the arrival of the new, there will be much chaos and the temptation to despair. Ours will not be a calm or gentle time, and change is permanent, here to stay. It is to be expected that at the great turning points in history, different parts of the body-politic move in opposite directions. The majority tries to hold on to the old ways, while a minority sets out to explore the new. You and I are destined to live out our years in the middle of the Great Paradigm War, a worldwide conflict between three mythic systems — the technological-economic myth of progress, authoritarian religion, and the emerging spiritual worldview.

Our situation is critical but not terminal. Neither apocalypse nor utopia is likely to appear in the near future. I see the first signs of dawn, a new unifying vision emerging from the quests of disparate men and women. In the long run the spiritual renaissance now in the bud will probably gradually change the way we conceptualize and experience the sacred, the way we organize our economic, political, and personal lives. I believe a new myth — with a new politics, new economics, and new forms of the social organization of cities, farms, and wilderness — is being born out of the twilight.

There is no way of knowing whether the emerging myth will thrive or perish, whether technocentric, urban modern nations have the will to survive and the capacity to move beyond the old ecocidal myth of progress, whether we have the resilience to re-form our uncivilization. It is sobering to remind ourselves that history is littered with the remains of great civilizations that chose to die rather than to change their organizing myth.

Hymns to an Unknown God is based on a hunch and a working philosophy I gleaned from a cartoon that showed a bearded prophet carrying a sign that said: "The world is not coming to an end. We will have to learn to cope."

I think that if we listen closely, the voice in the whirlwind will certainly tell us about the death of our old gods and may whisper something about new gods now being born.

INVITATION TO A JOURNEY

The task I have set for myself in *Hymns to an Unknown God* is to sketch a tentative map of our now-and-future spiritual journey, to chronicle the quest for a new organizing myth, and to suggest some of the resources and disciplines necessary for survival in these troubled times.

I undertake this, first, because it seems increasingly clear that the continued effort to build a society on a purely secular myth of perpetual progress will destroy us. Second, because the reactionary efforts of fundamentalists to establish Islamic, Jewish, or Christian nations governed by religious authorities threaten the civil liberties, women's rights, and sexual freedoms we have struggled so hard to achieve and lead back to tribalism, bloodshed, and idolatry. Third, I believe the emerging spiritual perspective on life is the most hopeful path open to our culture because it is truer than other alternatives.

But most important, I set out to map this way because it is the path I have followed. I was raised in a loving, nonconforming, conservative Christian home by parents who practiced what they preached and were strong and juicy people. The hymns we sang still echo in the corridors of my mind and memory. Once upon a time my God was a mighty fortress, the shadow of a mighty rock within a weary land, a help in ages past, a hope for years to come. Even though I no longer accept the authority of Bible and Church, the truths in back of the words still reverberate in the depths of my being. Often, in the quiet hours when I am filled with sadness or joy, a phrase from the old psalms and stories, a refrain from a hymn, or a line from a traditional prayer will swim to the surface of my mind and bring me a measure of peace that passes understanding.

I can't go back to traditional religion. Neither can I live within the smog-bound horizon of the secular-progressive faith. So I search for a way to unite the demands of the head and the heart. Without falling into mindless faith or surrendering to authority, I want to find a way to lean on the everlasting arms. And as I approach my inevitable end, I hope I may trust that the unknown God who has been the impulse and goal of my quest will abide with me.

In some ways *Hymns to an Unknown God* is a sort of philosophical sing-along. A soulful life is more about getting rhythm and tuning in to the music of the spheres than it is about getting the words correct. The truth of the spirit, as I know it, is better conveyed in song and poetry than by propositions. The best of the Christian tradition, which continues to nourish me, is expressed in the music it inspired. Often, my mind is uncomforted by any set of beliefs that can stand the test of doubt, but when I listen to Bach's "Sheep May Safely Graze," my soul lies down beside still waters and a mysterious Lord is still my shepherd.

The journey we are undertaking must contain a melodic element. We need to heed the advice of Socrates' daemon who advised that the practice of philosophy without musical accompaniment is hazardous to the soul. There is something essentially musical about the Western spiritual path. The most intricate forms of Tibetan Buddhism, Hinduism, and Taoism produced elaborate mantras, religious images, chants, and hauntingly simple melodies, but nothing similar to the intricate religious music of Bach, Handel, and Mozart. Why, I'm not sure, but it seems an important clue for Western men and women to follow our unique musical vocation.

The hymns, psalms, and poetry that unexpectedly invite me into the ambience of the sacred are echoes from my Christian heritage. (Those cited here are mostly taken from *The Hymnbook* of the Presbyterian Church.) If they are familiar to you, sing along with me. If not, substitute the music from your own tradition, or any music that conveys amazing grace to you. Under no circumstances should you proceed on the spiritual journey without reason or with reason that has been divorced from lyric. As Dudley Young reminds us in *The Origins of the Sacred*, the ecstasies of spirit must be disciplined by law — *nomos*. And the Greek *nomos* means both law and melody. There is no separation between the "lawlines" that keep the energies of music and spirit within bounds, and the rationality that allows us to understand the cosmos. The harmonious spirit, according to Pythagoras, Bach, and Einstein, is at once mathematical, reasonable, and musical.

Before we begin our journey, some warnings are in order. It is difficult to classify the method and style of this book. It constantly crosses the borders that conventionally separate psychology, philosophy, politics, and theology, and it dips time and again into autobiography. Be assured that there is a method in my madness. I am convinced that we suffer immeasurable harm from the usual academic, objective, anonymous ways of writing, talking, and thinking about our values and visions, our fears and hopes, our sexuality and spirituality. All too many books about the psyche and spirit appear to have been written by abstract authorities and professionals who give advice and offer conclusions from Olympus. I have come to distrust books in which the author lacks the courage to be vulnerable and share the story of his or her journey. Certainly, philosophy and psychology need to be more than true confession. We must think clearly about principles and evaluate evidence, build bits of information into reasonable worldviews. But there should be somebody at home in our reflections and theories — an identifiable human being who has come to his or her conclusions as the result of certain struggles and historical destiny. I write auto-biographical philosophy because I am convinced that it is only by allowing you to see the gnarls of my spirit that I may encourage you "to cherish the grain of your own wood," as Howard Thurman put it.

The story that unfolds here does not proceed in a straight line from beginning to end. Sometimes it meanders, sometimes it leads into blind alleys, sometimes it ascends to peaks from which we may see visions of distant countries in which we were once at home. Overall, it moves in a spiral direction, circling around and around the great mythic questions. The *spiral journey* may be the best metaphor for the spiritual life because we seem to discover what we have always known and forgotten. Gradually, we re-collect the fragments of our soul, which was "long ago and far away" single and whole. Everything happens *as if* we were moved by an unconscious vision, or a pre-conscious knowledge, that we are citizens within a sacred cosmos. But it is only as we explore that manner of living we call "soulful" that we discover, as Wordsworth said, "Though inland far we be / Our souls have sight of that immortal sea / Which brought us hither."

You will be disappointed if you expect that a spiritual quest will lead to certainty and possession of the truth, the whole truth, and nothing but the truth. Doubt and dialogue will always be with us. It is not necessary for us to find definitive answers to the unanswerable questions: Why are we here? Where do we come from? Where are we going? And how should we act in the meantime? But we do need to face into the wind and keep the great questions alive. It makes all the difference whether we remain open in wonder to the true mystery or surrender our discrimination and settle for the false religious mystifications of cult and tribe. The best hope we have for creating a sane future that preserves a sense of the sacredness of life will come out of a renewed habit of talking to each other about those things that can never be fully said but must never be forgotten.

Prior to our departure, we must undertake careful mental and emotional preparations. You will need to restrain your eagerness to be on the way, lest you jump on the horse and ride off in all directions into greater confusion. Americans have a distaste for preliminaries. We want one-minute solutions. But there is no instant spirituality. In the early chapters of this book, we will examine some of the dead ends and disastrous routes taken by other travelers on the spiritual path. We will study alternative maps and try to arrive at exact definitions of the goal we are seeking. We will do some stock-taking to find out what means of knowing are available with which we can stalk the elusive mystery of the sacred and make it a conscious part of our lives and relationships.

A kiss before leaving, a promise of things to come.

One day, as we move through the process of preparing ourselves, we will discover that, without realizing it, we have already come a long distance on our journey together. The preparations will have fused with the journey. Then we will find, to our surprise, that theory and practice have embraced each other, that our contemplation of self has become inseparable from our compassionate action for others, that our patient waiting in the fertile darkness has become our manner of trusting in the Unknown God, that our questions have become our joy.

CHAPTER 2

Living the Questions

Scene: The deathbed of Gertrude Stein. Stein's companion Alice B. Toklas is anxiously leaning over her dying friend and mentor. Toklas asks: "Gertrude! Gertrude! What's the answer?" Stein, opening her eyes, replies: "What's the question?"

"Be patient toward all that is unsolved in your heart and try to love the questions themselves like locked rooms and like books that are written in a foreign tongue. Do not now seek the answers. . . . Live the questions now."

RAINER MARIA RILKE,
Letters to a Young Poet

Monk: "All these mountains and rivers and the great earth — where do they come from?"
Master: "Where does this question of yours come from?"

CRISIS AND QUEST: AN OFT-TOLD TALE

An anonymous source reports that as they were leaving the Garden of Eden, Adam said to Eve: "My dear, we are living in an age of transition."

Twice-upon-a-time, near the border of the future-past, a story lies curled in the eternal kernel of always. It is Adam's tale of exile, Ulysses' saga of wandering, the search for the Holy Grail, my autobiography and yours. It is the Gilgamesh epic and it was first recorded four thousand years ago in what is now Iraq. It will be retold as long as we remember that human beings are homesteaders who have been dispossessed of our hearth, gypsies who long to live forever in a lush valley beside still waters. It is the recurring drama of crisis and quest.

Just yesterday, sometime around 2700 B.C., young King Gilgamesh, two-thirds god and one-third man, reigned in Uruk. Flush with conquest, proud of his walled city, he occupied his days with arrogant plans for war and his evenings with deflowering virgins and seducing the wives of his warriors. To contain his daemonic energy, the gods created his mirror image as a companion — Enkidu, a man of the wilderness, innocent of civilization — a stormy heart to befriend a stormy heart. After a great wrestling match, the men became the best of friends, and for a while Gilgamesh was content. But in time, he became oppressed by idleness. Driven by boredom and unsatisfied cravings to establish his name, he and Enkidu undertook an expedition into the forest to cut cedar to build a magnificent temple. There, they encountered and mercilessly killed the ferocious giant Humbaba, who was the gods' guardian of the forest. To punish them for their arrogance, the gods decided that Enkidu must die. Gilgamesh wept for his friend and fell into deep despair.

Haunted by his new knowledge that death would overtake him just as it had his friend, his life became as nothing. With mixed despair and yearning, he set forth on a long journey to the Faraway to search for Utnapishtim, to whom, alone of all men, the gods had granted everlasting life. After many trials and tribulations in the dark forest, he found Utnapishtim, only to be told that "there is no permanence" and that all men are fated to die. But, taking pity on Gilgamesh, Utnapishtim revealed how he might find a medicinal plant that grows under the water, with prickles like the thorn of a rose, that would at least restore his youth. Gilgamesh tied heavy stones to his feet, dived deep into the sea, and came up with the elixir that could make old men young again. Just as he was about to eat the plant, however, he saw a well of cool water and went down to bathe. Deep in the pool was a serpent that sensed the sweetness of the flower. It rose out of the water, snatched the plant away, sloughed its skin, and returned to the well.

When Gilgamesh realized his loss, he sat down and wept. At last, weary, wise, and resigned, he returned to Uruk. We may imagine that, disillusioned of false hopes, he reawakened to the ordinary pleasures of life, ceased to abuse his power, and accepted his destiny.

AWAKENING FROM THE DREAM OF PROGRESS

To understand the latest variation of the oft-told tale of the quester, we need to look at the kinds of questions we ask ourselves and the kinds that our culture calls forth. We need to distinguish between the values and visions to which we give lip service and those that are truly the basis for our actions. Like the medieval philosophers, we must distinguish between our beliefs and how we live — our operative faith. Beliefs are ideas in the head, cognitive expressions, maps of the world, our best conceptualizations of how things are, our credos. Faith is in the gut and the heart; it is trust-in-action, a disposition to behave as if something were true or valuable.

In a well-integrated person or culture, beliefs and faith may coincide, but in modern societies we have an increasing disassociation between the two. What we profess to believe has very little to do with the way we conduct our lives. Our religion and our faith, our belief-maps and our operating values, are widely separated.

On the surface, America seems fundamentally a very religious nation, although we may be experiencing some momentary economic and moral challenges. *Reader's Digest* assures us nearly every year that Americans still believe in God, that the family that prays together stays together, and that church attendance is growing. Religious leaders and politicians deny there is "a spiritual crisis" because the Gallup poll shows that 94 percent of Americans believe in God, 66 percent believe in the Devil, and 70 percent believe Jesus is God.

But look deeper. In *Religion in America*, Gallup lists the themes that emerged from fifty years of polling:

The widespread appeal or popularity of religion.

The gap between belief and commitment, between high religiosity and low ethics. (Only 2 percent of men and women talk with their best friends about religion.)

The glaring lack of knowledge. (Only 33 percent of those 70 percent who believe that Jesus is God can name the gospels on which this belief is based.)

The apparent failure of organized religion, in part, to make a difference in society in terms of morality and ethics.

In America, in other words, faith is as superficial as it is extensive. Nowadays, as in earlier times, few people have the honesty to confront the obvious. If the word *God* designates "that about which we are ultimately concerned" (as Tillich says), then we have only to look at the shape of our political, economic, and social systems to see where we really place our priorities and what we in fact worship. The symbolic centers of the modern city are not cathedrals but research and development institutes, industrial parks, financial institutions and the computer networks that link them all together. If our heart is where our treasure is, God is nowhere near as important as General Motors or any major oil-producing nation. What is the operative faith of a nation that recently slaughtered thousands of Iraqi citizens in the most lopsided war in recent memory? In Oil We Trust, because it lubricates the progress-machine, in which we live and move and have our being.

Our gut-level faith, our cultural belief, has been in the shared dream of perpetual progress. We have assumed that history is an unfolding story of progressive triumph that will bring abundance to all. We feel we are all entitled to affluence. We believe we live at the end of the age of scarcity and the beginning of the age of democratic luxury. The myth of progress pervades and provides the operating assumptions of both the 94 percent who believe in God and the 6 percent of us who do not. We may "believe" in God, but the forces, the institutions, and the myths that give shape to our daily lives are largely secular — money, markets, machines, media, and managers. In theory we are believers; it is only in practice that we are atheists. The religious right is correct in charging that secular humanism is an ideology and a faith. But it is wrong when it assumes that we can go back to old absolutes and the faith of our fathers.

But even while we continue to hope against hope that some technological miracle will create an ever-expanding economy and a better tomorrow, the foundations of our faith in progress have been slowly undermined and are on the verge of collapse.

I would date the beginning of the end of the old order to 1988, when the great parable of the garbage barge unfolded before our eyes. The barge from New York traveled from country to country, trying in vain to find some place that would accept its cargo of industrial waste, only to have to return finally to its home port. It became clear to those with eyes to see that industrial, technological, and economic "growth" inevitably creates pollution, and that we may have to choose between "progress" and the environment. Deep in the pit of our stomachs, we fear we have come to the end of plenty. Yet most politicians, whistling in the dark, still act as if we can have it all — an ever-expanding economy, universal prosperity, and a healthy environment.

The "American way of life" has always been based on the unconscious faith that each generation will surpass the generation that came before in standard of living. Every immigrant group that came to our shores toiled and sacrificed, sustained by hope for a better future. In 1988, however, for the first time, when asked: "Do you think life will be better for your children than it is for you?" a majority answered no. We are the first generation of Americans to live in a postprogressive age.

Here is how the *San Francisco Examiner* of October 6, 1991, reported the widespread feeling that the era of endless progress is over. In a story headlined "America Wakes up from Its Dream," the newspaper stated that "For many of us tomorrow may not bring a better day. Ken Bauer, forty-two, weighs the good with the bad and feels satisfied with his piece of the American Dream. But he sees no way to fulfill what most Americans have come to view as a precious birthright — the promise of a better life for his children, just as his parents passed a better life on to him. . . . Settling for less is a foreign notion to Americans who grew up in the years after World War II, a time of unprecedented and unchallenged growth. America was the only game on the globe and its people looked to move ever upward. That game is over now."[1]

As the twentieth century draws to a close, we must write the obituary for the great god Progress. We are living in the last days of the myth of unlimited growth and technoutopia, and the religion of the Mall.

Understandably, we are reluctant to give up our habit of overconsumption and our blind optimism. But the time has come for ego death and the long journey of transformation undertaken by Gilgamesh and others before us.

TO QUEST IS TO QUESTION

Crisis and quest are perennial. Sooner or later something occurs in all cultures and individuals to smash the accepted answers and leave agonizing questions in its place. Alexander the Great or world wars change the map; the Black Plague or AIDS shatters the fragile sense of the harmony of nature; the printing press or the computer revolution creates a new literate class; industrial technology dethrones agriculture and reshuffles the medieval social order or small-town America. Or it may happen that an individual's faith just vanishes. Like Gilgamesh, a friend or lover dies, a near-fatal automobile accident or an illness strips away our natural illusion of immortality, and we become painfully aware of the fragility of life. Or a firing or downsizing or retirement robs us of our usual work and its meaning. Suddenly the floor and ceiling aren't where they used to be.

The spiritual quest begins when we turn away from our standard answers and turn toward fresh questions.

Nothing shapes our lives so much as the questions we ask — *or refuse to ask*. We are all questioners, but the questions that animate us are profoundly different. Imagine the different type and quality of life you would have if the main question you asked was one of the following: Where can I get my next fix of heroin? How do I serve God? What will the neighbors think? What happened during the big bang when the world was created? Who will love me? How do I get power? How can we destroy our enemy? How can we end violence? Where will I spend eternity? How can I make enough money? Who are my friends? How can I be comfortable? Is my cancer curable? How can I become famous? How do we heal the earth? Where can I get food for my children?

At different stages in our lives, different questions come to the fore. A young child implicitly asks: "Am I seen and adored? Am I safe? Can I trust Mother and Dad? How can I please them?" If the parents are critical, blaming, angry, or abusive, the child asks: "What is wrong with me? How can I escape punishment?" By adolescence, our questions shift to: "How different am I from my parents? What do I want to do when I grow up? How can I be popular with the gang?" As we reach adulthood, we ask: "How will I make a living? Will I marry? Will I have a family? What is my duty? How can I be a good citizen of my community?" In the normal course of events most adults find more or less satisfying answers to their questions about the meaning of life and their ultimate destiny in the shared beliefs of the people around them. They most often adopt the accepted mythology and ideology of the religious and secular institutions with which they are most familiar.

Years ago, when I first "lost my faith," when the answers I had been given no longer satisfied me, I discovered a way to begin again. Searching out the primal questions that underlie all religious faiths, I began to interrogate myself to find out what I believed, what I found to be sacred, what story I was going to live. As I began to love the questions themselves more than the answers, I began to identify with a timeless community of questers. During my youth, I had kept the symbol of the cross before my eyes to remind me to keep my yet-untested Christian faith strong and pure. When I changed from being a believer to becoming a searcher, I had no symbol for my quest. Recently, I wandered into a jewelry shop on a small Greek island and found a silver question mark on a chain. Now I wear it next to my heart, where it reminds me daily of the need to allow questions to enter and be exhaled as naturally as the breath.

I have come to believe that "the quest" is a metaphor for the willingness to live and wrestle with the perennial questions that underlie the mythic answers that religion offers. My "question" is the "quest-I'm-on."

It's time to take our first step into the depths. Like spelunkers of the psyche, we must descend beneath the surface of the status quo, make our way through a dark cave, plunge into the river and allow its current to carry us we-know-not-where. Each primal question is like a weighted line thrown into the fathoms-deep waters to help us sound the dimensions of the soul.

As you work through the following questions, you may find it helpful to make a timeline of your life. On it, you can chart the points at which your desires, beliefs, and questions changed as you grew and aged. You may also find it helpful to keep another piece of paper that is divided into two columns in which you write your answers to the primal questions. Devote one column to your immediate or obvious responses to the question, another column to the deeper answers that most closely approach the values you hear when you listen to the still small voice of your spirit, the voice you may have tried to ignore or drown out in your day-to-day life. By keeping this written record and reviewing it, you may become aware of different patterns in your life. You will see two different shapes to your life, the linear and the multilayered columns. You may even discern a third shape wandering through, informing and uniting the other two — the spiral curving of the spiritual quest.

PROFOUND QUESTIONS: SPIRITUAL SOUNDINGS

What Do I Desire?

What would satisfy me? My desires seem endless. I want, I want, I want — food, love, sex, entertainment, fame, money, gadgets. I fill my life with things that excite me for a moment. Catalogues come in the mail — The Sharper Image, L.L. Bean — and I look for something new to desire. I am always wanting. No matter how much I get, I never seem to be satisfied. I am stuffed but insatiable. What would fill this void I stuff with food, sex, trinkets, addictions of one kind or another? How can I silence the concupiscent cravings within me created by the enticements of a consumer culture and follow the path of deeper desire for truth, for meaning? I suspect that when I purify my desires, they provide me with the most reliable clues to the spirited life.

The change begins the day you notice that you can never get enough of what you didn't want in the first place. You notice the fix doesn't satisfy, the craving is not relieved, the narcotic (alcohol, drugs, success, sex, power, fame, money, possessions) does not anesthetize your pain or restlessness. In the moment when you become disillusioned with your normal satisfactions and ask "What do I really desire?" your soul rather than your ego takes charge of your life.

The great pathfinders testify that the motive for the spiritual life is awakening desire rather than grim duty.

Don't do it if you don't want to.

Siddhartha, the young prince who was to become the Buddha, enjoyed all the luxury money could buy—sweetmeats, silks, vintage wines, and a beautiful woman. One day, venturing outside the walls of his pleasure castle, he encountered a sick man, an old man, and a corpse being carried to the burial ground. He suddenly understood that none of his pleasures could rescue him from the inevitable suffering of the human condition. At that moment the habitual pleasures that formerly moved him turned to ashes. The old story does not go into detail, but we can imagine that the young man fell into disillusionment and depression. Perhaps it was some time later when he saw the fourth sight—a wandering mystic with a peaceful face—and realized that all he really desired was to seek liberation.

Similarly, if we "listen with the third ear" to the story of Jesus' temptation, we can understand it as a dramatic report of an inner dialogue and struggle with desire. Rather than a factual encounter with a being called the Devil or Satan, it chronicles the same changing climate of desire in the life of Jesus as Siddhartha experienced. In Matthew's account (4:11), we read that the Devil first tempted Jesus to turn stones into bread to satisfy his hunger. He then suggested that Jesus try to manifest miraculous power by throwing himself from the pinnacle of the temple. When neither of these worked, the Devil offered the final human desire—power. "Again, the Devil took him to a very high mountain, and showed him all the kingdoms of the world and the glory of them, and he said to him, 'All these I will give you if you will fall down and worship me.' Then Jesus said to him, 'Begone, Satan! For it is written, "You shall worship the Lord your God, and him only shall you serve." ' " Jesus, unlike Siddhartha, was not born to power or luxury but was a child of poverty living among a disenfranchised people. He must have been greatly tempted to use his talents to gain political power but chose instead to follow his deeper vocation. This is a turning point that many of us face, and it is one that recurs every day, as old and new temptations emerge to divert us from our purpose.

Zen Buddhism couples the assumption that desires are endless with the vow to extinguish desire and reach Nirvana, bliss, enlightenment. The Stoics, likewise, preached the wisdom of attaining a condition where we accept what happens to us with equanimity. Augustine had another solution: "Thou hast made us for thyself, O Lord, and our hearts are restless till they rest in thee."

How do we winnow our desires, separate the wheat from the chaff, and cultivate the desire for wholeness, for compassion, for a quiet and centered spirit?

It helps me to do this by comparing spiritual and physical nourishment, the problem of appetite and diet. We all experience the conflict between the desire for foods that are good for us and the desire for others that merely taste good. I should eat my broccoli, but I want ice cream and chocolate. If we consider nothing but the satisfaction of the moment, Häagen-Dazs wins every time. But if I savor the complete experience of eating, from the taste to the long-range effect, I may have more sustained pleasure in eating a healthy diet than yielding to the impulse to gratify cravings of the moment for junk food.

Savor various satisfactions. Become a gourmet of desires. Cultivate what promises to make you most joy-ful.

Yesterday a man called me in an agitated state. For a year, he had been paying intricate attention to his dreams and engaging in almost constant self-analysis. Suddenly his dreams had stopped, and he was worried. What should he do? As I probed, I discovered that he was tired of looking inward, and he wanted to travel to India. I suggested that perhaps the disappearance of his dreams was a signal to him to forget the dramas of his inner world, follow his desire, and take an extroverted journey. With some surprise and relief, he replied: "You mean, it would be all right for me to do what I really want to do?"

"Almighty God, unto whom all hearts are open, all desires known, and from whom no secrets are hidden, cleanse the thoughts of our hearts by the inspiration of thy holy spirit that we may more perfectly love thee."

Why Is There Something Rather Than Nothing?

At the beginning and end of all our days is the great meta-question, the granddaddy of all riddles. A three-year-old boy is riding in a car through the countryside with his father, and he sees a herd of animals grazing on a hill. "What are those?" he asks. "Cows," his father replies. "Why?" the boy asks. "Why are there cows? Why is there anything?"

I am Everyman, Everywoman. Normally I am normal. I live in an ordinary domesticated world, sky above and firm ground beneath my feet. The sun rises and sets, and the stars move in their orderly courses. I am competent, sophisticated. I understand how to program the VCR and invest my surplus dollars in the stock market. But sometimes figure and ground switch, and everything familiar becomes strange. A black hole opens in the depth of my psyche, and all my certainties disappear. I suffer from ontological shock. I am thrown back into unknowing childhood, filled with wonderings. Why? Why? Why? Why is there a world rather than an infinite emptiness?

The best scientific explanations do nothing to quiet my mind or soothe my spirit. Tracing the chain of cause and effect backward to the big bang only leaves me standing between two mirrors in which I see an infinite regress of images of myself asking endlessly: "And why a big bang? Why is the cosmos so law-abiding? Why not a random chaos as impossible to predict and understand as the combinations that would emerge from a trillion dice thrown by a madman? Why should nature be so constructed that one bit of it — the human mind — can nearly understand the laws and uniformities that inform the rest of it?" How passing strange it is that even if we succeed in creating the ultimate scientific theory of everything, we will still be left with the unanswerable question — Why is there anything?

Frederic Spiegelberg, formerly professor of Indian culture and thought at Stanford University, now ninety-seven years old, was recently reminiscing about thinkers who influenced his life. "Something my mother said when I was quite young has continued to grow in significance as the years have passed. . . . She stood by the window, looking out upon the street underneath, horse carriages going by, and sparrows and other birds feeding on our balcony. After a silence, she spoke quietly — '*Was soll das Alles?*' These four words were the most powerful expression for theological search that I have ever heard: 'What is the meaning of all this?' There she stood, astounded, bewildered by the miraculousness, the immenseness, the unexplainableness of it all, standing there and asking that. And knowing at the same time that it is a 'stupid' question, for clearly she was aware she was pointing to something which cannot be answered but must be asked and lived time and time again. . . . Early in my academic career I made as a motto for my life a quotation from Goethe: 'Bewilderment about the fact that there is anything at all, and the curiosity about meeting that fact as a wonder, is the best part of man.' "[2]

Each of us must craft our splinters of experience into a model or map, a worldview and a philosophy of life to guide our daily decisions. Human beings are necessarily biomythic, narrative, or storytelling animals. We may uncritically accept the mythology of our culture, or we may borrow from the myths of the Aborigines or Hopi to cobble together our own world-picture. But either way, we never escape the condition of amazement. I suppose that is why I frequently hear the refrain from the Appalachian carol echoing in my mind: "I wonder as I wander, out under the sky."

Who Am I?

Do you remember how you looked in the mirror when you were a child and wondered who you were? And why?

I have a wallet full of identification. My curriculum vitae tells the basic facts — name, rank, date of birth, family, accomplishments. Beyond that, I can spin you a thousand stories that form my history into a unique autobiography. But no explanation or series of explanations insulates me from the shocking fact of my existence.

I play a thousand roles. To my parents, I am a son; to my children, a father; to my wife, a husband; to my neighbors, a responsible citizen; to God — ? I notice that I always seem to be performing for some audience, following a script that goes with the role I am playing. I try to look good for my audience. What will "they" think about me? Do I look right? Smell okay? Drive the right car? Drink the proper wine? Everybody is always watching and judging, and I want their approval. When I act inappropriately, I feel embarrassed, ashamed of myself, as if I am caught in the spotlight. I pretend I am a hero. I strut my stuff on the stage I erect, but when I watch myself closely, I see I am still performing for someone's eyes, wanting applause. Sebastian Moore, the English theologian, said, "Sin is seeing your life through somebody else's eyes." The current joke in the "recovery" movement echoes the same insight: "You know you're codependent when you're dying and somebody else's life passes in front of your eyes." You and I exist in an unholy symbiosis with our watchers. I know many men whose sense of self-worth depends on how they are valued by the women in their lives, and women whose self-worth depends on men's views.

Who would I be, how would I act, by what values would I abide if I had no sense that my life was a performance for various audiences?

Can I Love?

Sometimes it seems as if I am condemned to solitary confinement within the prison of my ego. Year after year, this tough ego survives underneath the pleasant mask of my personality. Look at me: I smile and have polite manners, but that is all a facade — a Potemkin village. Below the surface of my persona, I have hidden fortifications, a thousand defense mechanisms, a fortress. My self-importance, superiority, arrogance, and habit of judging others form walls that keep me safe. I am not like "them," I tell myself. I'm better, more cultured, work harder, have better morals. I dream of conquest, winning, vindictive triumph, being number one.

Secretly, I approach every situation in a calculating manner. What's in it for me? Do I stand to gain or lose power, prestige, time, energy, money? How can I turn this situation to my advantage? Who are my enemies and potential allies? Jean-Paul Sartre was right: "Hell is other people." Life is a battle in which we are either conquerors or conquered. Other people are either potential threats or useful objects. If they are more beautiful, powerful, smarter, or wealthy, I envy and fear them and find some way to flatter them and cut them down to my size. If they are inferior, I secretly despise them and use them for my purposes.

In the twisted recesses of our psyches, we all feel and act like this: ordinary people no less than famous politicians, actors, talk-show hosts, and athletes. The ego-war is everywhere, in high places and low. Observe the superstar evangelists, priests, ministers, healers, gurus, and "holy" men and women, and you will find even they compete for titles — the most saintly, the most wise, the most enlightened, the most free of ego.

Yet just when I am ready to despair of love, a Chinook wind blows through the window of my wintry fortress, and an unexpected thaw begins. Walking down Main Street, I notice the taut pain in the face of a homeless man — so like my own — and an arrow of compassion strikes my heart. Or after weeks of civil frigidity and polite warfare, my love and I lay down our arms and find delight in each other. Or the evening news brings me a picture of a Kurdish father holding his dying child, unable to find food or medicine, and my imagination begins to create a story. What would it be like if it were me and my child? Imperceptibly, imagination creates compassion, and I feel connected to another man's awful love and pain. Could my weather pattern change from frigid to warm? Could these rare zephyrs of compassion become the climate of my life? What alchemy would convert my leaden meanness into golden generosity? I am too thrifty with my love, always looking for good bargains.

I was amazed this morning by a posttrial television interview with Reginald Denny, the man who was pulled from his truck and badly beaten in the middle of the 1992 Los Angeles riots. I had witnessed the replay of the beating captured by television a dozen times, and I imagined that he would naturally want revenge. Instead, during the trial he embraced the mothers of his assailants and spoke with compassion of the suffering they had experienced in seeing their sons acting in such a brutal manner. Even though the men who tried to kill him expressed no remorse, he had forgiven them and pleaded for a lenient sentence.

What grace or effort makes such magnanimity possible? (Magnanimity: "a loftiness of spirit enabling one to sustain danger and trouble with tranquillity; a nobility of feeling that is superior to meanness, pettiness, or jealousy and that disdains revenge or retaliation, generosity of mind.") An essential element of the spirited life.

If you are ready for some radical — and possibly disturbing — self-knowledge, you might undertake an assessment of your LQ — love quotient. How much does the desire to be a more loving person figure in your life? How wide or narrow is the circle of those you love? How many of your daily activities are suffused with feelings of love? Which of the many varieties of love do you practice? (For suggestions, consult "Love" in Roget's Thesaurus.)

Am I Free?

I move through each day making all the customary minor decisions. I choose to get up when the alarm rings, drink tea rather than coffee, eat oatmeal rather than eggs Benedict, walk to work instead of taking a taxi. I don't even have trouble with the moderately important either/ors: Should I risk everything and buy a country property, or should I stand pat in the old suburb?

But I can't control my mind. At times my thoughts travel ten miles a minute around a half-mile track. Once I start worrying about money, my health, or my kids, I become obsessive.

Worse yet, I notice that I repeat certain self-destructive games, scripts, emotional patterns. In many respects, I first married a girl who was suspiciously like the girl who married dear old Dad, and I looked at my new wife through mother-colored glasses. I rebelled against my parents and got stuck in their countervalues. I'm the negative image; I automatically do what they didn't, and vice versa. It is as if I were a puppet moved by my parents' unconscious fears, by their unlived life. I must do what they didn't. Call this captivity to the past, or whatever you want — repetition compulsion, tape loops, neurotic obsessions, unconscious subpersonalities, engrams, archetypes. I feel as if I live in a haunted house. Phantoms from yesterday preprogram my daily life. I appear to be awake, but in reality I'm sleepwalking much of the time.

I am ashamed to admit it, but my unconscious is contaminated by all the standard prejudices and stereotypes with which my culture infected me. I am a product of a racist society that says: White is better than black, brown, yellow, or red; men are superior to women; rich is better than poor; heterosexual is normal, homosexual is perverse. I dislike these prejudices. I know them to be vile, inane, destructive, and wrong. I do not honor them when I find them crawling up from the slime of my unconscious. But these irrational and uncharitable prejudgments lie dormant like a virus in my mind, waiting to break out when I am weak.

How do we free ourselves from the unconscious forces that have conditioned us to behave in ways we consciously despise?

A man was recently executed in Washington State for sexually abusing and murdering several small children. He resisted every legal effort to save himself from execution because he felt there was no way he could possibly become free of his horrible compulsions. In a statement the night before his execution, he explained that when he remembered his crimes, he was simultaneously guilt-stricken and sexually stimulated, and he knew that given the chance, he would kill again. Tortured as he was by guilt and desire, death was his only path to freedom.

What kind of exorcism would it take to free our minds and spirits from the spell imposed on us by our parents and our culture? How do we overcome the wounds that have been inflicted on us in our youth, so that we do not perpetuate an endless cycle of revenge and retaliation? In what measure can we ever be free from our past?

The great metaphors from all spiritual traditions — grace, liberation, being born again, awakening from illusion — testify that it is possible to transcend the conditioning of our past and do a new thing. How this elixir of freedom is released is something we must discover as we proceed.

What Is Wrong with Me?

Like every human being, I am often ill at ease. Sometimes I am anxious without knowing why. Sometimes I feel ashamed that I have not lived up to the best in me, and I fear that I will be abandoned or punished for my failures. I worry about an endless list of possible catastrophes that may befall me.

More fundamentally, a fault line runs down the center of my being. There is a gulf between what I ought to be and what I am, between my potentiality and my actuality, between my essence and my existence, my ideals and my actions, my values and my behavior. The way I live is an insult to what I believe. Wrestling with my favorite addictions and long-standing compulsions, I have frequently felt my kinship with Saint Paul, who said: "I do not understand my own actions. . . . I can will what is right, but I cannot do it. For I do not do the good I want, but the evil I do not want is what I do. Now if I do what I do not want, it is no longer I that do it, but sin which dwells in me."

Some people suffer from a chronic sense of inadequacy, others from overweening arrogance. One woman wonders why she has settled for a marriage without intimacy, another why she has never dared to risk marriage.

Each of us must make a fundamental philosophical decision about how we are going to understand the flawed, faulted, broken character of human existence. How are we to understand our dis-ease? Is it due to hardness of heart, rebellion, and disobedience to the will of God? Have we betrayed ourselves? Is it neurosis, a split between grandiose and debased images of the self, that causes us to neglect our real self? Is it a wound that is the result of childhood abuse and faulty parenting? Is it because I am an adult child of an adult child of an adult child of an alcoholic, wealthaholic, workaholic, religionaholic? Is it a chemical imbalance or a genetic abnormality? Is it alienation that comes from living in a capitalistic, consumeristic, competitive economy? Is it due to maya, illusion, ignorance of my true (non-egoic) nature? Is it an ontological wound that comes with human self-consciousness, imagination, and inevitable self-judgment by standards we ourselves erect?

At the moment Americans are increasingly accepting a philosophy of entitlement that allows us to define ourselves as victims. We assume that we are entitled to a life without loneliness, anxiety, fear, want, or abuse of any kind. When, contrary to our expectations, we experience any dis-ease or unease, we must find somebody to blame. If there is poverty, it must be because there is a conspiracy of the wealthy. If we feel vague anxiety, it must be because we were abused as children.

The serenity prayer (attributed to Reinhold Niebuhr), "O God, give me the courage to change those things that can be changed, the patience to accept those things that can't be changed, and the wisdom to know the difference," reflects the spiritual imperative to distinguish between the psychological faults and failures we can correct and the essential suffering that belongs to the human condition that we must bear with dignity.

How do you think about the pain of your life? What is the cause of your mental anguish, your physical illness, your financial insecurity?

What Would I Be Like If I Were Healed?

What would I look like if my brokenness were healed? If I were whole? Actualized? What is my promise, my potentiality? What might I become? What vision of my ideal self should I hold before the eye of my heart? Is it realistic to aspire to a life without anxiety? Without fear? Without hate? Without ego-centricity? Should I be like the Buddha, or Jesus, or Gandhi, or just a stronger, more trustful, more loving version of Sam Keen, warts and all, still intact?

Pathology is an easy science. It is easy to see the myriad ways in which we are dis-eased and fail, how we are twisted, injured, and unhealthy in mind, body, and spirit. Unfortunately, we usually think of health as nothing more than the absence of disease. We lack a science of wholeness, of spiritual health.

We need spiritual heroes to give us working images of different types of sanctified lives that we can hold before our eyes for in-spiration. This is a ticklish business, dangerous but necessary. Religious believers easily fall into idealizing and idolizing heroes. Jesus, Mohammed, and Buddha, to say nothing of Jim Jones and Sun Myung Moon, are turned into demigods with magical power to save any who call their name. If you look carefully, you will discover that all authentic spiritual heroes and heroines have hearts of gold and feet of clay. Perhaps each of us needs to assemble a personalized image of the spiritual hero we need in the form of a collage. I might, for instance, construct the portrait of my personal saint by borrowing liberally from the great pathfinders of the world's religions, appropriating Georgia O'Keeffe's reverence for beauty, Paul Tillich's capacity for systematic thinking, Dorothy Day's eros for the poor, Vaclav Havel's political courage, and Wendell Berry's enthusiasm for the land, and add to them examples of daily acts of compassion and simple kindness that I have witnessed, as well as the sexual grace bestowed on me by a couple of earthy women who shall remain anonymous to protect the blessed.

What do you aspire to become? From what sources do you take your idealized image of yourself?

What Help Is There?

What means and medicines are available to heal our human dis-ease? So long as there is help, there is hope. But what spiritual resources and disciplines, what therapies, lead us toward greater wholeness? Should I pray, meditate, chant, go to Mass, fast, join a church, or go on a vision quest?

These days, something like a free market in religion and spirituality has developed. The plain vanilla, standard-brand religious denominations that once had a virtual monopoly on healing souls continue to preach the gospel of salvation in and through the word and sacraments of a church. But a thousand spiritual entrepreneurs are now competing for the loyalty of believers. We are suddenly in the middle of a spiritual freak-show.

Many of the new forms of spirituality are frivolous, undiscriminating, uncorseted mysticism. Some are pure money-making schemes. Some are political movements with power-hungry men masquerading as spiritual leaders. Some are silly, others sinister. We do well to remember Jim Jones and his faithful followers, all now mouldering in a Guyanese grave, and the FBI-assisted suicide of David Koresh and his followers in Waco. Some of the supposed physicians of the soul create iatrogenic dis-ease, sickening those they claim to cure.

The choice of a physician for the soul is a difficult matter. How do I know which medicines to take for my spiritual dis-ease, which healers to trust? The Dalai Lama himself exhorts Westerners to scrutinize their teachers, spy on them if necessary. Examine your beliefs about your teachers, idols, role models, and authorities. If you find yourself defending some of their behavior that you would condemn in others, are you doing harm to yourself? To travel into the wilderness, we will need a compass and some tools to help us measure and discriminate — that is, we will need to construct a spiritual bullshit detector (which we will do in a later chapter).

Who Are My People?

Who is the we of I? With whom do I belong? How narrow or wide do I draw my circle of care and commitment? Are my bonds only with my family and friends? With my immediate neighbors? With people of the same race and class? Does patriotism define who is inside and who is outside the boundaries of my community? Am I willing to kill or allow my government to destroy a class of people it has designated "enemies"? Are the socially designated scapegoats—the outsiders, queers, victims, public enemies—a part of my community?

What in my immediate community, my circle of friends and family is vital? Who in this circle is actually inimical to community-building? Who would support my journey and mission, and who must be left behind? What would a healed community, a healthy nation, an in-spirited world order look like?

What Is Evil?

Is evil an illusion, a kind of shadow that gives aesthetic depth to the picture? Is evil the result of the Devil, of human freedom, or is it a structural condition of life itself? Must the possibility of evil exist in order for goodness to exist? If there is a benevolent and powerful God, how can there be evil? If this God does not exist, is there any way evil can be redeemed? Even if we reject the idea of some metaphysical dualism—a struggle between God and the Devil, or light and darkness—how do we deal with totalitarian governments, tyrants, war-mongers, criminals, and violent men and women?

Is There a Meaning in My Life?

Does my life serve any transcendent purpose? Is there any value higher than personal survival to which I may commit myself? I want my small life to be encompassed within a larger context. I need to have my life make a difference. I want to serve, to create, to leave my mark in the sands of time. What gifts do I have that will allow me to leave the world a better place? How do I find my vocation? Do the so-called "accidents" of my birth, the gifts and wounds I received through no virtue or fault of my own—being born American, Chinese, or Bosnian, male or female, healthy or frail, privileged or impoverished—present me any special opportunities and responsibilities? Do my special interests and talents suggest a personal vocation?

How Do We Heal the Earth?

All of the questions I ask myself as I engage in my quest are perennial and ontological. They belong essentially to the human condition. Only this one is a new question. As far back into history as we can trace, humans have asked about individual and communal healing. But only in our generation has our diseased environment become a problem. Ecological anxiety is a new phenomenon. For the first time we are being forced to ask ethical questions about the ancient elements — air, earth, fire, and water. What are our obligations to what we previously considered "natural resources"? Should trees have (legal) standing? What moral obligations do we have to other species? Do we need an amendment to the Constitution, a new Bill of Rights, to protect animals, forests, and airshed? How do we end the anthropocentric illusion and rejoin the commonwealth of sentient beings?

There are many more great mythic questions we might ask: How close should men and women be? What foods can we eat, and which are taboo? How do we deal with suffering in a graceful way? By way of summary and preview, here is a chart that suggests the perennial mythic questions that animate the questing or spirited self and the perennial human experiences and emotions from which they arise:

In the end, as in the beginning, the great questions loom. Like Gilgamesh, we are destined to search in the Faraway for a balm to soothe the dis-ease of existence and to return home dis-illusioned but able to govern our lives with greater wisdom, compassion, and contentment.

In dealing with the quandaries of my existence, I will always remain an amateur. Every morning I awake from strange dreams, finger the silver question mark that hangs around my neck, and rise to face novel dilemmas and delights. I am sixty-two years old and well educated in philosophy, theology, and psychology. I have no severe neurotic problems. I am contented with my personal existence. Yet every day I wonder: Who am I? Why was I born? Why will I die? What can be done about evil? After toast and tea, I set forth into the morning with my compass and a few provisions to try, once again, to map the familiar-mysterious territory of my days and search out the Unknown God.

PERENNIAL MYTHIC QUESTIONS

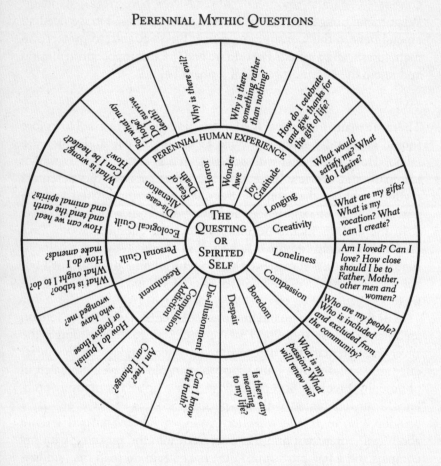

PERENNIAL HUMAN EXPERIENCE

THE QUESTING OR SPIRITED SELF

Why is there evil?

Why is there something rather than nothing?

How do I celebrate and give thanks for the gift of life?

What would satisfy me? What do I desire?

What are my gifts? What is my vocation? What can I create?

Am I loved? Can I love? How close should I be to Father, Mother, other men and women?

Who are my people? Who is included and excluded from the community?

What is my passion? What will renew me?

Is there any meaning to my life?

Can I know the truth?

Am I free? Can I change?

How do I punish or forgive those who have wronged me?

What is taboo? What ought I to do?

How do I make amends?

How can we heal and tend the earth and animal spirits?

What is wrong? Can I be healed? How?

For what may I hope? Do I survive death?

Horror
Wonder
Awe
Joy
Gratitude
Longing
Creativity
Loneliness
Compassion
Boredom
Despair
Dis-illusionment
Compulsion
Addiction
Resentment
Personal Guilt
Ecological Guilt
Dis-ease
Alienation
Fear of Death

CHAPTER 3

Autobiography: Your Life as Sacred Text

"Whither shall I go from thy Spirit?
Or whither shall I flee from thy presence?
If I ascend to heaven, thou art there!
If I make my bed in Sheol, thou are there!
. . . .
For thou didst form my inward parts,
thou didst knit me together in my mother's womb.
I praise thee, for thou art fearful and wonderful.
Wonderful are thy works.
Thou knowest me right well;
my frame was not hidden from thee
when I was being made in secret,
intricately wrought in the depths of the earth.
Thy eyes beheld my unformed substance;
in thy book were written, every one of them
the days that were formed for me."

PSALM 139

"It is private life that holds out the mirror to infinity; personal intercourse, and that alone, that even hints at a personality beyond our daily vision."

E. M. FORSTER

"Without going outside, you may know the whole world. Without looking through the window, you may see the ways of heaven."

Tao Te Ching

"Abandon the search for God and the creation and other matters of a similar sort. Look for him by taking yourself as a starting point. Learn who it is within you who makes everything his own and says, 'My God, my mind, my thought, my soul, my body.' Learn the sources of sorrow, joy, love, hate. . . . If you carefully investigate these matters you will find him in yourself."

Monoimus,
a gnostic teacher

According to the *Popol-Vuh*, the Mayan book of the dawn of life and the glories of gods and kings, the Makers and Molders formed the first four Motherfathers from white and yellow maize and gave them perfect vision and the ability to talk directly with the gods. "Perfectly they saw, perfectly they knew everything under the sky and everything was seen without obstruction. They didn't have to walk around before they could see what was under the sky; they just stayed where they were." And the first beings gave thanks to the gods: 'Truly now, double thanks, triple thanks that we've been formed. We've been given our mouths, our faces. We speak, we listen, we wonder, we move. Our knowledge is good. We've understood what is far and near, and we've seen what is great and small under the sky, on the earth.' " But the Makers and Molders, fearing the Motherfathers would become as gods, repented of the powers they had given to them and weakened the eyes of humankind. "They were blinded as the face of a mirror is breathed upon. Their vision flickered. Now it was only when they looked nearby that things were clear. . . . Now, to get any answers from anyone, up there in the sky or down in this ground, it'll have to be in our minds' ears, or we'll have to decipher an animal's ominous cry, or read an animal's sudden move, or smell the wind if it blows the smoke of our offering back in our faces, or feel an answer in our very blood."[1]

*   *   *

Where will we search, if not for answers to our questions, at least for some taste of transcendence of our brief moment in time? How are we to proceed? What territory will we explore?

Those of us who have lost confidence in the old authorized map of the path that leads to the kingdom of God, who have no guides or gurus whose footsteps we can blindly follow, who have no faith in the supposed revelations of God that are the property of church, mosque, synagogue, or sangha, necessarily begin our journey with a sackful of existential questions and a yearning to experience something more of the unknown totality that encompasses our partial lives.

Some, like a friend of mine named Susan, are able to find comfort from knowing that they are an integral part of an incomprehensibly vast cosmos.

At forty-two, two years after her divorce and the tragic death of her only daughter, Susan was painfully trying to begin again. In her grief, she retreated to a small cabin in the woods. One night she had an extraordinary experience: "I woke to the coolness of the cabin, the wood stove having spent its heat. I decided to start up another fire in the hope of keeping the room warm the rest of the night. It was so peaceful, both externally and internally. I was in love with the moment, standing in the dark, in this small cabin, in this quiet draw; waiting for the flames to make union with wood; looking out at the thin moon leading stars in a friendly night chase through the trees; listening to the waterfalls pouring over the rocks. I became aware that the song of universal grace was coming from the room, right where I was standing. It's a song felt more than heard, coming from even deeper than the heart. It was still with me when I curled down into the bed and cast off, smiling, into the gentle, dark river."

The sacred texts of almost all peoples contain some kind of creation story that suggests that we can infer or glean directly knowledge of God from the sun, moon, and blooming earth around us. The testimony of the ages is that within time and space and matter, we may find evidence of an immanent creative self-surpassing power that deserves the name "God." Once upon a time, the story of the coming to existence and the luxurious variety of the cosmos contained a sacred subtext.

THE STATIONARY JOURNEY

Supposedly, the cosmos has now lost its enchantment, and the weary sun displays only the relentless march of entropy. According to the accepted intellectual analysis, science has shown the planet Earth and its human inhabitants to be of minor importance in the scheme of things. The Copernican revolution removed the Earth from the center of the universe; the Darwinian revolution destroyed the illusion that the naked ape was a special creation; the Freudian revolution demonstrated that homo sapiens is governed more by folly than by reason. In the name of science, or science fiction, humankind has developed a strange kind of false modesty, a demeaned sense of its place in the cosmos.

In spite of all speculation about the varieties of life that might exist in other galaxies, however, in spite of the efforts to discover complex life-forms elsewhere in the universe, the best scientific knowledge we have at the moment shows us an infinite universe of uninhabited planets and burning stars. Earth alone manifests the fleshing forth of the creative power of Being in multiform life. *As far as we know, the planet Earth is the only place that contains a kaleidoscope of multifarious forms of life, many of which are conscious, some self-conscious, and one of which tells stories about itself.*

It requires little or no leap of faith to embroider this central fact with spiritual meaning. Only on our known Earth has Being issued forth as flesh and fowl and flora. Here alone, in all the black holes and infinite spaces of the universe, the Spirit (which the Greeks and early Christians identified as the Logos — the informing, creative rationale that forms every living thing from within) has assumed the flesh of dolphin, indigo bunting, and human being.

This is the scandal, the koan, the mind-shattering puzzle, that is the basis for the spiritual quest: Earth seems to be the stage where the central drama of the cosmos is being played out. How splendid and lonely!

When we begin to explore our place within the immensity of the evolving cosmos, we enter immediately into the paradox of spirituality. We are already within Being itself; thus, we have nowhere to go and nothing hidden to discover. We are what we seek and are in the midst of what we seek. An old Zen koan points to the dilemma: How can a man riding on an ox, looking for an ox, ever find an ox?

Our metaphors of "journey" and "quest" are somewhat misleading, because *we already know the basic spiritual truth.* At some level of our being, an implicit knowledge of our interconnection with the cosmos is programmed into our genetic makeup, and our carbon atoms are imprinted with the memory of the distant stars from which they came and whose substance they share. Our limbic brains incarnate the history of aeons of reptilian evolution that went into their making.

It is no exaggeration to say the Universal Energy — God — is bone of my bone. As many "primitive" peoples have said, the *axis mundi*, the world pole, the reverberatory center of the world, passes directly through our spines. Early Christians, struggling to define the nature of Jesus, said he was of the same substance as God. The identical eternal impulses that created the big bang flow through the synapses of our nervous system and beat in the chambers of our heart. My life, every life, is the site of the incarnation — inspired matter.

Even though we are integral parts of an elaborate universe that in some mysterious way existed prior to its parts, most human beings are shaped both by a knowledge of the truth and by self-deception. Every religion is based on the perception of this same complex truth. "The earth is the Lord's and the fullness thereof, and all those that dwell therein," but we usually see it through sin and ego-colored glasses as an arena for self-gratification. We exist within a sacred Buddha-field but act under the influence of our illusion of separation.

Albert Einstein stated our dilemma in this way: "A human being is part of a whole, called by us the 'Universe,' a part limited in time and space. He experiences himself, his thoughts and feelings, as something separated from the rest — a kind of optical delusion of his conscious- ness. This delusion is a kind of prison for us, restricting us to our personal desires and to affection for a few persons nearest us. Our task must be to free ourselves from this prison by widening our circle of compassion to embrace all living creatures and the whole of nature in its beauty."[2]

The quest for spiritual knowledge is a conundrum: We possess a treasure chest that contains the truth and a baffling variety of keys, any one or none of which might open it. The end is already in sight: We fit within and belong to the universe. But unfortunately, we do not know how to *appropriate* the truth that would comfort and heal us because we systematically delude ourselves and fall into the habit of pretending and acting as if we were separate from and superior to all of the other forms and life-forms — animals, vegetables, and minerals — that in concert make up the universal symphony.

How do we open the treasure chest and make use of the riches we possess? How can our feelings and actions become harmonious with our knowledge? How can our heads tutor our hearts? How can we develop the sense of connectedness and the disposition to compassion that are appropriate to our theoretical knowledge that we are integral parts of a universe? How can we transcend our self-encapsulating delusions of centrality? I *know* I am a part of the whole, but I *feel* as if I were an orphan abandoned in a careless and chaotic multiverse.

What we call "the spiritual life" and "the spiritual quest" are simply the ways we discover to transcend our delusions of our own separateness, superiority, or inferiority and gradually feel our identity with our fellow beings and compassion for them. The treasure in the chest is our heartfelt trust in that Totality that we may or may not wish to call God, *and* that assurance of our belonging that emerges only from compassionate action. As we approach the midpoint in our journey in this book, it will become increasingly clear that in the realm of the spirit the only truth we may claim is inseparable from love and action. We either do the truth in love, or we remain lost in care-less chaos. To paraphrase one of the early quantum physicists: We already have the truth. What we don't know is how to arrive at it. It takes a lifetime to find our way home. We all suffer from homesickness, a longing to return to a cosmic household we have never left.

To understand that we are stanzas within a universal song gives us necessary but not sufficient direction for our spiritual practice. Once upon a time, in a galaxy deep within our essence, we, like the original Motherfathers of the Mayan myth, may have been in immediate communication with the Creator and all of creation. But at best, our knowledge of the bonds that unite us with the sacred cosmos is now obscure. The mirror in which we might see the image of God in creation is clouded over. Knowing that we belong within a vast cosmos can leave us as much disturbed as comforted. Contemplating the beauty of the Earth may soothe us, but looking into the black holes in timeless space can overwhelm us with a sense of our insignificance. Nobody captured this sense of cosmic loneliness better than Blaise Pascal, the seventeenth-century French philosopher: "The eternal silence of those infinite spaces strikes me with terror. . . . When I consider the short extent of my life swallowed up in the eternity before and after, the small space that I fill or even see, engulfed in the infinite immensity of spaces unknown to me and which know me not, I am terrified and astounded to find myself here and not there."

But the cosmic story fails in an essential way to provide me with a map for *my* spiritual journey. It locates human beings in the grand scheme of things, but it does not locate that one individual who is the center of my quest for meaning — Sam Keen. My quest, like yours, is driven primarily by a personal-*existential* need to discover how I fit within the scheme of things, not by an abstract need to understand how human beings fit within the cosmos. I want to know if I have any gifts that serve a lasting purpose.

If I am ever to be at home in the world, I must discover how a single life fits into Life, how my story fits into the universal story. Perhaps it is a hidden blessing that the Maker, Molder, Bearer, Begetter, Sovereign Plumed Serpent should have breathed on the mirror and limited our vision so that we could see only what is nearby, only a small part of the face of the earth. By examining my own story, I can at least bring into focus one small part of the sacred whole.

JOURNEYING BEYOND EDEN

My story, like yours, is a unique variation of the universal myth of the Garden of Eden: "And the Lord God planted a garden in Eden in the east; and there he put the man whom he had formed. And out of the ground the Lord God made to grow every tree that is pleasant to the sight and good for food, the tree of life also in the midst of the garden, and the tree of the knowledge of good and evil. . . . And the Lord God commanded the man, saying, 'You may freely eat of every tree of the

Garden; but of the tree of the knowledge of good and evil you shall not eat, for in the day that you eat of it you shall die.' "

Read the myth carefully, and you will see that the Lord God, or his authorized earthly representatives, presents us with a double bind, a Hobson's choice, a lose-lose dilemma. Either: Be obedient to authority, remain in the Garden of childlike innocence, and receive the gift of happiness and immortality. Or: Exercise your freedom, gain bitter-sweet self-knowledge, judge good and evil for yourself, be expelled from the garden, earn a living by the sweat of your brow, and live with the awareness that you will die.

The story of the Garden endures because it captures something perennial about the human condition. We are all born small and helpless into a world ruled by adults who inevitably appear to us as visible gods and omnipotent authorities. We imbibe their mores with our mothers' milk and are informed by their myths in our fathers' arms. When their eyes shine on us, we bask secure within their everlasting arms; when they are displeased, we fall into disgrace and fear punishment, abandonment, and death.

In due time, some crisis presents us with the challenge to develop autonomy. But when we attempt to taste, sense, and discover what feels right and wrong, we come into conflict with the Rules. *Thou shalt. Thou shalt not.* The authorities say: *Nice boys don't . . . Good girls don't . . . Do as you are told. . . . Don't talk back to your father. Don't sass your mother. Because we said so — that's why. Because that's the way it's done. Don't ask so many questions. Yours is not to question why, yours is but to do or die.* And they punish us "for our own good."

Each individual is presented by family and culture with a double bind. The nature of parents and authorities (both good and bad) is to demand of us obedience to the norms, lifestyles, ideologies, and religions in which they believe. Their demands are enforced by the interior security forces of the conscience (the psychological equivalent of the KGB) and by invisible norms and visible laws. If we experiment and break the taboos, we may be punished and we will certainly feel guilt and be cast out of the Garden. But if we do not, if we remain obedient children, we will feel the shame that comes from never exercising our freedom and from living our own lives within the

Garden of the Authorities. If we disobey, we will have to wrestle with guilt and autonomy; if we obey, we will have to wrestle with shame and dependency.

Traditional religious life takes place within the confines of the Garden, within the worldview of the official myth. The spiritual quest begins when we resolve to taste the forbidden fruit and draw our own life-map based on what we have discovered in our explorations.

A second kind of double bind determines the itinerary of our spiritual journeys — call it a double-double bind. Parents give double messages to their children because of their own ambivalence about what is permissible and what is forbidden. To the degree that Dad and Mother have lived in thoughtless conformity to the rules they inherited from their own parents and other authorities, they will pass on to their children an unconscious imperative to act out their unlived rebellion. Far from having a simple set of unambiguous command-ments to obey, the Eden of family life is governed by contradictory injunctions. Consciously, Dad says: "Work hard and keep your nose to the grindstone." Unconsciously, he says: *Sow your wild oats (as I never did)*. Consciously, Mother says: "Act like a lady." Unconsciously, she says: *Be wild and sexy (as I wasn't)*. We inherit from our parents the unresolved contradictions that shaped their lives. If we decide to leave Eden, to seek self knowledge and grasp the authority for shaping our own lives, we have to wrestle with the values our parents overtly promoted and with the repressed possibilities, the disassociated op-tions that remained unconscious for them. Whatever is unquestioned and unquestionable for parents is (unconsciously) assigned to their children. To gain authority over our own lives, we must not only question the vision of good and evil that governed life in Eden but explore possibilities that our parents and society ignored or refused to consider. After rebelling against the familiar, we begin a journey into a remote wilderness that was forbidden and strange to the gods of Eden.

The details of these challenges vary from person to person. An abused child will have to struggle with low self-esteem, a sense of abandonment, and outrage; an overindulged child with an unrealistic sense of entitlement. A gifted and precocious child will struggle with an

inflated sense of self. Every style of parenting leaves children with
characteristic hurdles that they must jump in later life. Good parents
no less than bad ones inform and deform their children with values and
visions that they will have to test and either reject or affirm. Each family
sets the dramatic agenda for its members.

For my friend Cherif, a Berber from Algeria, immigration from
Africa to California prepared him for the more difficult journey he is
now beginning: from living within the myth of his family to creating
his own life-story. Recently he told me: "My father was a baker, and
he told me: 'You have a square head and aren't going to do much with
your life. Why don't you take the bakery over?' 'No way,' I said, and I
ran away because there was no example of anybody who took their life
in their hands. It was impossible in Algeria. I went to France and
worked in the food business, then came to the United States and got
married. I was working as a waiter, and one day the baker got sick and
I took over and started baking. Soon I opened my own place. I am
successful, but I feel uncomfortable being a shopkeeper and having
employees. It isn't an open relationship. I spend fourteen hours with
these people. I don't want to run this shop. I am at a crossroad. I want
to do something more meaningful with my life, something that has to
do with healing.

"When I was a kid, I had wide eyes, I could see through the bullshit,
the lies about religion. People went to the mosque, but there wasn't
much spirituality. Everybody thought I was inhibited, but it was because I was psychic like my grandmother. I knew when things were
going to happen and what people were thinking. Now I am going back
to those memories to give myself courage to make this jump. I owe it to
myself. I know my gifts, although sometimes I am ashamed of them.
One voice in me says: 'Who do you think you are to bring healing to
people's lives? You don't have credentials. You are condemned to be a
baker.' But another voice says: 'You have the gifts to be a healer. You
were not born to be just a body. You have something that carries this
body around, a soul.' Every time I ring my spiritual bell, I get over-
whelmed by another voice: 'How are you going to make a living? It's a
jungle out there.' But if I can't go through life playing my own guitar,
life isn't worth it for me. I can choose now."

A MODEST LEAP OF FAITH

Any effort to discover a purpose that transcends eating, drinking, and making money must begin with a leap of faith. But where religion requires a broad jump into the arms of authority, the spiritual quest requires only a short step over the void. Its basic assumption is: *My life is the text within which I must find the revelation of the sacred.* If there is some sacred ground and meaning of my life, it must be discovered here and now. If we have ears to hear, eyes to see, and bodies to feel, we are always being addressed. Certain moments, events, words, persons, or objects may suddenly become luminous to us. Where our lives seemed chaotic, a pattern emerges. A sign is no different from an ordinary event; it is the meaning we give to it that sacralizes it. As a believer in my personal life as a text, I can discern a hidden subtext that comes to light in special moments.

The experience of discerning the sacred is not available on the secondhand market. Without knowing how to calculate the odds on such matters, it seems improbable to me that God would have whispered the meaning of *my* life into the ear of some guru or authority. Likely, my best chance to hear the still, small voice is to listen carefully for a sacred echo in the voices and silences that resound within my mind, my body, my heart.

I believe the safest wager is this: I assume that my being is encompassed within Being itself. The mystery of the Self is part and parcel of the mystery of Being. The Unknown God for whom I search—the principle of unity—is not absent, only hiding in the substance of things. When we ignore our own intimate experience, we end up searching for God in all the wrong places. If I explore the depths of my being, I will discover the heights of Being. As below, so above. My life provides me with my only privileged access to the Unknown God and to the unknown but knowable sacredness of my own life. My autobiography contains the sacred story that will help me discern the path that leads toward a greater sense of the unity and holiness of life.

RE-COLLECTING YOUR PERSONAL HISTORY

Most religious traditions label autobiography as egotistical. The point of most religious disciplines has been to eradicate the ego, the illusion of the individual, the unique, historical self. Individuality is the disease, not the cure. Lately Don Juan, alias Carlos Castenada, echoed this theme of Eastern spirituality and made the idea of "erasing personal history" central to his project of becoming a warrior, a man of knowledge.

I believe that, far from being arrogant, prideful, or egotistic, the autobiographical path of seeking the sacred through the intimate experience of our own personal history is the essence of humility. All human beings have in common our uniqueness. Each of us can create an autobiography. It is our gift and task to explore our particular moment in history, the ground on which we dwell.

When I pay attention to the particulars of my life, I discover that no ready-made religious system fits the shape of my brokenness or gives a blueprint for the specific type of life that would be fulfilling for me. I need to discover how I have been wounded and blessed by my family and my culture, how I have been twisted and strengthened by the experiences I have endured. I need to learn about the gifts that I have to offer.

There is no one right way. The dignity and meaning of my life involve the discovery and creation of my way, my truth, my destiny. To have a spiritual vocation is to trust that my life is a gift to be unwrapped and enjoyed. I might adopt many stances toward my life. When times are bad, when an illness condemns me to pain, when tragedy strikes, when I observe senseless cruelty, I am tempted to conclude that life is an absurd joke. Sometimes it seems as if we are hurled into existence without our consent, hungry for meaning that is hidden from us, and sentenced to die for an unnamed crime we did not commit. But in good times and bad, I am pervaded by a sense that it is a privilege to exist. Between the void before and the void after, the few years of my life are an island in time given to me.

The autobiographical approach is not to be confused, however, with the emphasis of much modern psychology on self-esteem. Narcissism is the opposite of spirituality. On the spiritual journey, we explore the self so that we can go beyond the limits of our ordinary sense of ego and entitlement, beyond the illusion that "I am the center of the universe." Through remembering the relationships that have formed my being, I begin to discover a self that is not encapsulated. The isolated, self-sufficient, nondependent self is an illusion. Buddhists speak of enlightenment as involving the shattering discovery that the center of the self is void. I am no-thing that can be defined. The "spiritual journey" is a metaphor for the never-ending process of discovering the enormous range of connections and relationships that form the nexus of the self. In recovering my autobiography, I discover that I am and have always been plural. *I am forever defined by my interactions within a web of beings that extends backward and forward in time into infinity.*

Only by exploring and sharing my autobiography can I witness my discoveries of the sacred. My story is not normative. I am under no illusions that I am a saint, a hero, or a model for anyone. I do not write in order to say: Here is *the* map for you to follow. I only share some of the twists and turns in my journey in order to encourage you to take your own story seriously. Examine the sacred text of your daily experience, reconstruct the events and relationships that went into the creation of your being, re-collect memories, and form them into the narrative that makes your life a once-told tale.

The process of searching for the sacred dimension in our lives is similar to that which a novelist uses in constructing a character. "God lives in the details." The *details* make the story come to life. A novelist must know exactly what the protagonist eats for breakfast, how he combs his hair, how his father and mother treated him as a child. Just as the animating spirit of the character becomes clear through the specific details, the presence or absence of the sacred can be discovered only by examining the details of our experience. In remembering our personal history, we hope to discover that, as Plato said, "Time is the moving image of eternity."

Like an archaeologist, I will have to dig through layers of extraneous matter to reach the foundations. By excavating the myths that formed and misformed me, I hope to get nearer to my origins, my *primal* or *essential* self. While many contemporary social psychologists hold that the idea of an original self is a fiction, a questionable but useful notion,

I am encouraged to undertake this exploration by the generations of mystics and sojourners from many different traditions who testify that the prodigal self, having divested itself of the illusions and shortsightedness that family and tribe impose, can return to a homeland in which there is no alienation between self and other.

To discover my essence, the sacred intention that was inscribed in my DNA, the story before the story, my original face (as Zen says), I must re-collect the loom of myth on which my psyche was woven by my parents and the unquestioned early authorities. The stories of family and clan formed us before we became self-conscious and began to shape our own life-story. Before we could create our own life-story, the authorities inscribed the official myths on our skin. Keens, McMurrays, all white, American, and Presbyterian, first told me my story, my fortune. I am, as you are, a palimpsest — "a manuscript having besides its present writing one or two earlier partially erased writings."

My life, and yours, is a dance between destiny and freedom. My autobiography is not a monologue of a self-made man but a dialogue, a love story, that I co-author with God, Nature, Being-becoming-itself. My song is an antiphonal refrain, a hymn sung by a choir of many voices.

The co-creation of a life is terrifying and joyful. Freedom is a wild and loving thing. There are no certain guideposts in this forest, no official information booths for travelers to certify the way.

Sometimes at night, when I am tired of being forever a traveler, I look in through lighted windows and am nostalgic for the settled life. For a moment I long for a Bible, a Jesus, a guru, an authoritative word from beyond to guide me. But I know the price is greater than I want to pay. It seems less than gracious to abandon the authority I have been given for my life, frail and brief as it is. In this ordered and creative chaos that I will always be fashioning into the narrative of my life, I am sustained by an abiding trust that, as Isak Dinesen said, "God made man because He loved stories." Without my autobiography and yours, the story of the universe would be forever incomplete.

As I relate my awakening, let your mind spring back to your own earliest memories of self and (m)other or compliance and rebellion. Add to the memories that make up the timeline of your life. These are the keys to how your psyche was formed, to your first taste of freedom and the beginning of your quest.

BARE FEET AND LEVI'S: MY SPIRIT AWAKENS

As far back as I can remember, I felt the tension between religion and the spirited life, between Eden and the open road. From the moment of birth, I was wrapped in the swaddling clothes of Christianity. Before I was able to make up my own mind, I was encompassed in the matrix and maya of religion, taught the correct answers, and encouraged not to ask troubling questions.

Once upon a time in Sunday school in the basement of the First Presbyterian Church, I sat in a circle of small and shining faces listening to Miss McCelvey read Bible stories. After Joseph and Mary and the baby Jesus, there were milk and graham crackers, and the Lord's Prayer was recited in unison because none of us could remember all the words, and then there was singing: "Jesus loves me, this I know / For the Bible tells me so. / Little ones to him belong. / We are weak but he is strong." I was the first one to memorize my Bible verse: "For God so loved the world that he gave his only begotten son, so that we should not perish but have eternal life." When I recited it at Sunday dinner, my brother Lawrence thought I was showing off, but I felt warm and proud and basked in Mother's and Dad's approval. My Eden was warm and filled with love. And love weaves its constraints so sweetly, we hardly know we are being imprisoned by our efforts to be good sons or daughters.

But the human spirit is restless. It craves the excitement of the open road. It does not like the security and ease of life within the Garden.

One morning I set forth on my red tricycle in search of adventure. I was well provisioned, having stowed an adequate supply of candy in the kit bag in back of the seat. Moments before my leave taking, Mother appeared and set the limits of the permissible: "Sammy, you can ride up to the corner and around the block, but don't cross the street." No sooner had I escaped the eyes that watched over me than temptation appeared. Just across the street, the sidewalk ran into forbidden woods, whose mystery beckoned me with irresistible force. I looked and could see no danger. No cars coming. No Mother in sight. So I crossed over into freedom and anxiety. As I rode along, I was surprised and a little disappointed to find that the Land Beyond wasn't noticeably different from my home territory. Finding no monsters or enchanted castles, I turned back and crossed back into Eden. But in my brief absence, it had changed. Everything looked the same, but I was shrouded in guilt. What if *she* found out where I had been? I pedaled home as casually as I could. Mother met me at the door. "Sammy, did you cross the street?" Thunder and lightning seemed to come from the mountain and threatened to annihilate me. I was too small to cope with such power. No place to hide. With an instinct as old as Adam, I summoned up my courage and defended my vulnerable, borning spirit. "No, Mother, I did not." I still wonder if she knew that I lied and that if I was ever to become my own man, I had to lie to protect the sanctuary of my freedom.

The endless journey had begun — and the habit of questioning.

When I was four, spring burst forth with crocuses and cicadas singing in the long evenings. I wanted to put away the constraints of winter and go barefoot and run free in the woods, feel the red mud squishing between my toes and the pine needles tickling my arches. Not allowed — ringworms in the soil were rumored to lodge in the intestines of the unshod and produce that brand of "laziness" that Presbyterians were quick to notice in the poor. One evening before bed, Mother was conducting our ritual Bible reading (soon to be followed by Hardy Boys adventures). The story for the day was about Moses and the burning bush. I perked up my ears as I heard God's words: "Moses, take off your shoes, you are on holy ground." "Mother," I interrupted, "God created the whole world, didn't He?" "Yes, son," she replied. With impeccable theo-logic I sprung the trap: "Then why do we ever have to wear shoes?" I asked. Mother's answer is not recorded either in my memory or in family lore.

And I wondered about prayer.

We were instructed by word and example that the proper way to pray was with our eyes closed. No peeking. No sneaking food during the blessing. My greatest temptation came during the long pastoral prayers before the sermon, when the minister put on his special praying voice and a pious silence fell over the congregation. I was overwhelmed by curiosity. Did everyone really keep their eyes closed? Occasionally, my parents clairvoyantly sensed my waywardness and would open their eyes in time to catch me scanning the congregation. They would signal me by casting their eyes downward that I was to return to the sacred darkness. Thus caught and chastened, I assumed the proper posture for blind faith, but all the while within the sanctuary of my mind, the questioner was busy. Why should we close our eyes to pray? Why shut out everything except the minister's words? Why sing "For the beauty of the earth, for the splendor of the skies," and then close our eyes? Silently, I resolved that when I grew up, I would pray only with my eyes open. Or maybe I wouldn't pray at all. Why, after all, should I have to inform the Almighty about my needs or His duty?

And why did God need me to put on a pious voice and wear special clothes? When we were kids, we had clothes for Sunday, for school, and for play. Sunday vestments were our most splendid and most uncomfortable — wool pants that itched and starched shirts and ties that irritated the neck. In the 1930s in the South, ordinary wear for boys was floppy denim jeans that could be washed and didn't have to be ironed. One glorious summer, my father returned from the West with Levi's for my brother and me — miracle fabric, fourteen-ounce denim, riveted at the pockets, stiff with dye that turned your legs blue until they had been washed many times, guaranteed not to rip, tear, or wear out nearly forever. Perfect duds for running through briars and playing marbles in the dirt. Better than being naked, they armored us for the adventures we pursued once we escaped from the watching eyes of adults and our other natural enemies.

I might have escaped some of the constraints of religion earlier, but for my need to have a direct and personal experience of the faith that animated my mother and father. From the beginning my rebellious nature and questioning mind were mixed with an equally strong drive for mystical knowledge. I wanted to know what could and could not be known about God.

I can still picture the religious double bind in which I became trapped. When I was ten, living in Boaz, Alabama, a traveling layman from the Business Men's Council of the Pocket Testament League, Inc., visited. Before he left, he presented me with a small New Testament and asked if I would sign the pledge that committed me to read at least one chapter in the Bible each day and carry it with me wherever I went. I did. For a year I kept the magic book — my personal talisman and power object — in a niche in the limb in my tree house and read a chapter a day. I prayed to God to grant me a personal relationship with my Lord and Savior. Day after day, I waited for Jesus to come into my heart, but the more fervently I prayed, the more disappointed I became when the Lord tarried. My earnestness and effort only increased my sense of alienation. Doubt filled the space I had reserved for grace. I finally tired and concluded that although Jesus might be my savior, he was as remote as God.

Today, as I examine the childish signature on the pledge in the tattered New Testament, I understand the burden of righteousness that rested on my small shoulders and how inevitably I had to become a prodigal son in order to discover my own path. Likewise, I understand the motives that led me, against so many of my better spiritual inclinations, to seek full membership in the church when I was eleven. The split-screen image of that event remains vivid. On one screen I see the boy Jesus at twelve standing before the elders of the synagogue, instructing them. On the other screen I see myself in my Sunday best standing before the elders demonstrating my knowledge of catechism and creed. "What is the chief end of man? The chief end of man is to glorify God and enjoy Him forever." That these two images merge tells me that, in order to please my mother and grandmother and all the adoring elders, I made heroic efforts to pour myself into the preformed mold of the life of Jesus.

But no sooner did I make the effort to squelch my doubts and take comfort in the security of religion than the gypsy spirit emerged to disturb my false tranquillity.

The first time it happened, I was eleven years old, walking up Court Street in Maryville, Tennessee, on my way home from town. Pearl Harbor had been attacked, and loyal Americans were learning to hate "Japs." While playing with my friend Tommy Ganger, I wondered out loud whether Christians were also supposed to hate Japs. His parents forbade him to play with me because I was unpatriotic and was always making trouble by asking questions. Later, I was brooding about all this as I walked when suddenly I had the sensation of standing in a pool of light. I seemed to rise out of my body, and I could see myself standing at a crossroads where I was able to preview two scenarios that my life might follow, and I knew I had to choose. I could see that if I accepted what my friends, parents, and other adults said was true, things would be smooth and I wouldn't disturb people. But if I chose the other path, each time I questioned I would rise up higher on a mountain and be able to see farther and more clearly. I think the decision I made in that moment to search for understanding rather than security, to keep questioning rather than accept the faith of my fathers, was the beginning of my spiritual quest. Without knowing into what far kingdoms it would lead, I took the first step toward cultural disillusionment and waking from the unconscious spell my parents and culture had cast on me.

This momentary spiritual awakening at eleven left me with the disturbing knowledge that I could not be merely a faithful son of loving parents, a much-beloved grandson, an accepted member of the gang, and an obedient child of the covenant. I came to suspect that blind faith is cheap faith, and cheap faith is too expensive — it is purchased at the cost of giving up spiritual adventure.

On reflection, I realize that at an early age the principles of my spiritual credo began to emerge:

Go barefooted. "Feel the different philosophies of earth and pavement beneath your feet" (Heather Keen). Remain earthy and humble, of the humus. Try to understand the ground of your being.

Open your eyes. See all you can. Beauty is an intimation of holiness. Celebrate the gifts of the ears, eyes, nose, mouth, and skin. Be sensible. Taste the bitter and the sweet.

Speak with a single voice. Live in a single world. Don't dress in vestments that disguise your ordinariness. Wear Levi's whenever possible.

WRITING YOUR SPIRITUAL AUTOBIOGRAPHY

A guidebook is useless unless you want to take a journey. The purpose of *Hymns to an Unknown God* is less to share the details of my life than it is to give aid and comfort to those who are on a path similar to my own. It will work best if you pause at the end of each section or chapter and test what I have said against your own experience. In preparing to write this book, I spent two months gathering all the photographs I could find from every period of my life and placing them in order in large albums, in order to trigger my memories. I suggest that as you read this book, you pause to re-collect your own history and begin to write your own spiritual autobiography.

Some guiding questions and suggestions:

- What authorities, myths, stories, scripts have in-formed your life? Where did you get your first set of answers to the great questions about the meaning of life? What was your parents' credo?
- In what ways does your current religious faith, philosophy, and practice of life differ from that of your parents? How much continuity and discontinuity is there between the generations?
- In what measure do you still dwell, comfortably or uncomfortably, within the Garden of Eden, refusing to taste of the fruit of the tree of the knowledge of good and evil and judge your life through your own experience? Through whose eyes do you look at life?
- Assemble the stories of those events, words, persons, and objects that unaccountably became luminous and gave you a feeling of direction, purpose or sacred meaning. What peak experiences, revelations, openings, illuminations, and awakenings have punctuated the flow of your ordinary life?

CHAPTER 4

Approaches to an Unknown God

"Immortal, invisible, God only wise,
In light inaccessible, hid from our eyes."

The Hymnbook, no. 85

"You must go by the way which is the way of ignorance.
As we grow older the world becomes stranger, the pattern more complicated."

T. S. ELIOT

BASE CAMP, MOUNT ANALOGUE

"In the mythic tradition," wrote Rene Daumal in *Mount Analogue*, "the Mountain is the bond between Earth and Sky. Its solitary summit reaches the sphere of eternity, and its base spreads out in manifold foothills into the world of mortals. It is the way by which man can raise himself to the divine and by which the divine can reveal itself to man. . . . For a mountain to play the role of Mount Analogue, the ultimate symbolic mountain, its summit must be inaccessible, but its base accessible to human beings as nature has made them. It must be unique, and it must exist geographically. The door to the invisible must be visible."

So far, our journey, which began when we determined to escape the moral crisis and spiritual drought that afflicts our life and homeland, has forced us to take leave of our usual views of the secular city and the routines in which we live. Moved by our yearning, driven by questions, we have set out to explore the barely remembered foothills, the origins of the geography that forms our own inner landscape. We look anew at those events that have formed and distorted us, hoping to find some deeper meaning and purpose for our lives, a new map of basic beliefs and right action.

A motley group of adventurers, grail hunters, restless souls and seekers have found their way into the high hill country and have built a makeshift camp at the base of the Mountain with many names — Mount Analogue, Mount Sinai, the Mount of Olives, Mount Olympus, Mount Meru, Harney Peak, Mount Kailas.

Every night around the campfire there is endless discussion of the topography of the Mountain, the pitch of the slopes, the likely location of glaciers, crevasses, and avalanches, the most promising places for bivouacs and routes to the summit. Some climbers avoid the bull sessions and spend all their time checking equipment, studying their maps, and planning their assault on the Mountain. At high noon when the sun is brightest, and on clear nights when the moon shines, everyone gathers on a large promontory, hoping for a glimpse of the Mountain.

In reality, nobody even knows if the Mountain exists. The region in which tradition locates it is constantly obscured by low-lying fog that fills the valleys and by unbroken clouds that cover the heights. Occasionally, strong winds dissipate the fog and move the clouds in billowing tableaux of gossamer shapes — castles in the air, gigantic figures of animals and monsters. Some observers say they have had a clear vision of a well-defined mountain. But alas, those who claim to have had such revelations regularly produce very divergent sketches and topographical maps of the one true Mountain. Periodically, wild-eyed pilgrims from places with strange-sounding names arrive in camp and announce that they have climbed to the summit and seen the surrounding territory from the vantage of the highest peak. Inevitably, when one of the summit conquerors gives his account of the narrow but true route, he accumulates a group of disciples who resolve to follow in his steps.

Sifting through all the ambiguous evidence and conflicting claims, the more careful and open-minded adventurers realize they have a problem that blocks any direct approach to the Mountain. If the unknown peak cannot be located, it cannot be scaled.

It would appear that our journey has ended at the base camp.

But perhaps it is only the direct approach that is blocked. If we were to change our orientation and proceed in an inward rather than an outward direction, search the heights and depths *within the self*, we might discover a passageway to the Beyond. Maybe some hidden capacity for transcendence is homogenized into the essence of our humanness that may offer us a glimpse of the Mountain. An echo in the cave of yearning might bring us news of unfathomable depths. Exploring the geography of the inner mountain, the spirit or soul, may give us some clues about the best way to approach the holy Mountain.

INSPIRED LANGUAGE: THE POETRY OF THE SACRED

At this stage of our adventure, our best hope for moving forward is to begin with the working assumption that the human spirit or soul contains an image of God, an assumption that all religious and spiritual traditions share. Our spirit-mirror is undoubtedly fogged by the hot breath of the ego and the image of God is blurred, but it may nevertheless allow us to use something like a mental computer with image-enhancement to construct a rough map to guide us further on our quest.

To lay out this preliminary map, we need to agree on some common terms and meanings. The discovery of our freedom-spirit-ability-to-transcend involves an awakening from the entrancement of culture. Spirit is the universal solvent that cannot be contained in any social or psychic structure. Prodigal sons and daughters must leave home and travel into a strange land where names have not already been attached to all experience.

It should be obvious to everyone except those who believe they have God-in-a-box and cynics who have abandoned all efforts to talk about anything that transcends verifiable knowledge that authentic language about a spiritual experience of the world is necessarily highly imaginative, poetic, and inexact.

Inspired speech is language stretched to the breaking point, tumbling over itself, falling headlong into nonsense, bursting to reveal something that can't be said. It is alternately excessive and overly modest, speaking of archangels and taking refuge in the syllable *om*.

The best spiritual language is silence: "Be still, and know that I am God." "The Tao that can be spoken is not the eternal Tao." "God" is a symbol for the unspeakable — I Am That Am.

While culture-bound religion gossips about God and speaks knowingly about sin and the path to salvation, inspirited language is shy and reserved. It witnesses rather than preaches. As coyotes, mystics, and Zen masters know, a spiritual tongue is kept in cheek and in check.

Next to silence, the encounter with the holy is best expressed in song, dance, ritual, poetry metaphor, parable, koan, story, and myth. Perennially, men and women speak in tongues, dance in ecstasy, fall into trances, in order to dip down into the silence beneath language and express in sound or gesture an intuition too deep for words. In speaking about spiritual matters, we are always beating around the bush, albeit a burning bush.

Authentic spiritual language about God does not confuse the map with the territory, the symbol with the thing. Literalism concentrates on the letter and misses the spirit; it gets the words but never the music, creates a spiritual tone-deafness. You can starve to death trying to eat a cookbook.

In addition to protecting ourselves against the religious tendency toward literalism and idolatry, we need to guard against the secular tendency to lay claim to and demean the language of the sacred.

Desecration begins with the prostitution of language. Great words are captured and forced into the service of small intentions. Faith, hope, and love are used to create profit or to promote tyranny. Advertising, propaganda, and political double-speak systematically torture language, assassinate truth, and betray a passive public into believing that happiness can be purchased or a meaningful life be won by obedience to the proper authorities.

When *Joy* becomes a detergent, it no longer bubbles up from the depths to surprise us and wash us clean of our pettiness.

When *Spring* is a soap, lilacs no longer remind us of the promise that winter is passing and hope is in the budding.

When the names *Cougar* and *Lynx* are attached to automobiles, the machine becomes our totem and our bodies are no longer inspired by feline grace.

When we *destroy a city to save it*, we lose the meaning of healing, all distinction between the sacred and the demonic.

When *land* becomes synonymous with *property*, we fall into the illusion that we can own the Earth that was once "mother," and will forever be the substance of our embodiment, the iron in our blood, the oxygen in our lungs.

When something that is dirty is *soiled*, we forget the sacred cult that was at the heart of agriculture (a word that means "to till, to dwell, to adore") and we come to fear the humus that is central to the definition of human beings.

When *capital* comes to mean only "money," we have certainly lost our heads.

When our *investments* are in stocks and bonds, we have ordained Mammon and placed our hope for security in the abstractions of the market.

When *corporations* create the laws, products, and rhythms by which we live, we have emerged from the body of Mother Nature only to be engulfed by another body, and the corporation has become the male-womb from which all value flows.

When *love* is something that must be "made," we confuse fabrication with grace.

When alcoholic drinks are described as the "most-spirited" or as ways to get you "to the bottom of it all," spirit has been reduced to a means to achieve materialistic, egocentric goals and a spiritless oblivion.

IN SEARCH OF A DEFINITION OF SPIRIT

Confucius said that the task of a philosopher was "the rectification of terms." If, he said, we know the meaning of "father, son, mother, daughter," then families will be happy and communities strong.

To regain the spiritual depth of our lives we must renew our understanding of certain words that stand guard and form a perimeter around
human dignity. We diminish ourselves if we lose the meaning of: *spirit,
flesh, soul, body, sacred, holy, pleasure, promise, passion, suffer, repent,
forgive, reason, wonder, freedom, trust, evil, care, hope, heal, truth.* Each
of us must earn the right to use these words by discovering how they
express our experience. We renew ourselves by renewing our contact
with the sacred and struggling to coin the metaphors and make the
gestures that best distill our experience. To get the sweetest meat, our
language must slice near to the bone. When inspired, we speak with an
erotic tongue, we slide into the folds and crevices, and we caress our
inarticulate experience until it breaks into song. To re-collect our
experience of the sacred, like poets we make a raid on the inarticulate
and come back bearing metaphors. We stitch the word to the silent
fabric of our days and create meaning: old wine, new wineskins.

If we can continue to dissolve some of the false mystification and
dogmatic nonsense that cluster around a variety of accounts of what is
the nature of spirit, we can arrive at some working definition of spirit.
So let's discard some of the most prevalent, vague, crass, dogmatic, and
reductionistic definitions.

Spirit and *soul* are popularly used in such wishy-washy ways that it is
impossible to know what people are claiming or rejecting when they
use them. Among the pious, I often hear gossamer sentences such as,
"Spirit is elusive, ineffable, unbound. Soul is our point of connection
between self and spirit. It is a quality of consciousness. Spirit is the
nonphysical essence lurking in our hearts. Soul is what survives when
all the rest of me dies." A sign posted at the trail head that leads toward
the Mountain cautions us against such fuzzy-headed mysticism:
"Warning! Lack of clear thinking about the spiritual life is likely to land
you in a murky swamp, in the company of muddled minds, surrounded
by an obscure cloud of occult claims and false mysteries."

We can also reject out of hand definitions of the kind we hear on
Sunday morning from the televangelists who rule the airwaves, which
have the questionable virtue of being tight to the point of rigidity. By
spirit, they mean one and only one thing and it excludes most of us.
The gift of the Holy Spirit is from God to His people who have

accepted Jesus as Lord and Savior. If you accept such a definition, you need only have faith and wait.

My approach to a working understanding of *spirit* is to look at it in the context of the other words that belong in the same family of ideas, such as *ego, personality, sacred, holy.*

The word *spirit* originally referred to breathing or breath. It designated the animating or vital element in humans or animals, in contrast to the purely material element. Often *soul* has been regarded as an immortal spiritual entity that is distinct from the body, an elusive quality that animates humans and animals, and gives human beings the unique capacity to transcend mere animality. It is easy to see that both words arise from the primal experience of trying to figure out the difference between the living and the dead. Immediately after death, a person still looks the same as he did in life, but something is missing. His breath has vanished, and with it all the energy, vitality, and special qualities that made him recognizable — loved or hated — by others.

It is inevitable that we try to understand and name this essential mystery that separates the living from the dead. We can't help wondering whether an *entity* (called soul) animates and breathes us, enters our body the moment we are born and departs when we die, and perhaps survives in some nontemporal and nonspatial realm (heaven) or returns to reanimate another body (reincarnation). Or whether, as in the case of Adam, a creator God molds the human body out of clay and breathes His spirit into it. Further: Observing two living persons, one of whom is dull, depressed, and lacking in energy and animation, and another who is lively, passionate, energetic, and full of enthusiasm, we naturally wonder what makes the difference.

Clearly, our social self — the face we put on to meet the faces we meet — can be distinguished from our spirit or soul. The problem comes when we overidentify with our personalities and roles and forget to search for and deepen our relationship to that mystery that constitutes our spirit or soul. Without the quest for spirit or soul, we become superficial. Our egos and personalities are inevitably too constricting and need to be modified by a spiritual perspective. Certainly, we need a strong sense of self. But if we don't see ourselves as including our family, the ecosystem, the community, the Ultimate Being-Becoming-

Itself whose most appropriate name is God, then we betray the magnificent complexity that is named in the ancient words *spirit* and *soul.*

Spirituality or the soulful path is the quest to discover our "higher" selves and explore the "depths," to allow ourselves to be moved-animated-inspired by that sacred "no-thing" that keeps us human, the Unknown God within whom we live and move and have our being but may never fully comprehend. The animating principle in a human being is *the spiritual instinct,* the impulse to go beyond the ego to explore the heights and depths, to connect our individual life with something beyond the self, something more everlasting (even if ever-changing) than the self. Ultimately, our self-esteem comes from our discovery of a purposeful source of deathless meaning that transcends the self.

Finally, *spirit* and *soul* are not occult entities but are the ways in which we define the essence of our humanness when we transcend our social and psychological conditioning and experience ourselves as being encompassed within a cosmos we perceive as sacred or holy.

A SPIRITUAL COMPASS AND SOUL-DETECTOR

Oftentimes, all we need when we have encountered barriers to our journey is a very rough indication of a direction. Something as inexact as "Go south rather than north" may suffice, as a rough compass to guide us toward the sacred, on the model of the game we played as children. *You're getting warmer. You're getting colder.*

Just as there are physical symptoms of health and illness — blood pressure, heart rate, or energy level — we have an inner compass that can tell us whether we are moving in the direction of the spirited or dispirited life. Even an agnostic can explore what Gabriel Marcel, the French philosopher, called "concrete approaches to the mystery of being." There are, he says, certain dispositions such as wonder, fidelity, love, and hope that lead us in the direction of the sacred, and others such as betrayal, hatred, and despair that lead toward a desecrated world.

For all the differences in the world religions about the path to God, a near-universal agreement holds that certain ways of acting lead away from God. For instance, at the center of the Buddhist wheel of life there is this warning: If you try to grasp and possess the world (symbol: the cock) or if you shrink from life and yield to fear (symbol: the snake), you will fall into greater and greater delusion or maya (symbol: the pig) and you will progressively sink lower and lower, being reborn as an animal, a hungry ghost, or a citizen of hell. Judaism, Christianity, and Islam portray "sin" in a similar manner, as the effort to possess and dominate life, and warn that it leads to the alienating illusion that the self rather than God is the center of the universe. From here it is only a short step to lording it over other people, treating them as objects, as soulless "its" rather than sacred "thous," and from there to villainy. The meaning of salvation is moot; sin is obvious.

We can determine whether we are approaching or retreating from a spirited life by recognizing that greedy (and therefore fearful) egocentricity leads to a deluded and alienated style of life, away from the self-transcending path of spiritual awareness. Based on this fundamental principle we might make the following distinctions between the spirited and the dispirited life:

Spirited life	*Dispirited life*
Disarmed psyche	Armored psyche
Porous	Self-sealing
Inclusive	Exclusive
Compassionate	Totalitarian

No matter how lost we become in chaos, anxiety, meaninglessness, and despair, we can always consult one absolute point of reference to determine the direction in which we should travel. In the spiritual journey, the compass unfailingly points toward compassion. This spiritual compass is the equivalent of the satellite Ground Position System that pilots and ship captains use to discover their exact location. Inscribe this single word on your heart— "compassion." Whenever you are confused, keep heading in the direction that leads toward deepening your love and care for all living beings, including yourself, and you will never stray far from the path to fulfillment.

EVIL AS A LANDMARK

Paradoxically, it is much easier to detect the absence or perversion of spirit than its presence. The recognition of evil is one of the most certain landmarks on our spiritual journey. There are ways of being in the world that destroy all access to anything we might legitimately claim to be the realm of the sacred.

Extreme examples, parables of horror — the Nazi extermination camps or the Soviet gulags — place us immediately in a landscape that is without question desecrated and demonic. Anyone whose spirit is alive and well knows instinctively that whatever attitudes, values, and behaviors led toward Auschwitz lead away from the sacred. Identifying such a clear and distinct instance of evil and desecration provides the spiritual searcher with the equivalent of a compass on which true North has been indicated. The spectacle of raw and indisputable evil is a signpost that says in bold letters: *Wrong direction. Do not enter! This way leads toward self-destruction and desecration and away from the realm of the spirit.* And if we may be certain that wanton cruelty and senseless violence result in desecration, we may begin to trace the first outline of what it is like to live in a sacral world. In violating what ought not to be violated we sense a silent testimony to the essential sacredness of living beings.

We recognize the existence of raw evil in the brutalizing of what ought to be sacrosanct. (This morning, it was babies killed by Serbian snipers in Sarajevo.) If we reverse Dostoevsky's famous warning, "If God is dead all things are permitted," we get a formula for a completely dispirited landscape. *When torture, genocide, and ecocide are permitted, the sacred and the human spirit are absent.* We may be uncertain about God, but it is very clear when we are in the presence of idolatry, desecration, and betrayal of the promise of human beings.

The presence of evil gives us a moral compass not only because it points clearly toward desecration but because it shows that developing compassion for our neighbor and undertaking some action to lessen the quantity of evil in the world is a necessary part of the spiritual life.

It is easy, even "normal," to look across the river and see our neighbor first as a rival, next as an aggressor, and finally as an enemy of God whom we are justified in destroying. But, without denying that we must struggle against social and political evils, the spiritual tradition makes it very clear that the only true holy war is one that begins within the soul of the individual. The battleground between good and evil, that terrifying place "Swept with confused alarms of struggle and flight, / Where ignorant armies clash by night" (Matthew Arnold, *Dover Beach*), is within me and you. The "face of the enemy" is one we construct from the disowned parts of our self-righteous ego.

Inspired teachers admonish us to remove the beam from our own eye before we attempt to take the splinter from our brother's eye, to descend into hell before we try to storm heaven, to become acquainted with our demons before we try to become angels.

The most certain mark of spirited men or women is their willingness to view the world through the lens of their own brokenness and to wrestle with their own tendency toward selfishness, greed, cruelty, arrogance, hate, apathy. If the spiritual life is visualized as a journey, as much of it is struggling to get out of the mud of sin-alienation-illusion as it is ascending to the peaks of insight and enlightenment. To ascend the sacred mountain be prepared to descend again and again into the dark valley.

SNAPSHOTS AND PORTRAITS

Louis Armstrong was once asked for a definition of jazz. "Man," he replied, "if you don't know, I could never tell you." It is difficult to offer any more than a working definition of spirit, but in certain instances the needle of my soul-detector indicates that I am in the presence of the phenomenon.

Spirit, like wind, is visible only in the movement that results from its presence. We see the trees swaying, the breath moving through the cycle of inspiration and expiration, but we do not see the thing itself. Soul, like light, can be detected only by what it illuminates. We must creep up on the intangible quarry, and when we are in its vicinity we can detect its presence or absence.

One of the most ancient and universally recognized signs of spirit is involuntary movement. In Bali, Haiti, or Woodstock, the drums sound a hypnotic rhythm and the dancers move like people possessed by an alien spirit. The Siberian shaman rides the beat of his drum, falls into a trance and soars with the wild yonder high above the village where he can see the causes and cures for illness, or descends into the underworld to search out the names of the demons who are troubling the community. The Holy Spirit is shed abroad in a Pentecostal congregation, and a dozen men and women tremble and begin to speak in tongues. The sedate silence of a Quaker meeting is interrupted as a Friend is moved by the spirit to speak. A Sufi teacher's words begin to fall automatically into the orderly cadence of poetry, form themselves into a chant, and, finally, burst out in a spontaneous song of praise to God. The choir in a black Baptist church begins to swing the hymn, the congregation takes up the beat, clapping and swaying as the spirit moves among them.

But, every trance, every instance of being swept away by an overpowered emotion, should not be taken as evidence of the working of a healing, whole-making, or holy spirit. Plato warned that there were both divine and demonic forms of possession and madness. The author of the first Letter of John cautioned early Christians that they should "test the spirits to see whether they are of God." There are many kinds of counterfeit or perverse spirituality that seduce individuals into making a premature surrender of their will and personal responsibility to a destructive cause or organization. The frenzy of a mob of English soccer fans on a rampage is a cruel parody of the ecstatic communion of Hopi Indians engaged in a rain dance. In the Nuremberg rallies, thousands of Germans, inspired by the ritual and promise of the Third Reich, surrendered their consciences and conspired with a single will to commit mass murder.

The best test of whether a particular instance of self-transcendence, or entrancement, is apt to be creative or destructive is to see if it leads to compassionate action and a more inclusive communion. John puts the matter simply: "He who says he is in the light and hates his brother is in the darkness. By this we know the spirit of truth or the spirit of error. Beloved, let us love one another; for love is of God."

An inspired life is marked by an increase in the power-in-love and a decrease in the will-to-power.

If I could capture spirit or soul on film, it would be in incidents in which a man or woman acted in a heroic or grace-ful way that went beyond what we would have expected or predicted based on what we know of their personality or character. Two famous snapshots make visible the invisible movement in which ego is transcended and transformed into spirit — the one of the Vietnamese Buddhist monk immolating himself to protest the war, and the one of the young Chinese man standing quietly in front of the oncoming tank in Tiananmen Square.

For a more complex portrait, I would point my camera at a bedroom in Cambridge, Massachusetts, where my old friend Dick Ruopp lies nearly immobile in a hospital bed in the advanced stages of Lou Gehrig's disease. He is hooked to a respirator that helps him breathe and to tubes through which he takes his liquid meals. His arms are supported by a harness that allows him to type on a computer keyboard on a bedside table, and a voice synthesizer turns his written thoughts into spoken language. All the roles, behaviors, status symbols, and pleasures that once characterized the man are now missing. The former president of Bank Street College, gourmet cook, bon vivant, sailor, carpenter, and educator has been stripped of everything that usually makes life worth living. Yet everyone who enters the room recognizes immediately they are in the middle of a great drama in which love and spirit are being made visible. Between Dick and his wife, Pat, who were married after they discovered he had the disease, a constant liturgy of love is enacted. Care is offered and accepted as naturally as the smiles that pass between them. Teasing and easy banter are mixed with serious conversations conducted in an antiphonal dance of gestures and eye movements, of a synthesized voice and a New York accent. I have never heard a complaint! Once when my wife, Jan, and I were visiting, Jan said, "You are doing beautifully with all your difficulties." Dick replied, "Nothing else I can do." Jan said, "You could piss and moan a little." Dick replied with a wicked grin, "I never thought of that." My camera would finally come to rest on the face of the man — gaunt beneath the well-trimmed gray beard, eyes sparkling and beatific — where we could see the incarnate definition of "an inspired life."

Next, I might film the moment of inspiration and transcendence when Larrick, now a master electrician, musician, and sailor, was liberated as he sat in a jail in Iran, convicted of smuggling hashish. "What can I say? I was young and foolish, and I got caught in Iran with fifty-five kilos. I had already served fourteen months of a two-year sentence when I was hauled before the court again and given five more years. At that point I knew this would probably happen again and again and I would never get out of prison. I wrote to my wife and told her it was no use waiting for me. After a while I went on a hunger fast because I would rather die than spend the rest of my life in prison. One night I got down on my knees. This was incredibly hard for me to do because I was raised in a Mormon family and was turned off by organized religion. I am an agnostic. But I prayed to an Unknown God. It was sort of 'let's make a deal.' I made a solemn oath that if I got my freedom, I would right all the wrongs I had done and get a handle on my drug abuse. After twenty-four days without food, suddenly I realized it didn't matter whether I was in prison or out. *Freedom is an inside job.* I had to find it within myself. Not long after that, the guards came and told me to gather my belongings because I was going to be set free. I didn't believe them — they did this kind of thing all the time to torture prisoners. Sure enough, an amnesty had been declared and they let me go. But it didn't matter. I was already free. It took me ten years after that to kick my addictions, but as of next month I have been clean and sober for eight years."

I would also film an incident that happened a few years ago when I witnessed the spirit of a woman — I will call her Betty — emerge and blossom under difficult circumstances. I was one of the leaders of an Outward Bound group that trekked for several days through a narrow canyon in Arizona. Betty had signed up for the trip on the recommendation of her therapist but was totally unprepared. At thirty-eight years of age, she was bland, passive, and in poor physical condition, a woman who had conformed to what was expected of her, worked as a clerk, and retreated from the world. She reported that she was a virgin, had no romantic relationships or close friends. By the end of the first day, she was a pathetic mass of sore muscles and blisters. By the end of the second day, her feet were covered with open sores. To everyone's amazement, however, the more difficult things became, the less she complained. At dusk of the third day when we reached our campsite, other members of the group gathered around and bathed and bandaged her feet and made her as comfortable as possible. On the fourth and fifth days, Betty was surrounded with care as she walked in constant pain. With every mile, she seemed to be leaving her old personality farther behind, and her face grew more defined and radiant. By the end of the journey, she emanated toughness, self-confidence, pride, and determination to change her life. We all felt honored to witness her metamorphosis and graced by her presence. I learned later that when she returned home, she immediately quit her job, enrolled in an advanced degree program, and emerged from her cocoon.

THE UNFATHOMABLE SPIRIT

Gazing deeply into the soul, hoping to find mirrored there an image of God, what we discover is that the human spirit itself is unfathomably high and deep. The inner Mountain is as obscured by clouds as the holy Mountain we yearn to climb. The soul-mirror reveals the indefinability of a human being. The reality of who I am can never be entirely captured or exhausted by any set of predicates that describe me. At the heart of my most intimate knowledge of myself, I know myself to be unknowable, forever a fugitive, escaping my best efforts to entrap myself in a web of language and consciousness.

Only I can discover my spirit and make myself free. Only I can take the existential leap, make the decision that carries me beyond what I was yesterday (and what every expert would predict I would be tomorrow) and do a new thing. The unique human capacity we call spirit can also be called freedom. It is the capacity to transcend our biological, psychological, social, and political conditioning. It can never be discovered by science, since it is not allowed in the laboratory.

We discover freedom and spirit only in the first person singular, in the solitary and risky moments when we cease to consider our life as an impersonal phenomenon and inhabit the particularity of our unique experience. A man I know who had been addicted to drugs and alcohol from the age of thirteen to twenty-seven described his recovery in a way that offers a good description of the discovery of the spiritual dimension. "I was," he said, "required to stretch further than I thought possible."

Gabriel Marcel, whom I met when I was writing my doctoral dissertation, *The Idea of Mystery in Gabriel Marcel*, made a distinction between problems and mystery that I have found essential to under-

standing the nature of spiritual life. Problems may be solved by accu-
mulating data, but genuine mysteries cannot be eliminated by any
conceivable increase in knowledge. At first a mystery seems to be only a
difficult problem that could be solved if we had additional information
of some kind. But it is different. For instance, scientists can eventually
solve the problem of curing a disease because the virus exists "out
there," apart from the investigators. A sophisticated psychological test
may determine the probability that a marriage between Linda, who
tends toward hysteria, and me, who tends toward the obsessive-
compulsive side of the scale, will succeed or fail. But it can never tell
me whether I should marry or divorce Linda.

When I seek the meaning of my life, freedom, God, evil, spirit, there
is no objective standpoint from which I could gather evidence that
would be apart from my willing, feeling and deciding self. Whenever I
ask about matters that involve my existence, I am inseparable from the
"data." A mystery is something in which I myself am involved, and
therefore the distinction between what is in me and what is before me
loses its meaning and its initial validity. Each of us must make awesome
decisions about whether we are or may become free, what we value,
when and to whom we make commitments, whether we trust or
mistrust the mystery that encompasses us, how we will tell the story of
our life.

The most important decision we ever make is about whether we can
make decisions. Freedom is born in the moment I decide I am free to
move away from what has previously imprisoned me. Because I am
free, because I am spirit, I transcend all that I or anyone else can know
about me. When I have added all that biology, sociology, psychology,
and any other science might tell me about myself to the self-knowledge
I accumulate by observation and meditation, I remain a profound
mystery to myself.

So, not even self-knowledge is the goal of the authentic spiritual life.
Pursuing my spirit, I have gradually divested myself of the garments of
identity with which my family, culture, and myself clothe me. I have
been dis-illusioned, dis-identified, and radically de-mythed, left with
the sense that I can no more comprehend the limits of this strange
being I call myself than I can understand the stranger who is my
neighbor or the weird wombworld that nurtures me.

In spite of psychology's claim to the mantle of the soul doctor, spirit is not the same as the unconscious. The unconscious is the ignored or repressed side of the psyche that is formed by family and culture. It is the proper function of psychotherapy to make the unconscious conscious, to deal with the repressed shadow-knowledge, to make knowable what is in the unconscious. Psychoanalysis can potentially help me understand how my psyche, my persona, and the character armor of my gender were formed, how I was in-formed and mis-in-formed by my familial and cultural mythology. Ideally, psychoanalysis helps us to demystify and de-myth the illusions of persona and psyche, so that we do not carry over unresolved familial conflicts into the spiritual quest, so we don't need gurus and authorities to replace parents. Too often, though, it substitutes therapist for personal authority and holds up the ideal of self-understanding — which can never be total — as motivation, thereby cutting off a greater sense of self and connection.

A kind of systematic unconsciousness is built into the structure of consciousness. An important, non-psychological reason I can never exhaust all that could be known about myself or the world is that every act of knowledge involves ignorance. When I "pay" attention to any aspect of my self, another part of me remains in the shadows. Sometimes I turn around as fast as I can to see what is in back of me, but my shadow moves faster than I can. And when I observe myself most closely I fall into the quantum dilemma — I change the self I am observing by the act of observation. Every time I take a picture of myself, I find I was posing for the camera. I can't seem to catch myself unawares.

To live by the sign of the spirit is to give up the illusion that life, the world, other people, and the self can ultimately be known, predicted, controlled, pigeonholed, and rendered secure.

I am a dangerous character. Always becoming. Beneath my persona-psyche-gender (all of which are proper objects of self-knowledge), I extend fathoms deep into the measureless, the undefinable, into the unknowable totality. The unfathomable spirit and the unknowable God are inseparable notions.

TRUSTING AN UNKNOWABLE GOD

"The idea of God can become the final obstacle to God."

MEISTER ECKHART

"Darkness within darkness. The gateway to all understanding. . . . The Tao that can be told is not the eternal Tao."

Tao Te Ching

"If a man wishes to be sure of the road he treads on, he must close his eyes and walk in the dark."

SAINT JOHN OF THE CROSS,
The Dark Night of the Soul

If you are beginning to experience metaphysical vertigo, a fear of falling into the endless interlocking mysteries, don't worry. At this point in our journey you should be feeling light-headed, weightless in the void. We are not on firm ground. We are standing between two mirrors, each of which contains an image that dissolves into a mysterious background. When we look at the inner Mountain, ourselves as spirit or soul, we see an inexhaustible vista. When we look in the direction of the Holy Mountain, the cloud cover lifts only long enough to allow us to see that there is no single Mountain that we might climb. We are encompassed by mountains. Our base camp appears to be only a valley in a vast surround. To complicate matters further, since we are standing between the two mirrors, the images reverberate and mingle to form an infinite regress in which we can no longer distinguish what is within and what is without. The ground on which we stood that separated us from the Mountain has just disappeared from beneath our feet.

Relax. Yield to the vertigo and the falling will become the flying, the no-thing-ness will become the sanctuary.

*   *   *

If we probe deeply into the history of theology, we discover that the most profound religious thinkers have suffered (and enjoyed) the same vertigo we are experiencing. Most seminal theologians and philosophers, after straining every muscle of the mind in an effort to define God, have come to the conclusion that the ultimate One remains shrouded in mystery. As the Negro spiritual said, God is "so high can't climb over it, so low can't crawl under it, so wide can't get around it, got to go in by the door" (and we are not certain which, if any, of the doors lead to God). God is not an object to be known or a problem to be solved by human intelligence, but is the ground beneath our capacity to understand anything, the totality within which we live, move, and have our being.

In the end, religion collapses back into mysticism as it recognizes that after we have said all we can say about God, we are still surrounded by an impenetrable silence. Thomas Aquinas devoted his most rigorous thinking to trying to establish how we could speak about God based on analogies taken from human experience. But after our minds have erected the ladder of analogy as high as possible toward God, he concludes, "we remained joined to Him as to one unknown." Augustine, after writing endless words trying to explain the Trinity, admitted in the end, "I only write in order not to be silent." Mysticism counsels us to follow the *via negativa*, to honor the infinite distance that separates the finite and the infinite, to live within "the cloud of unknowing" (Jakob Boehme), to respect the silence of the Godhead where nobody is at home (Meister Eckhart), to recognize the hiddenness of God (Martin Luther's *"deus absconditus"*), to understand that we can only speak about God in symbolic, parabolic, and poetic ways.

We are caught in a paradox called the human condition. Our spiritual instinct drives us to connect with the whole of being, but the structure of our minds, limited by the conditions of our mortality, frustrates our desire. In truth, we cannot *know* enough to be either theists or atheists. We have no alternative except to *decide* whether to trust or mistrust this encompassing mystery.

It seems to me that the best theological position is one that combines agnosticism with trust. I choose to trust the surrounding mystery out of which I emerged and into which I will disappear in death and to rest secure within the darkness of the unknowable One.

The first spiritual virtue of this position is humility, the willingness to remain earthy, a creature of the humus. This odd virtue involves the commitment to live joyfully with what we can know, not to cheat, not to pretend to be able to throw a bridge over the chasm that separates us from knowledge of the whole of Being.

Each time I abandon the quest for certainty and embrace the essential endarkenment of the human condition, I find it is a good thing to be a citizen of earthy multiplicity, ignorant of the One.

Accepting endarkenment may seem like another odd virtue. But it has a healing power as an antidote to the pride and hidden idolatry that comes with the claim to "know" the will and ways of God. There are many tragedies we do not invite when we remain true to the Earth. The moment any people lay claim to the privileged status of "a chosen people" or claim to possess the only true revelation of God, they provide themselves with a theological justification for war. There is a high degree of correlation between true believers, known gods, and high body counts.

In practice, the only way to love our neighbor — the great commandment of every religion — is to give up the claim to privileged knowledge of the one true God. A new Golden Rule should be stated: Love your neighbor's truth as much as your own. Love demands humility. The essence of arrogance is to believe that we have a monopoly on truth and that our neighbor is in error. Love involves repentance, recognizing the fallibility of my truth claims, listening and learning to cherish the truth of the stranger.

Each of us creates a picture of our world by connecting only a dozen or so of the trillions of dots that would have to be connected to make a "true" portrait of the universe (if, indeed, the notions of *knowing* the universe and *the truth* make any sense at all). Considering the inherent limits of the finite human mind and our nearly inexhaustible capacity for self-deception, we may actually be closest to the truth when we remain acutely aware of our ignorance.

Faith is dancing in the dark.

AN AGNOSTIC'S PRAYER

As a modern American, my mentors in manhood have taught me by word and deed that I am expected to be self-sufficient. From Emerson I learned self-reliance. Erich Fromm taught me the virtue of autonomy. Gary Cooper, Clint Eastwood, and all the heroes of those great morality plays — the Western movies — showed me that a Marlboro man stands tall and goes it alone. Most recently, a gaggle of pop psychologists have warned me against the terrible danger of codependency. No crutches, no leaning. I am a free-standing, self-supporting individual.

It is with some embarrassment that I admit that on certain occasions I have been unable to keep myself from praying. Like a shipwrecked sailor, I have hurled my petition into the void:

> Almighty Father, strong to save,
> Whose arm hath bound the restless wave,
> Who biddest the mighty ocean deep
> Its own appointed limits keep:
> O hear us when we cry to Thee
> For those in peril on the sea.

Don't misunderstand me. I don't *believe* in prayer. I only *do* it. Or perhaps, it does *me* in spite of myself. I can't make intellectual sense of prayer. If the careless universe operates clocklike following the lockstep laws of cause and effect, what will be will be — *Que será, será*. And no willfulness or entreaty on my part will change anything. If there is a caring, knowledgeable, and powerful God, He-She-It keeps His-Her-Its eye on the sparrow and, surely, watches me too. In which case, prayer is redundant. Nor would any God with self-esteem need me to sing praises to His-Her-Its holy name. Nor would a provident God, like a forgetful CEO, need to be reminded to intercede and grant clemency to some little one caught in the pain and tragedy that are an inescapable part of the human (God-created) condition.

Nevertheless: Thursday night before Christmas, my daughter's lifelong friend, Wiyanna, was found unconscious and rushed to the hospital. Through the long hours of Friday and Saturday, she remained in a coma, and none of the tests showed anything. The doctors were baffled. All we could do was sit and wait with her parents. As I watched our daughter, afraid and uncomprehending, holding the hand of her inert friend, from the depths of my being I cried out: "No! God. No! Please!" I don't know what I expected. But sorrow, outrage, and hope mingled and uttered forth a cry for mercy into the encompassing darkness. Much as my mind rebelled against prayer, my spirit could not abide living in a world where science and self-sufficiency were the last word.

I report, with enormous relief, that on Sunday morning our sleeping beauty awakened and asked for her mother. On Tuesday, she was discharged from the hospital, fully recovered. The doctors still have neither a diagnosis nor an explanation. Nor have I any needles on which to knit the experience, no categories that allow me to understand what happened or why. Only this: My spirit, like love, cannot be contained within the horizons of my mind. It soars above reason and swoops down into the chaos beneath rationality. It travels with its own passport and freely crosses the frontiers of the known and explainable world.

"We may be compared to owls trying to look at the sun; but since the natural desire in us for knowledge is not without a purpose, its immediate object is our own ignorance."

NICHOLAS OF CUSA

"Living is a form of not being sure, not knowing what next or how. The artist never entirely knows. We take leap after leap into the dark."

AGNES DE MILLE

CHAPTER 5

In the Presence of the Holy

"Holy, Holy, Holy! Though the Darkness Hide Thee
Though the eye of sinful man
Thy glory may not see
Only Thou are holy; there is none beside Thee
Perfect in power, in love, and purity."

The Hymnbook, no. 11

It is in plain sight, but cannot be seen.
It is never silent, but cannot be heard.
It is not lost, but cannot be found.
God is unknowable, the soul unfathomable.
But the Holy may appear in any moment.

As we set out into the wilderness, we can find some guidance about where and how to look by examining the maps and travel reports of some of the great spiritual explorers, even those from other religious traditions.

I would be less than honest if I suggested that the division between the traditional religious and the spiritual paths is equivalent to a separation between the lambs and the lions, the timid and the courageous. Church, mosque, synagogue, and sangha have treasures that can and do transform the lives of those who discover and make use of them. There is no denomination that does not contain a leaven of saints of the ordinary life — radiant, wise, and compassionate men and women, overflowing with generosity and joy. The spirit, like the wind, blows where it will, within and without the walls. It may come upon you as you sit in a stained-glass sanctuary surrounded by all the symbols of your faith, or as you stand on a high ridge in the Cascade Mountains when the lightning strikes a tall ponderosa a heartbeat away from where you are hiking, or as you stand in a picket line protesting the unjust ways of the powerful.

SALVAGING TREASURES FROM ANCIENT TRADITIONS

Not one of the founders of the great religions was orthodox. Jesus wasn't a Christian, Gautama wasn't a Buddhist, Mohammed wasn't a Muslim. All were charismatic spiritual seekers, mystics, prophets, troublemakers, critics of the establishments of their day. As Emerson said, speaking about religion, "In the first generation, the men were golden and the goblets were wooden. In the second generation, the men were wooden and the goblets were golden." Charisma is bureaucratized, the spirit is forced to punch a time clock and answer to the authorities.

Recognizing there is a hidden spiritual treasure within the maze of every religion, the smart seeker will make use of the maps that have been drawn by great pathfinders. Treasure hunters would be foolish to burn down the library.

Every religious tradition has cartographers who chart the geography of the metaphysical realms, mark the stages on the journey, and explain the techniques and disciplines necessary for getting to Heaven, Nirvana, or Shambhala. If you are looking for a Baedeker to guide you on your pilgrimage, you will do well to examine both the simple and the intricate guidebooks.

The classical minimalist religion, elegant and simple, is outlined in the *Tao Te Ching* (*The Classic Book of Integrity and the Way*) and in *The Way of Chuang Tsu*. Since the Tao, the Mother of all things, is unnameable and cannot be grasped, we should be soft and flowing, like the water that wears away the hardest rock. The Way is easy. Give up conscious striving, yield and become as supple as a baby. Empty yourself, avoid conflict and attachment. The great discipline is to learn the way of non-action. Chuang Tsu advises: "If fishes, born in water, seek the deep shadow of pond and pool, all their needs are satisfied. If man, born in Tao, sinks into the deep shadow of non-action to forget aggression and concern, he lacks nothing, his life is secure.

Within the Christian tradition, the Bible, creeds, dogma, moral teachings, and sacraments of the Church provided a relatively simple, officially authorized, map for the majority. In the allegory *Pilgrim's Progress*, the single most influential book apart from the Bible, Christian follows the path through Vanity Fair, into the Slough of Despond, climbs the Delectable Mountains, and makes his way toward the Celestial City. For the literal minded, the authentic life was supposed to be an "imitation of Christ," a following "in His Steps." The Christian mystics created more elaborate schemes. Bernhard of Clairvaux, like Plato, envisioned a ladder that led from the impure love of created things to the pure love of God. John of the Cross charted the passage through "the dark night of the soul" in a way that anticipated modern psychology's understanding of the healing journey through depression. Teresa of Ávila likened the stages of the spiritual journey to a progression through many mansions of an interior castle. In this journey, we gradually move away from nonreflective living and reliance on our external spiritual side — teachers, books, verbal prayers — and turn inward to explore our innate divinity and cultivate inner authority, until we, finally, experience a mystical marriage with God. Hildegard of Bingen, a twelfth-century contemporary of Bernhard, left one of the more amazing accounts of the mystic life in her *Illuminations*, a verbal and pictorial account of her visions. In her highly original theological imagination, sin is conceived as the drying up of the sap of life. When we are unjust and uncaring, we become cold, hard, brittle, and dusty. Salvation is verdancy, greening, juiciness. Jesus, the juiciest of the juicy, is Greenness Incarnate. The Holy Spirit is the greening power that makes all things grow and sends merciful dew into the human heart to overcome dryness.

Of the major world religions, Tibetan Buddhism has created the most intricate maps and elaborate spiritual technologies: chants-mantras, gestures-mudras, pictorial schema-mandalas, and different forms of meditation. The great Wheel of Life that is painted on the walls of temples, monasteries, and many public buildings depicts the causes of misery (Desire-Hatred-Delusion), and the karmic realms through which creatures must evolve — the realms of the gods, the Titans, the hungry ghosts, hell, the animal realm — before they reach the human realm and have the chance to attain enlightenment. In the

Tantric forms of Tibetan mysticism, the pathway toward liberation is said to run directly through the human body. The quest for enlightenment involves making use of breath control, meditation, visualization, and compassionate action — to raise the primal energy (prana, kundalini) up the spine, through the various psycho-spiritual centers (chakras) until the entire body is infused with divine light, wisdom, and compassion. (See *Foundations of Tibetan Mysticism*, by Lama Govinda, and *The Tibetan Book of Living and Dying* by Sogyal Rimpoche.)

In making use of traditional religious maps, or more modern ones, keep in mind that "the map is not the territory," and that you are the final authority, the cartographer, and autobiographer of your life-journey. By all means, consult the classical accounts of the experiences of the great religious pilgrims. Make use of them, but don't try to follow them exactly or you will get lost.

It is especially important to search for the jewels that are hidden in your birthright tradition. In the beginning of our quest we often become exiles, but eventually the spiritual journey circles round toward home. If you were raised in a Jewish home you may become a sojourner in a Buddhist land, but eventually you will need to return to your native holy land to rescue the spiritual treasures that are still buried there under a mound of toxic trash. The same principle applies to all seekers, regardless of race, color, or creed.

RELIGION AND THE SPIRITUAL QUEST

To oversimplify slightly, there are two paths we might take that promise to lead us in the direction of the holy, two different ways to seek answers to the perennial existential questions that face every human being — the path of the religious pilgrim, and the way of the spiritual seeker.

Religion offers authorized *answers* to life's most agonizing questions — creeds and catechisms. I was visiting Mother the other day, and she told me a joke that characterizes the nature of religion. "A Sunday school teacher asks his class: 'What little gray animal climbs trees, gathers nuts, and has a long bushy tail?' A little boy answers: 'I know the answer is supposed to be Jesus or God, but it sounds like a squirrel to me.' " No matter what the question, the answer for Christians is always Jesus or God.

Every religion claims to possess a revelation of God, divinely inspired scriptures, rituals, and priests. I can think of no better illustration of this than an incident that happened to me years ago. I was engaged in a public debate about the question of authority with Herb Richardson, a friend who was a conservative Christian theologian. He said, "I will tell you what it means to believe in the authority of the Bible. If you ask me if I believe what is on page 313 of the Bible, I will say yes. And then I will see what is on that page."

Religion presents the faithful with an authorized map of life — precepts to be followed, the example of lives of saints, saviors, and bodhisattvas to be imitated, taboos to be avoided, commandments to be obeyed, traditions to be respected. Thus, the religious life is a *pilgrimage* to a known destination. The end is given as well as the means. God is the goal of the search. Church, bible, guru, and the accepted disciplines of the spirit are the means.

An individual believer may suffer from a crisis of faith, a dark night of the soul, but the way, the truth, and the life have already been set forth. The pilgrim's progress will be marked by moral struggles, failures, moments of disobedience, and backsliding, but the path itself is well charted by those who have gone before: "Brothers, we are treading where the saints have trod." The religious life is a repetition of a sacred way once and for all revealed to our fathers. The official story, the ritual, the authorized pattern of life, is supposed to be repeated. Improvisation, novelty, doing things in a new way, are eccentric, taboo. As the hymn says, it will "be my theme in glory, to tell the old, old story of Jesus and his love."

Obedience is the chief religious virtue: "Not my will but Thine be done." And the will of God is defined as the commandments, laws, rules, and disciplines that are sanctified by the authoritative texts, institutions, priests, and kings.

The spiritual quest is the reverse of the religious pilgrimage. The quest begins when an individual falls into a spiritual "black hole" in which everything that was solid vaporizes. Certainties vanish, authorities are questioned, all the usual comforts and assurances of religion fail, and the path disappears. A spiritual quest is the effort to discover the meaning of life. It is experimental, an exploration of a country not yet mapped, whose boundaries are not yet known. The spiritual mind lives in and loves the great mythic questions.

A man or woman on a spiritual quest makes a virtue of what religion considers a vice (and vice versa). The quester cultivates the discipline of doubt, affirms agnosticism as a badge of courage, delights in the darkness, finds freedom in unknowing, seeks dis-illusionment, descends voluntarily into the land of shadows, probes the unconscious, explores the profane, and prefers ordinary to sacramental places.

In summary, the contrast is:

The Religious Life	The Spiritual Quest
In the beginning is the word, the revelation, the known God.	In the beginning is the question, doubt, the Unknown God.
The path of life is well mapped.	The adventure is uncharted.
Chief virtue is obedience to the will of God.	Chief virtue is openness, waiting, listening.
Repeat the sacred ways.	Choose, create, invent.
Religious life centers on sacred objects and places: churches, shrines, texts, sacraments.	Spiritual life centers on profane experience, existential questions, ordinary moments.
Ascent	Descent
Revelation	Awareness
Based on miracle, mystery, authority, a revealed scripture.	Based on searching for evidence of sacred in events of my life.
Institutional, corporate.	Individual, communal.
The Gothic urge to rise above it all.	The incarnational thrust to get to the depth of things.

Every culture, nation, tribe, family casts a spell over individual members. Our identity, our values, our worldviews, and our stories are assigned to us unconsciously by an accident of birth. Our geographical destiny makes us Christians, Muslims, or Buddhists. We are all condemned by birth to be indoctrinated, mystified, and shaped by authorities we did not choose. And each of us must review this personal history to set ourselves free.

It is time to follow the twisted path that wends its way through the mountains of the mind.

DOUBT, DIS-ILLUSIONMENT, AND LOST FAITH

I was baptized into a community of faith, surrounded by Christians who assumed that faith was the single virtue that made hope and charity possible.

Ironically, my parents' strong faith and loving kindness sent me contradictory messages that sent me on a quest that would carry me far from home: "Think for yourself. But believe in the fundamental truths God has revealed in the Bible."

Knowing that I did not have unwavering faith, I often repeated the prayer: "I believe, O God, help Thou my unbelief." But the more I tried to silence my doubts, the louder they became. Just try not to think of a monkey! It was to be years before I discovered that the doubt I despised was a treasure that would enrich me in the absence of faith.

But the more I exercised my will-to-believe, the more doubt gained control over the strongholds of my psyche. With the onset of adolescence, troubling questions began to bloom in my mind like pimples on my still orthodox but troubled face. As my hormones raged, I was flooded with questions about sex. If God was the creator of my body as well as my mind, why shouldn't I follow my urgent impulses? Were my sexual drives, like my doubts, to be repressed? What should a Christian do if he found himself in the back seat of a 1948 Ford with Jane Derickson? Seeking guidance, I tried to imagine Jesus masturbating or making love to Mary Magdalene. But in the same measure that the fantasy aroused me, it made me feel guilty. Since there was no one I could talk to about the spiritual dimensions of erotic acts involved in the exchange of bodily fluids, I postponed radical questioning about sexuality for two decades.

Because I was still trying to fine-tune rather than reject the religion of my childhood and yet had doubts I could not silence, I soon reached a fork in the road where I had to choose between having faith in "revelation" and trusting the integrity of my mind. Why should my doubts and questions upset the faithful? If God created me, did He not also create my mind? And if He created my mind, wouldn't it be irreverent to refuse to question and think clearly?

I decided I would try to resolve my doubts by studying theology, but much to the distress of the elders of the Presbyterian Church, I enrolled at godless Harvard, where as one of my classmates was to say, "We come to study religion, not practice it."

At Harvard I fell under the spell of two giants who showed me how to think with passion and stretched my mind to fit the reach of my spirit — the theologian Paul Tillich and the mystic Howard Thurman.

There were profound differences between Tillich and Thurman. You can write about some thinkers with crisp, declarative sentences. Hemingway, for instance, had a clean, well-lit mind surrounded by paranoid darkness. His masculine ideal of grace under pressure produced a style that has an excess of clarity at the expense of depth. For Tillich one needs more complex syntax, sentences that include *both/and* that counterpose freedom and destiny, faith and doubt, existence and the Christ. His Germanic spirit insisted on ideas marching neatly in columns of two. To speak about Howard Thurman, one needs Byzantine sentences that weave together the priorities of the head and heart, that pause to dip into experience, that stop in the middle to listen to the silence, and that end tentatively with *perhaps* or *maybe*. Thurman's mind was filled with commas, semicolons, long dashes, parentheses, and subordinate clauses — no periods. I remember in particular one sermon in which he reached a tentative conclusion after following an idea down a twisted path to a dead end. Turning back to explore a side path, he paused for a long time and ended with question marks in his voice: "I don't know. I don't know. It may be."

Tillich held us spellbound by two-hour lectures, intellectually tight, footnoting all major philosophers, answering all possible objections. Thurman always began his probes with a baffling contradiction of common experience — a moral paradox, a conflict between duty and desire, the dilemma of suffering. Each session of his course began at 6:30 A.M. in the cool of Marsh Chapel at Boston University. After a time, Howard would begin to read slowly, often from Psalm 139: "Search me, O God, and know my heart . . ." Or we would listen to "Air on a G String" or "Deep River," and we would sit in silence for an hour. Later in the afternoon, we met again and talked about the insights and questions that had come to us. While he had a profound respect for the architecture of thought, Thurman insisted on meditative thinking that was connected to its roots in the feelings, images, and intuitions that spring out of our daily experience.

It was while I was being so tutored by great teachers and excited by the intellectual ferment of Harvard that the shriveled umbilical cord that had bound me to orthodox Christianity fell away. During my second year of graduate studies, I married Heather. Within a year she was converted to Christianity by the kindness and powerful example of my mother. I, needless to say, was ambivalent about her new-found faith, since I was in the process of losing mine and was experiencing the first thrill of thinking with head and heart. At Mother's request, we were invited to have dinner and conversation with Dr. Donald Barnhouse — at the time the most respected intellectual among fundamentalist Christians — who was in Boston to conduct an evangelistic service at Park Street Church. During dinner, I voiced many of my doubts and tried to share some of the ideas I had gleaned from Tillich, only to be informed that "Harvard and its theology has never saved a sinner." Heather, bless her inquiring heart, weighed in with her most agonizing questions, to which Dr. Barnhouse always gave proof-text biblical answers. Finally, with all the sincerity and pain that comes from wanting a secure faith and being unable to silence doubts, Heather asked: "How can you know? How can you be so sure?" Barnhouse replied by appealing to the Bible to prove that the Bible was an authority to which we should submit our wayward minds. With genius born of frustration, Heather then uttered what could well be an epitaph for fundamentalism: "I wish I could be as certain of *anything* as you are of *everything.*" Dr. Barnhouse took this as a compliment. Our dinner ended, and we accompanied him to Park Street Church for the evening meeting.

The sermon, appropriately enough, had to do with the virtues of faith as opposed to the pretensions of the mind. As Dr. Barnhouse built his case against the arrogance of the intellect, he began to mock Heather, reproducing her tone of voice and exact words. "They [intellectuals] say with supposed sincerity: 'How can you know? How can you be certain?' " Heather and I looked at each other in disbelief. I don't remember whether we walked out of the church immediately or waited until the end of the service. I do remember that later, as I held her crying in the darkness, she kept asking, "How could he be so cruel?"

That evening my mind opened wider, and I understood how I had been held by chains of love in a prison that did violence to my mind and spirit. Because I had been raised by gentle and kindly Christians, I had never seen clearly the hidden cruelty implicit in dogmatic religion. Dr. Barnhouse showed me the unloving logic of fundamentalism that allows true believers to love and respect only those neighbors who believe in their version of the revealed Truth. The multitudes who call God by another name, who worship in "strange" ways, are dehumanized by being called "pagans" or "unbelievers." In the name of God, they are consigned to error, to outer darkness and the fires of hell, unless they convert to the true religion.

When I ventured beyond the familiar territory in which I had lived as a child and young man, the first guide who appeared to help me identify the raw phenomenon of the experience of the holy for which I was searching was Rudolf Otto.

In his classic book *The Idea of the Holy*, Otto sets out to resolve the seeming contradictions between various religions. If we concentrate on the exterior — the rituals, creeds, dogmas, and symbols — the world's religions present such diverse claims that no reasonable person could take any of them seriously. Moses, Jesus, Buddha, Confucius, Mohammed, and Lao Tzu all seem to make contradictory claims about God. But if we concentrate on the *experience of the holy*, we find there is near-universal agreement. According to Otto, all encounters with the holy — an Aborigine dreaming in the Australian outback, a Jew at the Wailing Wall in Jerusalem, a Christian having a vision of Christ at the cathedral at Chartres — contain three elements.

The holy is always experienced as a mystery that is at one and the same time awesome-majestic-overpowering and fascinating-promising-desirable.

Let's consider each of the three elements of the experience of the sacred.

MYSTERIOUS BLUE FLOWERS

Several years ago, I was invited to dinner with Willy Unseld, the first American to climb Mount Everest. I had always been interested in mountain climbing and had read the account of the American expedition with rapt attention. Imagine my surprise when I was introduced to Willy Unseld, and his first words to me were, "You are one of my guides." "Why?" I asked. "After the climb," he explained, "I was being carried down from the mountain because I had severely frostbitten toes. We came to a snow-covered promontory that overlooked the vastness of Everest and stopped for a rest. I looked down, and there sticking out of the snow was a single blue flower! To this day I can't describe what happened to me. It was as if some infinite space opened up around the flower, and I stood transfixed, gazing at it. I have no idea how long in clock time I stood there, or how the vastness was both within and around me. Later, when my feet healed, I kept going back to the mountains, trying to recapture this experience that I had no way of naming or understanding. One day somebody gave me your book *Apology for Wonder*, and it helped me to understand what had happened to me. I know now that I will always return to the mountains, no matter what the cost, because that is where I find this kind of experience."

Only the wondering eye sees the sacred horizon enfolded within the petals of a blue flower.

Most often we fail to realize we are in the presence of the holy, either because we are too preoccupied with practical matters or because highfalutin religious language, with its false mystification, seduces us into believing that the holy is revealed only by supernatural and portentous events — virgin births, appearances of choirs of angels, visions of the seven heavens, the resurrection of the dead. Many people conclude that, since they have never seen miracles or heard the voice of God, they have never had a mystical experience. Recently, a friend described for me how a series of seemingly coincidental events — the availability of a sailboat, a perfect wind, a sunset — converged to allow him to scatter his father's ashes in a manner that became a sacred ceremony. He explained: "I would say it was a spiritual experience, but I have always been an engineer, and I don't think engineers can have a spiritual experience."

The paradox of authentic mysticism is that something as ordinary as the first blue flower of spring growing out of the snow, or a serendipitous wind, suddenly opens a vista onto eternity. In the twinkling of an eye our perspective shifts, and we see that *the ordinary is miraculous*. Buddhists speak about this experience as the oscillation between form and emptiness. Any flower, any English sparrow, any field of grass blowing in the wind can suddenly change from being an object in a landscape to an epiphany. One moment the flower is a known example of a classified species, an item we take for granted. Then figure and ground switch, and we are shocked into the realization that everything is radically strange and ultimately beyond our understanding. Why should there be flowers? The fundamental spiritual experience of ontological wonder does not depend on any special "miracle" or revelation.

Understanding that the ordinary *is* the miracle changes our fundamental stance and disposition. Life is no longer a problem to be solved but a mystery in which we may participate fully. It is the experience of the sacredness of everyday reality that allows a man or woman to answer yes to the philosopher Ludwig Wittgenstein's question, "The solution to the problem of life is seen in the disappearance of this problem. But is it possible for one so to love life that life stops being problematic? That one is living in eternity and not in time?"

The word *spirit* refers to the way we perceive the world and the self in the moment when our perspective shifts from observing the blue flower as object and specimen to encountering it as a transparent instance and symbol of Being-becoming-itself. My life is "spiritual" insofar as the rigid boundaries of my identity become porous and transparent to the Being, Energy, God from which and whom all blessings flow.

I confess that I have always longed for a glimpse of the One, but what I come up with time and again is a small revelation contained in some particular. A single forget-me-not, a hawk, a gnarled oak suddenly becomes luminous, weighty, saturated with meaning. (Why is it not sufficient to revel in the Many? Why the impossible drive, the unconscious obsession, to know the One who cannot be known? Strange creatures we humans, longing to see with our eyes that which lies in back of our eyes.)

The God-game is hide-and-seek. He-She-It-They always seems to depart just before I get there, leaving a trace of glory behind, like the track of a mountain lion never seen. Earth is full of footprints; it is the multifleshed incarnation of the *Logos*, the intentionality of God.

An encounter with the holy is mysterious because it shatters our normal habits of thought. It jars our categories of understanding because a starry sky, or the birth of a child, or a text we have heard a hundred times, or a high Mass, becomes transparent to a depth beyond itself. But the medium is only a symbol, a finger that points beyond itself, a container, a metaphor, a momentary incarnation of the mystery that can never be fully grasped or comprehended. An experience of the holy, unlike scientific investigation, does not give us verifiable knowledge about objects or events. It is not about facts but meanings. Spiritual experience has no factoids — no shrouds of Turin, no special miracles, no data unavailable to the skeptic. It is about experiencing the ordinary as miraculous.

TIGERS AND OTHER HOLY TERRORS

Because any perception of the sacred shatters the false security of common sense, it is accompanied by profoundly opposite emotions. The mystery of Being is terrible and fascinating, dreadful and desirable, threatening and comforting.

If we swallow the opiate of popular religion, we easily fall into the sentimental belief that spiritual awareness brings us only faith, hope, love, salvation, comfort, and peace of mind. But awareness of the mysterious dimension of the ordinary is inevitably accompanied by the terrifying awareness that life is ultimately beyond our comprehension and control.

Everything solid melts the moment our perspective changes from commonsense understanding to wonder. We become like the physics professor who was so awed by the vision of the insubstantiality of atoms that he walked around wearing snowshoes so he wouldn't fall into the void between the whirling electrons. Once we see the universe as a never-ending process and ourselves as ever-changing moments within that process, it is difficult to get too excited by the daily fluctuation of the Dow Jones averages. When we touch the no-thing-ness "beneath" all things, we become weak-kneed. We tremble and are struck dumb by the intense awareness of our creatureliness, our absolute dependence, and the contingency of the world.

If we want spirituality without illusion, we must face the fact that the incomprehensible ground of our Being is also a killing ground. Mother Earth is also Kali the Black with her necklace of skulls, and Cronus devours his children.

Ernest Becker, in *The Denial of Death*, presents the vision of the dark side of the Force in its starkest form: "What are we to make of a creation in which the routine activity is for organisms to be tearing others apart with teeth of all types — biting, grinding flesh, plant stalks, bones between molars, pushing the pulp greedily down the gullet with delight, incorporating its essence into one's own organization, and then excreting with foul stench and gasses the residue. . . . Creation is a nightmare spectacular taking place on a planet that has been soaked for hundreds of millions of years in the blood of all its creatures."

The poet William Blake, meditating on the dreadful, amoral power of a tiger, shows us the same terrible face of the holy:

> Tiger! Tiger! burning bright
> In the forests of the night,
> What immortal hand or eye
> Could frame thy fearful symmetry?

In what distant deeps or skies
Burnt the fire of thine eyes?
On what wings dare he aspire?
What the hand dare seize the fire?

And what shoulder, and what art,
Could twist the sinews of thy heart?
And when thy heart began to beat,
What dreadful hand? And what dread feet?

What the hammer? What the chain?
In what furnace was thy brain?
What the anvil? What dread grasp
Dare its deadly terrors clasp?

When the stars threw down their spears,
And watered heaven with their tears,
Did he smile his work to see?
Did he who made the lamb make thee?

Tiger! Tiger! burning bright
In the forests of the night,
What immortal hand or eye
Dare frame thy fearful symmetry?

It is a fearful thing to fall into the hands of the living God.

FASCINATING BLESSINGS AND POSSIBILITIES

No argument can neutralize the corrosive power of the dark vision. Reason cannot manufacture an antidote for the temptation to despair. Philosophers and theologians have labored in vain to explain the cruelty of nature and justify the ways of God to man.

But there is an antiphonal refrain that is both less and more than the voice of reason, that accompanies the cries of panic we hear on the killing ground of life. The dirge and the alleluia chorus reverberate back and forth when we remain true to the full mystery of Being.

In the same measure that we shudder and recoil from the raw, majestic power of Being, we are drawn toward the infinite source of beauty, nurturance, and creativity from which we emerged and which sustains us in life (and possibly in death). Alongside Blake's vision of the terrible tiger, we must place the rhapsody of Saint Francis of Assisi, who called himself a brother to the wolf.

> All creatures of our God and King,
> Lift up your voice and with us sing
> Alleluia, Alleluia
> Thou burning sun with golden beam
> Thou silver moon with softer gleam,
> Oh, praise Him! Oh, praise Him!
> Alleluia, Alleluia.
>
> Thou flowing water, pure and clear,
> Make music for thy Lord to hear. . . .
> Thou fire so masterful and bright,
> That givest man both warmth and light. . . .
>
> Dear mother earth, who day by day
> Unfoldest blessings on our way
> The flowers and fruits that in thee grow
> Let them His glory also show. . . .
>
> Oh, praise Him! Oh, praise Him! . . .
> Alleluia, Alleluia.

In all encounters with the holy there is a promise of comfort, fulfillment, harmony, and love that fascinates, en-courages, and calls us to trust in the ultimate benevolence of Being in spite of appearances to the contrary. But the echo of dread and breathless panic can always be heard in the background of the hymns of the spirit. It was precisely in the valley of the shadow of death that the fascinated psalmist was able to proclaim that "the Lord is my shepherd." It was in the midst of their afflictions that Black slaves could sing, "There is a balm in Gilead, to make the wounded whole." It is when all the careless power of the universe tempts us to despair that we touch the vernal impulse at the heart of Being that opens our hearts and minds to possibilities that transcend our immediate experience of the possible. And then we may wonder: Perhaps, there is something deathless at the heart of my Being; perhaps tragedy, although real, is not ultimate; perhaps the alienation, the sin, the brokenness of the human condition can be healed; perhaps I am not alone in a careless multiverse.

The fascinating dimension of the experience of the holy has often been expressed by the use of erotic language and sexual metaphors. From the Song of Songs to the poetry of Rumi, the relation of the soul to God has been likened to sexual intercourse between lovers. Looking carefully at the face on Bernini's famous statue of Saint Theresa, it is impossible to tell whether the ecstasy is spiritual or sexual. All of the kindly metaphors of religion, the promise of succor, mercy, grace, refuge, abiding in the everlasting arms, spring from the primitive feeling of being drawn toward the inconceivable source from whom all blessings flow.

SACRED CONCERNS

Mircea Eliade and Paul Tillich are spiritual explorers who have suggested some notions that will be useful as we try to distinguish between hopeful and disastrous paths, creative and demonic ways of surrendering our autonomous egos to something larger and more enduring than ourselves.

Eliade gathered evidence from a wide variety of cultures and showed in *The Sacred and the Profane* that an experience of the sacred creates a special way of organizing life. To illustrate, he cited the practice of Australian Aborigines who carry with them a ritual world-pole, a symbolic way of proclaiming that no matter where they are, they live at the center of the world. All life is organized around the sacred. We can see the same thing clearly in medieval European cities. The Gothic cathedral, the sacred space that housed the symbols of the sacred, stood at the center of the city. All life was organized in relationship to this pivotal point.

Whatever we consider of central importance, whatever provides the organizing principle for our life, we experience as holy. This functional definition allows us to understand that we may misidentify the holy. We may easily create idols by becoming ultimately concerned, placing our faith in, and giving our life-commitment to, a person, a cause, or an institution that should receive only our tentative loyalty. For instance: Paul Tillich showed how the Nazi movement in Germany took on all the characteristics of a religion. It demanded ultimate loyalty; it promised complete fulfillment; it created quasi-religious rituals and ceremonies; it produced transcendent experiences for its followers; it elaborated a complete worldview and apocalyptic program. Nothing centralizes and organizes life more stringently or produces quasi-religious experiences more easily than fanaticism and idolatry. Arthur Koestler's brilliant portrait of a true believer in *Darkness at Noon* showed the great surrender of ego and mind that was involved in making a complete commitment to Communism.

Tillich's translation of the pivotal experience of the holy into psychological categories gives us a benchmark we can use to discern when our commitments cease to be creative and become demonic, when the good destroys the best. When, for instance, does the pursuit of money stop being a means to enable us to live in a whole-some way and become an end in itself — worship of the Almighty Dollar? When does the effort to be the best figure-skater in the world become a destructive obsession? When does a drive for personal growth destroy a marriage, a home, and weaken the community? When does a commitment to a church or cult destroy the ability to welcome truths from wherever they arrive?

Considering our capacity for misplaced loyalty to demonic causes and institutions, it is essential that we pause frequently throughout our lives to take a critical look at our values, our priorities, and our commitments and consider whether we are moving in a direction that promises fulfillment or disaster.

Armed with working definitions, some rules of thumb about how to recognize an inspired or dis-spirited life, and a description of the experience of the holy, you are well prepared to look with new eyes at the uncharted territory of your life.

As you re-collect and re-member pivotal events and peak experiences, you will discover that sometimes you have been on a path that took you in the wrong direction, deep into a dis-spirited place. You may discover that you encountered the holy in religious settings, or at moments of crisis when you became aware of the awesome mystery of your freedom. Or you may find it was present when you were changed in the twinkling of an eye by love, or when you danced in unison with a congregation of thousands at a Grateful Dead concert, or when a meadowlark cut loose with a cosmic chorus.

CHAPTER 6

The Path Through the Mindscape

"God be in my head, And in my understanding;
God be in mine eyes, And in my looking;
God be in my mouth, And in my speaking;
God be in my heart, And in my thinking."

The Hymnbook, no. 395

"O the mind, mind has mountains; cliffs of fall
Frightful, sheer, no-man fathomed. Hold them cheap
May who ne'er hung there. . . ."

GERARD MANLEY HOPKINS

"I think in order to recover what I already know, to re-collect my essence, to savor the promise that has been unfolding since my birth, to see my cosmic face in the mirror of my mind."

SANDOR MCNAB

"A Soul met an angel and asked of Him: 'By which path shall I reach heaven quickest — the path of knowledge or the path of love?' The angel looked at him wonderingly and said: 'Are not both paths one?' "

OLIVE SCHREINER

THE HEROIC QUEST FOR CONSENSUS

We have already made a few exploratory hikes to reconnoiter the paths beyond base camp. Thus far, we have gathered questions that will guide us, proposed a method for our quest, made some preliminary definitions of that for which we are searching, examined the maps of the sacred drawn by some great explorers, noted a few landmarks we can trust to guide us, and constructed a makeshift compass that will tell us whether we are approaching or moving away from our objective. Those of us who have made our way to the base camp are a solitary lot, rugged individuals who have forsaken conformity and security in order to escape our dis-ease and follow our unique callings.

As we prepare to set off into the trackless country that surrounds the valley, we must proceed as a group. *From this point forward, the heroic journey is no longer a solo adventure but a communal undertaking.* The dangers we will encounter are unpredictable and varied. There may be swamps, quicksand, impenetrable rain forests, glaciers, ice falls, sudden storms, avalanches, paths that dead-end at the base of unclimbable cliffs. Should we make our way into the higher altitudes, some of us will begin to have bizarre visions and hallucinations (the equivalent of the rapture of the deep, from which divers suffer when they remain too long below two hundred feet).

Those who would attempt the ascent of literal or metaphoric mountains should be forewarned. "The extreme conditions encountered on mountains — wind, clouds, fatigue and altitude — predispose climbers to having visions or to seeing unusual phenomena in a visionary light. . . . High on Mt. Everest, his mind wandering from the effects of extreme altitude and fatigue, Frank Smythe had the distinct impression that someone else, a 'third man,' had joined him on his climbing rope. The feeling was so real that at one point he even turned to offer his mysterious companion something to eat. . . . Reinhold Messner . . . had this vision high on Kangchenjunga: In the last camp near the summit, I had a very strange vision of all the human parts I am made of . . . I could see a round picture with many pictures inside — not only of my body, but of my whole being . . . like seeing my life and my body and my soul and my feelings inside a mandala. But I was not even sure if it was only mine or generally human, yours or anybody's. . . . It was very, very strange."[1]

The idea that the heroic journey must be taken by a solitary individual fits neatly into the modern ideology of individualism. But it is a very dangerous half-truth that applies only to the first phase of the spiritual journey in which we explore the illusions of the psyche and our autobiographical truth. Those who try to go it alone end up isolated, alienated, and prey to all forms of madness. Every week, I receive a letter from some lost soul who is convinced that he or she has discovered the Secret Key. Usually, the letter contains an elaborate diagram of the System that explains how the hidden meaning of everything is revealed by adding certain numbers or dividing certain words. On occasion, you can see full-page advertisements in *The New York Times* for grand schemes to save the world and bring universal peace through a macrobiotic diet, transcendental meditation, or doing away with the IRS and the Trilateral Commission. As a general rule, the systems created by solitary individuals are not only idiosyncratic but paranoid.

From here on, the only way we can avoid the dangers and illusions to which solo climbers are susceptible is to rope up, stay in communication with each other, search for consensus, and reflect on our common experience. The lifeline that protects individuals from falling into the abyss of solitary madness or sinking into the quicksands of the shared folly is reason. And reason is nothing more or less than the commonly accepted rules of clear thinking that have emerged from the consensus of the widest and most inclusive community of men and women over the ages.

Some travelers who have come this far will grumble when they hear that our itinerary calls for us to proceed along the path of reason. They will complain: "I'm tired of head trips and mind games. I want to go directly to the path with heart. Thinking is a drag. No amount of analysis is going to bring me peace and contentment. Why don't we begin with prayer, or rituals, or chants, or acts of devotion? I want to be done with complexity, ambiguity and doubt, and take a leap of faith, commit myself, surrender."

There is no way we can or should prohibit individuals from pursuing their solo quests. But we are obliged to warn them that those who cut themselves off from the feedback and discipline of consensus are in constant danger of falling into spiritual narcissism and losing the link to the community of human experience that is necessary to create a compassionate mind and heart. Their failure to submit their beliefs to the court of universal experience condemns them to solitary confinement.

Somewhere along the way, each of us must make our leap of faith. When that time comes, our best hope for a safe landing is the rope that joins us to our fellow travelers.

The first requirement for a modern spiritual practice is to create a clearheaded theory of what it means to live within a sacred cosmos. We have no more urgent priority than to reunite intelligence with the experience of the sacred so that we may think about our political, economic, ecological, and psychological problems with inspired minds. Currently, we are in the middle of an epidemic of thoughtlessness, a resurgence of religious fundamentalism that has defined "faith" as the property of religious institutions, and a mindless march of abstract intelligence on a drunken binge that produces progress at the cost of destroying the environment. Humankind is suffering from a tragic divorce of reason and faith, from dis-spirited thinking. A spiritual lobotomy is not going to cure us of the consequences of blind faith and thoughtless action. To find our way through the thicket, we need the courage to think carefully, to reexamine our beliefs, to know on what they are founded. My own rules of reason follow the next brief section, which recounts how I came to terms with the absence of authority.

MY CONVERSION TO PHILOSOPHY

My disillusionment with my parents' religion left me with a void, an urgent need for some worldview and life-map to replace the shattered "faith of my fathers." As it turned out, the gift that has marked my life was the result of the wound—the loss of my original certainty. My disenchantment with Christianity was simultaneously a *conversion to philosophy*.

The moment I abandoned the effort to hold back the tide of doubts that were washing away the sand castles of my childhood faith, I dived gleefully into an ocean of questions. Like Renee, the protagonist of Rebecca Goldstein's novel *The Mind-Body Problem*, I stepped from one worldview into its mirror-image opposite. And I felt, as she did, that "My moral weakness became my moral strength, the barrenness of my belief was in truth the fertility of my rationality, and I was saved at last. . . . Can you imagine what it was like to turn from the spirit of religion to the spirit of philosophy, or, as I liked to call it in those days, the spirit of rationality? For here, reasons for beliefs are never beside the point but are the entire substance of the matter. The distinction between the mere belief and the reasoned belief is the distinction that grounds all philosophy. If truth is our end (and what else should be?) we must reason our way there."[2]

Freed from the struggle to believe what I found unbelievable, I began to explore many new paths. But like a child once burned, I was determined not to fall into overbelief. I wanted an intellectually responsible belief-system, not blind faith. If I were to commit myself, I wanted it to be with mind and heart. I vowed not to fall again into religious illusion.

My first plunge into the major world religions—Hinduism, Islam, Buddhism, Taoism—and the study of anthropology presented me with a baffling variety of gods, goddesses, angels, demons, and spirits—and a new set of questions. Do the competing visions of God invalidate each other? Since they cannot all be true, are they all false? Is there an evolution of religion from primitive polytheism to monotheism in which we might discover an unfolding revelation of the nature and will of God? Or were the radical critics of religion like Feuerbach and Freud right when they said that all gods are dreams, illusions, imaginative projections conjured up from our fear and our desperate need to believe that some fatherlike or motherlike being watches over us? Is religion only a prescientific effort to explain the universe that must be abandoned by anyone who is committed to think clearly about the nature and origins of the Earth? To be honest, did I have to return the wintry smile on the face of truth and embrace the sterile world of secular humanism?

As a graduate student at Harvard and Princeton and later as a professor of philosophy and Christian faith at Louisville Presbyterian Seminary, I wrestled with the question of how worldviews and religious visions can be tested, validated, or invalidated. I became fascinated with the first of what Immanuel Kant said were the three great questions of philosophy: "What can we know?" (The other two are, "What ought we to do?" and "For what may we hope?") I also continued to ask, "Can we know God, the sacred, the holy? If so, how?"

In the 1950s and 1960s the dominant mood in philosophy was set by A. J. Ayer, who decapitated all traditional theology with a single blow. In *Language, Truth and Logic*, Ayer maintained that the meaning of a proposition can be tested by its method of verification. If we want to know if there are mountains on the dark side of the moon or if God is omnipotent, we must find out how to go about verifying the truth of each statement. We might, for instance, send a satellite probe around the moon to verify or falsify the claim about the existence of the mountains. But how could we possibly verify the claim that God is omnipotent? There is no place outside the totality of reality or beyond the shoulder of God where we could conceivably stand to judge whether God is or is not omnipotent. Therefore, says Ayer, statements about God are neither true nor false but meaningless. They appear to make a claim about a reality out there—God—but they are really covert statements about our feelings. To say, "The Earth is the Lord's and all they that dwell therein," is like saying, "Every cloud has a silver lining." Theology, like poetry, only tells us how we feel or what we wish. It does not give us knowledge. Religion may be useful as a glue to keep society together; it may comfort us amid the frightful darkness of our days. But according to Ayer, we have no reason for thinking it is true.

My intellectual quest for a reasonable approach to matters of faith led me to Ludwig Wittgenstein. In his earlier years, Wittgenstein was one of the architects of an overly restrictive, scientist view of knowledge, verification, and language. Later in life he decided that there are different language games, methods of verification, and criteria for evidence. Religious statements, such as "In the beginning God created . . ." and "The Lord is my shepherd, I shall not want," are not isolated truth claims that can be checked by using the same method of empirical verification as science. They are part of an intricate web of metaphors, symbols, liturgies, hero stories, gestures, songs, dances, ethical demands, prophetic challenges, and promises of comfort that forms a perceptual screen through which we see the world. When we look at the world through religious glasses, we see everything in a different light from when we look through scientific glasses. When I affirm, "The Earth is the Lord's," I experience myself as a creature of God rather than as an accidental product of a happenstance process.

All worldviews, mythologies, and ideologies, whether they are religious, secular, or spiritual, are perceptual screens through which we filter our experience. They are handles that allow us to grasp and manipulate the baffling complexity of our world. None of them can finally be verified or falsified.

Imagine that three persons are standing in an old-growth forest of redwoods. The lumber contractor with a purely secular mentality sees only the economic possibilities — board-feet of redwood, jobs, and profit. The biologist with a scientific orientation sees the long evolutionary history of the interaction between the tree and its environment that has produced the intricate ecosystem of the forest. The person approaching the forest with religious or spiritual sensibilities experiences the redwoods as part of a created world. No one of these three worldviews is true or false. Each is a way of viewing things that involves a different response. The lumber contractor is galvanized into action to secure timber rights and "harvest" the forest. The scientist probes the depth of soil, measures the accumulation of humus, factors in data about climate variations, and produces a natural history of the forest. The religious or spiritual person typically is awestruck, reduced to a reverential silence by the numinous power of the towering trees, and feels gratitude for their beauty.

Taking some leap of faith is an inevitable part of the human condition. In a sense, each person's existential situation is like a courtroom in which the world is on trial. Faced with chaos, we are forced to search for evidence that we live in a cosmos. Is there a hidden order beneath surface disorder? Does God play dice with the universe? Faced with tragedy, evil, and death, each of us must ask whether there are grounds for hope. The mind is the prosecuting attorney, the defense attorney, the jury, and the judge. Any belief-system must make its case before the court of reason and present evidence to support its truth claims. While we can never offer certain proof for the absolute truth of a worldview and philosophy of life, we can establish that it satisfies or fails to satisfy the minimal requirements of reason.

For me, the discovery that no worldview can be proved was a relief. Finally I could abandon the impossible task of constructing an airtight belief-system and get down to the possible task of formulating a reasonable philosophy of life.

Even though we are in a universe that does not satisfy our need for certainty and that sometimes seems absurd and chaotic beyond measure, we can and must collect *evidence* for the reasonableness or unreasonableness of our belief-system. The alternative is folly — and not the fun kind.

Nothing reflects our dilemma so clearly as the emergence of television as a major determining event in our lives. Today we exist in a media-created environment in which we are besieged by competing truth claims. It is as if we were locked in a room with a hundred secular evangelists shouting at us, bombarding us with images of the good life, promises of salvation through free trade, full employment, and universal health care. Year by year, we grow more cynical because we know that our opinions are manipulated by sound bites and attractive images. What can we believe? How are we to decide what to believe, and on what basis?

In the course of my trek, as I have tried to make sense of what I see, hear, and feel, I have accumulated a number of rules of thumb that protect me from intellectual foolishness and that help me mold my experience into a reasonable philosophy of life. I think of these not as dry rules of reason but as a kit that contains both destructive and constructive tools — a file, hacksaw, and cutting torch to free me from belief-systems that threaten to constrict and imprison my spirit; a hammer, saw, and plane to fashion the raw material of my experience into a dwelling.

COMMON GUIDELINES: THE RULES OF REASON

Think as an Existing Individual, with Heart, Mind, and Spirit, Not as an "Objective" Intellectual or Professor.

The existentialist philosophers were my first heroes of the journey through the mindscape — Kierkegaard, Nietzsche, Dostoyevsky,

Camus, Sartre, and Marcel. They gave me the clue to the nature of a passionate mind: You have to think as *somebody*, not as anybody or nobody. I am embodied in a specific historical time and situation, born into a certain family, informed by idiosyncratic experiences. I must think as that singular man who wrestles with the problems, gifts, and wounds with which his life has presented him.

Question Authority.

The path to personal freedom involves two long and terrifying steps across the void. Step one: Question authority. Step two: Overthrow authority.

Church, cult, and state easily imprison believers within a self-sealing system of self-defined authority. Much as they would hate to be included within the same congregation, well-scrubbed Roman Catholics, plain-vanilla Southern Baptists, and Presbyterians are no less captivated by a circular logic than are the followers of the Ayatollah or Guru XYZ. All authorities claim: We are the repository and guardians of the Truth; therefore we are the Authority. If you question Authority — Truth (Us) — it is evidence that your mind is clouded, your faith is weak, and you stand in Error.

To question the authority of pope, bible, synod, guru, or party, a believer must leave the security of the group-mind, venture out onto the quaking ground of personal doubt, and issue this declaration of independence: Henceforth my experience of life will be the jury, my mind and heart the judges, that will determine what is true and sacred. I am the author and the authority in my own life.

The nature of our life-journey will be shaped by whether we take these two decisive steps. Many pastors, priests, and true believers are tortured by doubts but refuse to take the radical step and sever the umbilical cord to exterior authority. I have a friend who was for years a disciple of Bhagwan Rajneesh. Every year he would come to visit and proclaim that the guru was freeing his mind. All the while he was wearing the red and orange uniform and making apologies for Rajneesh's habit of collecting Rolls-Royces and for the bizarre goings-on at the cult headquarters in Antelope, Oregon, that included plots to murder disloyal disciples. In like fashion, the majority of Roman Catholics in the United States recognize the moral imperative to control population growth and use birth control, but they refuse openly to question the authority of the church.

To my mind, a kind of mild-to-severe schizophrenia results from trying to keep one foot in and one foot out of an authoritarian church or belief-system. A person, like a nation, cannot long exist half-slave and half-free. If we nibble at the fruit of the tree of knowledge but still cling to the security of Authority, we are caught in the impossible position of trying to take a journey and stay home at the same time.

Gather and Evaluate Evidence.

Perhaps miraculous healings take place at Lourdes; perhaps Allah is calling for a holy war; perhaps Sai Baba materialized diamonds from thin air; perhaps Jesus is the son of God. But to be intellectually responsible, we need to investigate and evaluate the evidence for such religious claims. Obviously, this task is not as easy as gathering the evidence for claims for stock-market offerings or hypotheses in the natural sciences. Nevertheless, it is always appropriate to ask: "How do you know?" "What is the evidence?" and "How would I go about establishing the truth or falsity or the reasonableness or unreasonableness of this?"

Subject All Hearsay Evidence to Cross-examination.

No authority, no revered tradition, no unquestionable revelation has any automatic standing in the court of reason. The utterances of Moses, Buddha, Jesus, or Mohammed, no less than the religious claims of Swedenborg, Sun Myung Moon, David Koresh, or the Pope — and the pronouncements of political leaders — must be tested against the minimum standards of reasonableness. All truth claims are subject to the same rules of evidence. We need to be vigilant, remembering that sincere believers can be mistaken. History is full of disastrous examples of blind faith, overbelief, and gullibility; it is littered with gods who have failed. Followers of Christ and Communism and Capitalism alike have conducted cruel crusades, and blood is a poor argument for truth. That billions of people have believed in reincarnation or in the resurrection of Jesus or in witchcraft does not exempt these beliefs from the requirement of producing evidence for their validity.

Be Internally Consistent.

The minimum requirement for any belief-system is that it be internally consistent. An inconsistent system is an oxymoron, a contradiction in terms. Self-contradiction, like the sound of metal grinding against metal in an engine, is a symptom of an impending breakdown. It is, for instance, inconsistent to claim that (1) God is love; (2) we, being created in the image of God, must love our neighbors as ourselves; and (3) God orders his chosen people to slaughter the inhabitants of the Holy Land. (Blessed shall you be when you dash their little ones' heads against stones.) Only by betraying intellectual responsibility can anyone believe all three of these statements, even if all of them are contained within the "revealed" text of the Bible. When we insist on believing contradictory assertions, we settle into a condition of spiritual schizophrenia in which faith and reason live in exile from each other.

I came upon a humorous instance of inconsistency early in my teaching career. Several young professors and I found out, after we had arrived at Louisville Presbyterian Seminary, that faculty members were expected to sign a pledge to refrain from alcohol. We refused, and the rebellion of the Young Turks began. During long faculty meetings in which the issue was debated, the New Testament professor, Dr. Love, argued that grapes are a gift from God but fermentation turns them into ungodly wine. During the supper break in our final meeting, we were standing in line at the salad counter of the cafeteria. I asked casually and as innocent as a viper, "Dr. Love, do you like blue cheese dressing on your salad?" "Yes," he replied. "It's fermented," I said. After midnight, the meeting ended with a victory for the forces of consistency and several of us adjourned to a nearby public house to enjoy blue cheese and the fruit of the vine.

To witness the emotional and moral consequences of a more serious failure to practice the intellectual virtue of consistency, visit a site where "pro-life" and "pro-choice" advocates are confronting each other over the issue of abortion. Each side maintains that it is motivated by reverence for life. But by a strange twist in logic, each side maintains its self-righteousness through a failure to be consistent. Most pro-life advocates are in favor of the death penalty, and most pro-choice advocates are against it. Those who favor abortion protect themselves from awareness of their inconsistency by insisting that the fetus is not a life to be reverenced, while those who favor the death penalty insist that the criminal is not a life to be reverenced. The result: sustained conflict.

Check to See If Your Core Beliefs Are Consistent with Known Facts.

Reasonable metaphysical speculation must conform to the same rule of external consistency that governs theoretical physics. As stated by the physicist Richard Feynman, "The essence of the scientific imagination was a powerful and almost painful rule. What scientists create must match reality. It must match what is already known. Scientific creativity is imagination in a straitjacket. . . . Whatever we are allowed to imagine in science must be consistent with everything else we know."[3] Metaphysics and theology must necessarily have a speculative and imaginative element, but everything they posit must be consistent with what we know. We can believe in supposed miracles that violate known laws of nature only if we are willing to suspend all critical judgment. We know enough about water to know that men do not walk on it, and we know enough about virgins to know they do not give birth. However, although we do not understand the mechanisms involved, we also know that spontaneous remissions of cancer occur, that poisonous snakes can sometimes be handled safely, and that there are instances of clairvoyance and ESP.

Strive for Coherence.

A reasonable belief-system must strive for coherence. Beyond the minimal requirement that it not be self-contradictory, a belief-system needs to hang together and present a unifying picture of the seen and unseen world. Human rationality is a process of creating a narrative from a chaotic mass of facts. Reason aims at connecting a bewildering variety of dots into a single picture, molding a diverse experience into a single story.

At the moment, a radical pluralism traveling under the label "the postmodern mind" is in fashion in intellectual circles. The feeling is abroad that nothing adds up, that there is only randomness. The contemporary style in the arts, in morality, and in politics is to abandon the traditional search for coherence and settle for making collages. Life has become MTV — one image, one experience placed alongside another without any connection. All dots and no connecting lines.

Anyone seeking wisdom is well advised to be skeptical about the latest styles. In intellectual life as in ladies' clothes, there are regular swings in fashion. Hemlines go up and down. In one decade we strive toward synthesis; in the next we deconstruct that synthesis. First, we make one big picture out of little bits of data; then we smash the picture and examine the component parts. Currently, empires are disintegrating, syntheses are coming apart, walls are tumbling down, and diversity, chaos and the rights of ethnic minorities are the news of the day. Day after tomorrow, new ordering principles, empires, and unifying stories will emerge.

In *The Sentiment of Rationality*, William James identified this rhythm as inherent in the nature of mind itself. To think is to try to bring order into diversity and vice versa. Too little order, and we have schizophrenia; too much, and we have tyranny. Madness comes in opposite varieties — incoherence and supercoherence. The ravings of an alcoholic with delirium tremens are a spewing-forth of unconnected sentences that don't add up. By contrast, the conspiracy theories of a paranoid are airtight. Rationality is the mind breathing in and out, constructing parts into wholes, then taking apart the whole into its components.

The inspired mind, like God, is always in the process of creating order out of chaos. Being partial and frail, humankind can never entirely see life steady and whole. But we lose something essentially human if we cease aspiring to center and unify our experience into a single vision. Classical Greek thinkers, religious apologists, and philosophers of science agree on little else except that the human mind is able to discern the rationality and order that runs through things. The microcosm is part of the macrocosm, the human *logos* grasps the divine *Logos*, the holographic mind reflects the holographic universe. Mind is stretched to its limits only when it strives to achieve coherence.

Strive for Completeness.

Completeness, like coherence, is both a necessary and an impossible requirement of thought. No one can possibly embrace the totality of knowledge, but a reasonable worldview cannot ignore entire domains of knowledge or experience. At the moment we are in deep trouble because the technological-economic paradigm ignores the ecological evidence that the Earth has limited natural resources and carrying capacity.

A worldview needs to address itself to the great mythic questions that are perennial because they reflect the struggle to come to terms with unavoidable elements in the human condition — birth, sexuality, politics, haunting beauty, heartbreaking evil, decisions, work, suffering, tragedy, and death.

The failure to strive for completeness is probably the most common failing in the thinking of all individuals and organizations. Something like tunnel vision seems to affect our thought processes. We focus our eyes on one small truth so hypnotically that we neglect all other truths. Like horses hitched to a wagon, we plod forward, seeing only the narrow swath of reality that is within the field of vision permitted by our blinders. As the German philosopher Goethe said, "Most sects are right in what they affirm and wrong in what they deny."

The result of thinking with blinders on is a very lopsided life. We become true believers rather than explorers, propagandists rather than philosophers, fanatics rather than lovers.

Many New Age spiritual groups so overfocus on willpower, on creating our own reality, on total responsibility and absolute freedom, that they become blind to the tragic destiny that condemns a labor organizer in El Salvador to be killed by a death squad, or a child born with AIDS to die at an early age.

At the opposite extreme, we are increasingly subscribing to a social philosophy that denies freedom and individual responsibility. The rush to claim victimhood is becoming an epidemic. Criminal behavior is forgiven because experts explain that deviant behavior is caused by hidden social and psychological forces. We are victims of family, gender, class, economics, or hormones. PMS, post-traumatic stress syndrome, or hypoglycemia induced by eating too many Twinkies becomes the cause and excuse for murder. Anything that can be named a syndrome creates a new class of victims.

Prefer Simplicity.

Other things being equal, reason strives for the simplest explanation. In metaphysics as in physical science, the most beautiful and elegant explanation is the simplest. Occam's razor — Don't multiply entities or explanatory principles beyond what is necessary — helps us to avoid overbelief. The traditional pantheon of demons, angels, witches, and ghosts; the sorcerers with whose antics Carlos Castenada filled the heads of a generation; and books like *Rosemary's Baby* seem more appropriate subjects for fantasy films than for serious spiritual consideration. Authentic mysteries are everywhere; we need not create occult entities. The manufacture of supernatural miracles is growing in direct proportion to the decline in the sense of wonder. An actual wolverine is far more miraculous than a nonexistent werewolf. The benevolence of good men and women is far more astonishing than dreams of angels.

For some people, there seems to be no end to the search for occult explanations. No amount of evidence will ever convince a true conspiracy buff that Lee Harvey Oswald killed President Kennedy, or that a small congregation of bankers is not controlling the United States government. If all else fails, we should conclude that sometimes things *are* what they appear to be. A rose is a rose is a rose. Even Freud, who had a taste for elaborate theories of dream interpretation, said that sometimes a cigar is just a cigar.

Respect Complexity.

Seemingly, this rule contradicts the previous one. But the virtue of simplicity rapidly turns into the vice of oversimplifying when we try to homogenize complex phenomena.

Sometimes clear thinking requires using the knife — either/or. At other times it requires us to arrange a complex marriage between both/

and. An apparent contradiction may be a fundamental paradox that cannot be dissolved by thought. For instance, quantum physicists can begin to understand the strange way light behaves only by dealing with it as if it were both wave and particle. When we are dealing with the human psyche, we can assume that only the contradictions are true. Because we contain an amalgam of conscious and unconscious motives, our feelings toward others are ambivalent, a complex compound of love and hate, desire and fear. Likewise, each person's freedom and destiny are so intertwined, it takes a lifetime to discover what is within our power and what is not.

Engage in Deliberation, Dialogue, Conversation.

An inspired life requires a community of dialogue and conversation because the treasure is always in earthen vessels. All encounters with the holy are mediated through the distorted medium of some local culture — Christian, Jewish, Muslim, Hindu, or Hopi. The perspective of every believer is biased. The only way to protect ourselves against the idolatry that creeps into culture-bound religion is to solicit the perspective of the wider community. Conversation creates community and compassion. Monologue creates dissension and fanaticism.

Reason is the name we give to the consensus that emerges from the conversation between persons and communities of widely divergent life-experiences. To the degree that reason has any influence on the conduct of life, it represents the triumph of a human community formed by a million individual conversations between people of different faiths and belief-systems. It is also unspoken testimony to the faith that we can figure out the rationale of things together better than we can individually.

Spiritual discrimination, like reason itself, grows out of dialogue. Wilhelm Pauck, the Reformation scholar, used to say, "Luther believed that something happened in gab. The word, talk, dialogue are important." It is only by talking about the things that matter most that an individual and a community develop wisdom. When we trust our neighbors and friends enough to speak about the mysteries, we learn to distinguish between responsible belief and credulity, between faith and fanaticism. Authentic faith always seeks a dialogue with reason because the knowledge of the heart and the head must be in harmony, or the psyche will remain dis-eased.

Submit Your Beliefs to the Test of Moral Action and the Requirement of Compassion.

Once the formal requirements of reason have been satisfied, the ultimate test of a religion or spirituality is the kind of life it produces. "By their fruits you shall know them." William James said that it is easy to produce religious experiences but hard to produce religious lives. The mark of an authentic faith is whether it inspires an ongoing effort toward the moral transformation of the self and a habit of care-ful social action. An authentic spiritual quest should lead to joy and compassion. As the hymn says: "Take from our lives the strain and stress, / and let our ordered lives confess, / the beauty of Thy peace."

At the heart of every spiritual tradition is the realization that only those who are willing to *do the truth* are undergirded by trust in the unknown God and achieve that "peace that passes understanding." *In the realm of the spirit, revelation is inseparable from action.* I know of nowhere this principle is expressed more poignantly than in the concluding passage of *The Quest for the Historical Jesus*, where Albert Schweitzer says of Jesus: "He comes to us as One unknown, without a name, as of old, by the lake-side. He came to those men who knew Him not. He speaks to us the same word: 'Follow thou me!' and sets us to the tasks which He has to fulfill for our time. He commands. And to those who obey Him, whether they be wise or simple, He will reveal Himself in the toils, the conflicts, the sufferings which they shall pass through in His fellowship, and, as an ineffable mystery, they shall learn in their own experience Who He is." For Schweitzer, who was already a famous biblical scholar, expert on Bach, and organist, the ineffable mystery of Jesus only became clear when he committed himself to the life of a medical missionary in Africa.

Hold Your Beliefs in an Open, Flexible, and Light-Hearted Manner.

The protagonist of Norman Rush's novel *Mating* suggests two interesting ways we can check our belief-systems. He says: "I am not an enemy of any system per se. I collect systems. I am an agnostic about systems, but I love them. What I say is we should ask the same questions of any system we consider. What are its fruits? . . . How much compulsion is required to keep it working?"

The test of "how much compulsion is required to keep it working" is an interesting guideline for belief-systems. Airtight ideologies have a way of turning into tyrannical political systems. As a worldview and philosophy of life, Communism satisfied many of the theoretical requirements of reason, but it became morally corrupt since a compulsive output of propaganda, double-think, force of arms, and political repression became necessary to keep it afloat. By contrast, Tibetan Buddhism, as exemplified in the life and teachings of the Dalai Lama, involves a rigorous ordering of every detail of life and constant attention to the quest for enlightenment, but it seems to produce a high degree of compassionate action. The more completely a worldview and life-map structures time and directs our energies, the greater certainty it offers. But any system that we must serve in a compulsive manner destroys wonder, imagination, and freedom.

CONSTRUCTING A SPIRITUAL BULLSHIT DETECTOR

Circumstances led me to go beyond assembling a tool kit for assessing the reasonableness of belief-systems to construct what I like to call my spiritual bullshit detector, a series of caution signs to help guard against overbelief, irrational and destructive worldviews, and idolatrous commitments.

In 1969, I was given a sabbatical and left the academic world where classical questions were debated in a decent and orderly manner. I packed up the family and went to California to study the human potential movement, where I became engulfed in intoxicating madness and creative ferment. I went to encounter groups where "head tripping" was not allowed and strangers demanded to know what I was *feeling* right then and there. Fritz Perls, the master of Gestalt therapy, challenged me to give up remembering and anticipating and to live in the here and now, to lose my mind and come to my senses. I submitted my body to Alexander Lowen and Stanley Keleman, bioenergetic therapists who urged me to allow the flow of sensual-sexual energy to charge my body with vital feeling. Ida Rolf manipulated and realigned my muscles and softened my character armor till I stood tall and loose and breathed deep. I hung around the edges of a New Left group of revolutionaries who were, any day, going to bring down "the establishment" and usher in the Age of Aquarius and the politics of love. I sampled some of the minor psychedelics. I inhaled. I frequented the infamous but innocent hot baths at Esalen. I surfed and ran on the beach and paid far too little attention to my children.

Before the end of the whirlwind year, I knew I could not return to my old manner of life. One morning in May, I called and offered my resignation from Louisville Presbyterian Seminary. Graciously and wisely, the faculty accepted. In a single moment I ceased to be a full professor with tenure and lifetime economic security and became a free spirit on an uncharted path with a family and no visible source of income. I was frightened and elated.

As it turned out, my transition from academic to freelance philosopher was relatively easy. At the time, I was living in Del Mar, which, serendipitously, was where the fledgling magazine *Psychology Today* was located. One day I received a call from the editor, T. George Harris, who asked: "Could you possibly hurry up to Santa Cruz and try to complete a conversation with Norman O. Brown that's bogged down for the magazine?" I could and did, and without noticing I made a segue into journalism. For the next twenty years I did many feature conversations with some of the seminal thinkers of the time: Herbert Marcuse, Joseph Campbell, John Lilly, Carlos Castenada, Stanley Keleman, Ernest Becker, Roberto Assagioli, Ivan Illich, Robert Bellah, Elisabeth Kübler-Ross, Michael Murphy, Rollo May, and Susan Griffin. I investigated and wrote about the consciousness movement, the new therapies, and the emerging psychological and religious cults. I interviewed some of the better-known gurus: Guru Bawa, Oscar Ichazo, Arthur Janoff, Muktananda, Chogyam Trungpa, and Werner Erhart. I investigated the Arica Institute, Primal Scream Institute, Naropa Institute, est, Wellsprings, Silva Mind Control, Psychosynthesis, and Scientology.

In the milieu of what has variously been called "the New Age movement" or humanistic psychology, I found an uncorseted spirituality that abandoned the classical effort to open a path between faith and reason that had been so important to me. No one in the Age of Aquarius seemed concerned to offer reasons for what they believed, much less to gather evidence to support their conclusions. The New Age was credulity gone wild—belief in healing crystals, channeling of entities, out-of-body experiences, pyramid power, sorcery, and prosperity for all. LSD visions were assumed to be true. est offered enlightenment in two weekends. Swamis, enlightened masters, and neoshamans spoke knowingly of the being of the One and *the* Truth. Channelers in trance gave voice to Seth, Ramtha, or other four-thousand-year-old entities. Light therapists cleaned your aura, realigned your chakras, and purged you of negative energy. Mystic Traders advertised that "you will enter into Nirvana with one endless step if you wear the Zen Enso T-Shirt ($18.95) and you can tune your Body, Mind and Spirit to the Universe with the fabulous Cosmic OM Tuning Fork ($34.95 plus handling and shipping)." The creators of new therapies promised that their nostrums and theirs alone would heal the alienated. *Common Ground*, a catalogue of resources for personal transformation in the San Francisco area, lists hundreds of spiritual technologies, therapies, and self-proclaimed healers, most all of them making superlative claims. The good, the bad, and the ridiculous advertise their spiritual wares side by side.

In my journeys around the new frontier, I saw many examples of destructive spirituality, false mystification, gross abuse of power, hidden tyrannies, and cultic fanaticism. Uncritical belief, misplaced faith, and excessive loyalty to gurus and groups were rampant. Personality cults formed in which loyal disciples overlooked or excused obvious sexual and financial misconduct, drunkenness, and tyrannical behavior. Werner Erhart's shady financial dealings are a matter of public record. Trungpa Rinpoche, as well as practicing the "crazy wisdom technique" of having orgies with selected students, drank himself to death. Ozel Tenzin, his successor, continued to have sexual relations with his students, even when he knew he had AIDS. Muktananda also had sex with young disciples. Psychosynthesis in the hands of Jim Vargu perverted the gentle teachings of Assagioli and expelled members who were not willing to swear absolute loyalty to the group and put "the work" above friends and family. The list of gurus and groups who practiced tyranny and thought control in the name of "spirituality" could go on and on. The followers of Fritz Perls, Carl Rogers, and Arthur Janoff did little mischief other than imitate their masters' style in ways that were semicomic. The followers of L. Ron Hubbard (Scientology) and Bhagwan Rajneesh usually lost both their money and their discretion. The followers of Jim Jones took the full dose of poison. Overbelief can be deadly.

It is in this ambience of uncorseted "spirituality" that I wrestle with the problem that has come to haunt us all. As California goes, so goes the nation. On the Western edge of things the extremes are the norm and moderation is rare. The rise of competing spiritual visions and new religions that is now so obvious on the Pacific Rim portends the future. Radical pluralism is here to stay. And in a pluralistic society we have to find a way to discern the difference between gullibility and responsible belief, between creative and destructive commitments. It is probably true that the great unanswered question of the twentieth century is "to what may we surrender"? Yet we need a set of rough principles to guide us lest we surrender to something too small, to false gods, gurus, and groups.

Think of these signs as similar to the warning label on a cigarette package. Caution: These practices may be hazardous to your spiritual health.

Be careful of charismatic leaders, unquestioned authorities, enlightened masters, perfect gurus, reincarnated teachers, and therapists who claim to have discovered the only valid therapy.

Avoid authorities who offer a universal blueprint for salvation or a map of your spiritual pilgrimage. Be suspicious of anyone who claims to have esoteric knowledge of the hidden truth, God's will, the outcome of history, or why we should bomb Iraq back into the Stone Age. The great spiritual secrets, like the Purloined Letter, are hidden in plain sight (although you may have to turn yourself inside-out to find them).

By all means, make use of the spiritual wisdom of teachers, therapists, friends, and pathfinders — the more the better. But follow Rumi's advice: "Learn about your inner self from those who know such things, but don't repeat verbatim what they say."

Be wary of anyone who fascinates, captivates, overwhelms. When you can't tear your eyes away from someone, you probably have begun to look at your life through their eyes rather than your own.

Avoid anyone who demands obedience. Obedience is a virtue for children and a civic obligation, but not a good way to spiritual maturity.

Look carefully at a spiritual teacher's personal life. Does he or she deal with money, power, and sex in an open and admirable manner? Spiritual leaders should be held accountable. No double standards. A great deal of mischief is excused under the guise of "crazy wisdom."

Check to see if a spiritual leader has friends, peer relationships, and a community of equals, or only disciples. I distrust anyone who claims to have achieved universal compassion but lacks the capacity for simple friendship. Friends keep us honest. When a leader has only disciples and devotees, he or she gets very little honest feedback or criticism. The ability to deal with others as equals is a necessary element in any authentic spirituality.

Observe whether difference of opinion, challenge, criticism, and discussion are encouraged or discouraged. Can those in charge acknowledge they don't know the answers to important questions? Does the leader ever admit that he (it is almost always a he) can be wrong and his critics right? A spiritual community should be open to whatever truth comes knocking on its door.

Do not commit yourself to any leader or group that demands that you place loyalty to them higher than your loyalty to your mate, your family, or your friends. Appeals to "a higher loyalty" to a church, a corporation, or a nation are suspect. It is much better to concentrate on learning to love those who are near to you than to commit yourself to a remote organization or future utopia. Charity begins at home. If a belief-system doesn't encourage us to strengthen our bonds with family and friends and to seek a wider community, it is a form of paranoia, not of good faith. If a group demands that you withdraw from the world at large, pack your bags and leave on the midnight train.

Reject *immediately* any leader or religion that identifies the homeland with the holy land, the folk with the people of God, the enemy with the evil empire. If narcissism is micro-idolatry, then nationalism is macro-idolatry.

Test how much humor and poking of fun about beliefs, slogans, and dogmas is permissible. The absence of humor is an almost certain sign of psychological rigidity, fanaticism, and impending spiritual and political tyranny. The first thing deadly serious leaders and organizations do is forbid satire, repress the clowns, silence the jesters, and kill levity. By contrast, the deepest spiritual traditions have always recognized that the sacred and the profane, like wisdom and folly, walk arm in arm, and therefore true piety must be seasoned with irreverent laughter. In sacred ceremonies in Bhutan, a disreputable clown with a wooden phallus held aloft shadows and parodies the actions of the "serious" dancers. Among the Pueblo people of the Southwest, the Koshares, the sacred clowns, accompany the kachina dancers and seem to interrupt the ceremony by making fun of serious matters. Mirth and merriment save us from taking ourselves too seriously and protect us from the idolatry of assuming that our churches, rituals, and formulas are themselves sacred rather than symbols that point beyond themselves to the unknown God.

Several examples of the kind of levity that diffuses false piety, as a sea breeze blows away the smog, occur to me.

During one of Paul Tillich's very abstract lectures at Harvard on the nature of God, a woman rose to ask a question: "Dr. Tillich," she said, "it is well known that psychoanalysts have an exceedingly difficult time with patients who know psychoanalytic theory. Do you think God has the same problems with theologians?" Momentarily, the audience was stunned by the question, until Tillich replied, "I am sure He does." He began to laugh in a way that set off a tidal wave that swept away the overserious mood of Systematic Theology 101.

The story is told that at the University of Chicago a famous debate was held between Charles Hartshorne and Paul Holmer. Hartshorne, a metaphysician in the tradition of Alfred North Whitehead, took more than an hour to construct an elaborate ontological argument for the existence of God. Finally, Paul Holmer, a philosopher convinced that common language contains the essence of wisdom, arose to give his reply. He paused a long time and then very slowly said: "God is great. And God is good. And we thank Him for our food. And that is all I have to say about God." And he sat down.

Over the years, friends of Joseph Campbell, all of whom were serious students of mythology and spiritual searchers, created alternative verses to the old revival hymn "Give me that old-time religion" that expressed a light-hearted irreverence for gods and goddess from different eras. (To the best of my knowledge the following verses should be blamed mostly

on George and Gerry Armstrong, Fred Holstein, Stephen and Robin
Larsen.)

Chorus:
Give me that old-time religion
Give me that old-time religion
Give me that old-time religion
It's good enough for me.

Let us worship Zarathustra,
Just the way we used to.
I'm a Zarathustra booster.
He's good enough for me.

Let us worship like the Druids,
Drinking strange fermented fluids
Running naked through the wood.
That's good enough for me.

Let us meditate on Buddha
There is no god that's cuter
Comes in silver, brass, and pewter.
And he's good enough for me.

I'll invoke the triple goddess
When she wears her Cretan bodice.
No, she isn't very modest
But she's good enough for me.

I will honor goddess Isis.
Of Egypt's gods she's nicest.
Her husband is in slices,
But she's good enough for me.

There's Rhiannon or Epona
No man could be her owner
If he tries, he'll be a goner
She's good enough for me.

Like Epona there's Athena
Only dignified but cleaner
Maybe also slightly meaner
She's good enough for me.

Shri Shiva, he's a dandy
With his old bull-buddy Nandi
And his mountain-mama handy,
He's good enough for me.

One of the things that has given the idea of "spirituality" an unpleasant odor in recent years is the obsessive manner and humorless style of some of its practitioners. I frequently run across true believers in Christianity, Zen, psychoanalysis, homeopathy, astrology, or artificial intelligence who have an explanation for everything that, unfortunately, blinds them to anything that does not fall within their belief-system. To make matters worse, this is often accompanied by a set of disciplines that encumbers them with themselves and makes them unavailable to others. I once heard a woman who lived with a man who devoted most of his waking hours to religious practices aimed at raising his consciousness and cultivating his relationship to God say in exasperation: "It is a lot easier to be a saint than live with one." At the very minimum, an authentic spiritual manner of life should dissolve the rigid boundaries and defense mechanisms of our egos, allow us to take ourselves more lightly, and make ourselves available to others.

As you make your way through the hazardous paradigm wars of this era, through the chaos of competing myths and belief-systems, keep your sense of humor intact, your heart open, and your wits about you. And every morning before you set out on your journey, check the batteries on your spiritual bullshit detector to make certain it is in good working order.

CHAPTER 7

Graceful Sensuality: Embodying the Spirit

"For the joy of ear and eye
For the heart and mind's delight
For the mystic harmony
Linking sound to sense and sight.
Lord of All to Thee we raise
This our hymn of grateful praise."

The Hymnbook, no. 2

"You do not have to be good.
You do not have to walk on your knees
for a hundred miles through the desert, repenting.
You only have to let the soft animal of your body
love what it loves . . ."

MARY OLIVER, *Dreamworks*

REORIENTATION: THE QUEST FOR GLORY IN THE LOWEST

In the beginning, spiritual quests nearly always follow the path we have thus far explored—the high road that leads toward the summit of the Mountain, toward some direct knowledge of the distant God. The traditional metaphors of the religious life suggest that our focus should be upward. God is "high and lifted up," in heaven, above all things. To have a peak experience we must "lift up our eyes into the hills from whence cometh our help" or ascend his holy Mountain.

The metaphors that suggest God is somehow "up there" may have originated in a time when people believed the gods actually lived on the tops of mountains. These metaphors are, however, misleading because they suggest that the spiritual life should be an upward thrust, a rising above the realm of the senses. The result is that much of what passes for spirituality is contaminated with hostility toward the body and a rejection of the common life of commerce and politics. But, as we will discover in the subsequent chapters, in the same measure that our spirits are inseparable from our bodies, our bodies are inseparable from the body-politic and our private devotions are inseparable from our political actions.

The public is mirrored in our private and familiar drama. Examine an individual psyche under the microscope, and you will find engraved there the myth of the polis, the values, worldview, and ideology of the culture. Autobiography is inseparable from politics, and vice versa. Our historical situation demands that we respond to some new, crucial question:

Can we discover a healing relationship between sense, sex, and spirit, between carnal and sacred knowledge?

Can we change our relationship to the Earth and our industrial-economic mythology to recover a sense of belonging within an inspired Earth?

Can we create compassionate communities? Is a politics of the spirit possible?

To answer these, our journey must abandon the heights and plunge into the depths. In the next chapters we will explore the path of carnal knowledge. As I come down from the Mountain, disillusioned in my quest for the exalted God, and return home to my mortality, the questions that touch my heart and direct my feet on a new path are: Is there glory in the lowest? Can my eyes see, my ears hear, my nose smell, my tongue taste, my skin feel the sacred?

Even to ask such questions may seem surpassingly strange. It is almost as if the moment we leave the rarefied air of the heights behind, we plunge into a swamp seething with confusion. Something crazy happens when we place the words *spirituality*, *sensuality*, and *sexuality* in the same sentence. It's as if they shouldn't be allowed to associate with each other. We seem to be mixing the pure and the impure, the sacred and the profane, in the same container. There is something shocking about this. The same impulse that leads us to search for God in the heights leads us to segregate the sacred from the sensual and the sexual. One belongs to the "higher" realm, the other to the "lower" realm; one is exalted and concerns our salvation, the other is base and tempts us to sin.

So long as we allow sensuality and spirit to remain so segregated, we create a condition that might best be called stabilized schizophrenia. Some people manage to live with the split by repressing either their sensual or their spiritual impulses. But the price is often high, as illustrated by the Roman Catholic Church's cover-up of sexual abuse by priests and by the tawdry conduct of Protestant evangelists Jimmy Swaggart and Jim Bakker.

The separation of spirit and flesh that pervades our culture confuses us all the more because deep down we know it is wrong. Each of us has a drive toward integration and wholeness, an insistent desire to celebrate the world of sense, to honor our flesh and to be joined with a loved one in the sacrament of sex.

Compounding the cognitive and emotional dissonance we feel about flesh and spirit, our cultural environment sends us mixed messages. In practice, we keep sensuality and spirituality dissociated, but *in theory*, the central religious myth of Western culture actually celebrates an integration of flesh and spirit. In spite of its promise for healing, few of us dare to explore the radical implications of what is perhaps the most audacious religious affirmation of all time: "And the Word became Flesh and dwelt among us, full of grace and truth."

We turn now to explore this clandestine path of carnal spirituality in search of grace-ful sensuality, inspired flesh, sacramental sexuality — glory in the lowest.

FOR THE BEAUTY OF THE EARTH

The crazy civil war between sense and spirit is all around me — and within.

I was lucky, or maybe graced, early in life to have a guru, a living exemplar of the link between sense and spirit, who tutored me in the dharma of enjoyment and enthusiasm. Cutting an apple and handing me half, he would say, "Look at the color of that winesap." Taking a spoon and dipping deep into the simmering pot, he would present me with a taste of chicken cacciatore and ask, "Does it need a pinch more basil or pepper?" Coming into a well-lit room at midnight, he would interrupt my reading with a command, "Go out and look at the full moon playing with the clouds." Rubbing several pieces of cloth between his fingers, he would test my discrimination, "Can you feel the difference between poplin, linen, and Egyptian cotton?" Turning up the volume on the record player so loud that it reverberated throughout the neighborhood, he instructed me, "Listen to the way the themes recur in Bach's fugues."

His teachings on the adoration of wood extended over a period of years. It began when he cut a walking stick from a hickory tree. First he peeled the bark and whittled the ends to the proper length, taking special care with the gnarled burl that was to fit within the palm of his hand. He then sanded the staff with the finest paper until its irregular contours were smooth to the touch. Next, over the course of several months, he rubbed the wood with kernels of wheat that he had gleaned from a nearby field, until it achieved the right hue. As the wood aged, there followed libations of olive oil, wax, and other substances that increase the raw beauty of hickory.

For three decades, my teacher — my father — instructed me in the five imperatives of carnal spirituality: taste, touch, smell, listen, and look. By his irrepressible enthusiasm, he taught me to savor, to appreciate, to pay attention, to adore, to rejoice in the open secret of this world's beauty. Each time that I am startled by beauty, I hear the echo of the old hymn, "This is my father's world / And to my listening ears / All nature sings and around me rings / The music of the spheres." Is it the earthly or the heavenly father who speaks to me from the mouths of orchids and the song of thrushes? I can't tell. Even thirty years after my father's death, the one who speaks to me everywhere has a voice that is both familiar and sacred.

And yet the landscape of my spirit was also swept by an opposing wind. Many nights, I lay awake and wondered whether I should pursue my interest in birds, whose kaleidoscopic beauty delighted me, and become an ornithologist, or set my mind on "higher" things. Perhaps I should study theology, I mused. In the snippets that remain from my adolescent journals are many references to my conflict between sense and spirit, body and soul, beauty and piety. I was convinced that to be a good Christian, I had to be more ascetic and repress my enthusiasm for pleasure. Too much enjoyment of "the things of this world" was the mark of a darkened pagan mind.

But the impulses of my body kept leading me down the pagan path to perdition. I tried to be a Christian, but my sensuality kept breaking through. No sooner would I vow to be more abstemious than I would be off to the Penny Hill doughnut shop to consume half a dozen warm honey-glazed, jelly-filled, cinnamon-coated doughnuts, or to the few woods that remained around Wilmington to spy out the hidden beauty of the wild. Asceticism and the pursuit of disembodied truth have always been against the grain in my wood.

Throughout my life beauty, more than any argument, has persuaded me of the blessedness of this world. My mind, swarming with doubts, is often grasped and silenced by a wild orchid hiding in a moss-covered nook by the creek. And when I despair of understanding the horrific face of history, my spirit is unexpectedly lifted by the adamantine song of a wood thrush piped into my ear by a passing wind. When I am stripped of argument and doubt, of all the theology I have learned and unlearned, I am left with that strong sense of the connection between beauty and holiness that is central to Navajo religion. Some of this connection is conveyed by their prayer from the Night Way ceremony:

In beauty may I walk.
All day long may I walk.
Through the returning seasons may I walk.
Beautifully will I possess again.
Beautifully birds.
Beautifully joyful birds.
On the trail marked with pollen may I walk.
With grasshoppers about my feet may I walk.
With dew about my feet may I walk.

With beauty may I walk.
With beauty before me may I walk.
With beauty behind me may I walk.
With beauty above me may I walk.
With beauty all around me may I walk.
In old age wandering on a trail of beauty, lively, may I walk.
In old age wandering on a trail of beauty, living again, may I walk.
It is finished in beauty.
It is finished in beauty.

THE DISEMBODYING OF SPIRIT

What has happened to us? Why are we so conflicted about sensuality
and sexuality? What diseased, disembodied idea destroyed our delight?
How did the world become disenchanted, unsound? When did it cease
to chant and speak sacred messages?

In contemporary life, two forces conspire to desensitize our bodies —
bad religion, and the madness of getting and spending. We begin our
quest disabled, our bodies injured, our senses dulled by the dual
burden of an antisensual religious tradition and a consumer culture.
The unlikely alliance of religion and economics encourages us to
sacrifice our bodies to serve a "higher" cause — God or Commerce. We
suffer from sensory deprivation, sensory overload, and dispirited senses.
We are out of touch. Things don't make sense.

Each time I have traveled to Athens and climbed the Acropolis, the
place where Western culture first celebrated the link between sense and
spirit, I am saddened to realize how far we have fallen from grace. On this
holy hill, it is still possible to see in the ancient statues of men, women,
animals, and gods, and in the magnificent columns of the Parthenon and
the surrounding temples, a celebration in marble of the faith that the
highest expression of the sacred is found in harmony and beauty.

There is no doubt that the sweet contours of human anatomy, no less
than the starry skies above, have filled men and women with wonder
since the beginning of human history. The Greeks first argued that
beauty is visible evidence of the divine. Had you asked Socrates and
Plato how they knew the cosmos was infused with divinity, they would

have pointed to the orderly movements of heavenly bodies. It was an axiom of ancient thought that the order, and therefore the rationality, of nature was a model and guide for ethical life and the governance of the ideal republic.

In the *Symposium*, Plato proposed that there is a ladder that leads from sense experience to the highest mystical vision. Begin by loving a beautiful object, he said, and you will gradually ascend on the wings of Eros to the love of beauty itself. And, he argued, beauty, truth, and goodness are inseparable. When the physical eye adores, the eye of the mind is gradually opened to behold the beauty of the divine ideals, forms, and archetypes that both transcend and inform the material world.

Classical Greek thought both glorified and devalued the realm of the senses. On the one hand, the life of reason was supposed to help us rise above the gross material world and transcend the unruly passions of the body. Yet nowhere has the beauty of the human body been so celebrated as in Greek sculpture, so cultivated as in the gymnasium, and so honored as in the Olympic games. It is said that Socrates, who was ugly and wished to appeal to young men, invented the dialogue in order to create the spiritual equivalent of wrestling.

The Greeks also created an elaborate therapy to reconcile body and spirit. To witness the practical application of the belief that beauty is necessary to restore the harmony to body and soul, we might travel from Athens to Epidauros — the healing center sacred to the god Asclepios. For nearly a thousand years, well into the fifth century A.D., the cult of Asclepios spread throughout the Greek and Roman worlds. It had over four hundred centers located outside cities, where there were fresh breezes and flowing springs. At the most famous of these, Epidauros, men and women in search of healing made use of a repertoire of techniques that rivaled any of those currently being used at "holistic" healing centers. At night, a suppliant would sleep in an open-air dormitory — the Abaton — and await a healing dream, often brought by one of the sacred serpents that crawled around the grounds. During the day, prayer and sacrifice were offered in the temple. In the four-thousand-seat amphitheater there were competitions in music, poetry, and athletic games. Tragic and comic theater presented a vision of nobility and provided the catharsis of laughter and the noble tears that purge the mind just as hellebore purged the stomach and bowels.

Exercise, hot and cold baths, massage, drugs, herbs, diet, or surgery might be prescribed.

Socrates speaks for all time the axiom that is the foundation of spiritual healing: "You ought not to attempt to cure eyes without head, or head without body, so you should not treat body without soul."

Gnosticism: The Body as Prison

How did we lose the ancient faith that flesh is an incognito for the spirit? Somewhere in the few hundred years that separated classical Greek culture from the Christian era, there was a fundamental shift in worldview, attitude, and feeling about the body.

In the turmoil following the conquests of Alexander the Great and the breakup of the Greek city-states, the Western world underwent a massive paradigm change, a transmutation of values. We can see this reversal of philosophical mood best in the emergence of untold numbers of new sects and philosophical schools that are lumped together under the name of gnosticism. Sects such as the Essenes and the Neoplatonists in Alexandria, and quasi-Christian theologians such as Marcion, all shared a gnostic view that the body and the material world are a filthy prison, a dark cave, in which the pure soul is trapped. Gnosticism involved a radical rejection of the body and a search for a divinely revealed *gnosis*, or secret knowledge, that would awaken the soul and cause it to remember its divine origins.

In an effort to escape the alien material world, many gnostic sects practiced severe asceticism. Because this world is the creation of a demiurge or an evil spirit, they believed, the desires of the body for sensual and sexual pleasure are evil impulses that should be denied. A passage from *The Book of Thomas the Contender*, which was found at Nag Hammadi, typifies the rejection of the flesh: "Woe to you who put your hope in the flesh and the prison that will perish. . . . Woe to you who are captives, for you are bound in caves." Perhaps the most telling metaphor for the gnostic feeling about the body is the one that suggested the soul is like a pearl — pure and immortal — that has been dipped into the excrement and slime of matter. The spiritual path, in gnosticism, involved acquiring the secret *gnosis* and the disciplines necessary to cleanse the soul of the taint of its immersion in time and matter.

Christianity: Incarnation and Ambivalent Carnality

This climate of gnostic rejection of the senses permeated the ancient world at the beginning of the Christian era. The mood of Saint Paul and the early church was one of apocalypse. The world is coming to an end soon, they believed. Time is short. The situation is urgent. Christ will come again at any moment, and everything will be destroyed and transformed in the twinkling of an eye. We are only sojourners here, so we should not settle down to cultivate and enjoy the earth. Time spent in dalliance is inexpedient, stolen from the serious business of preparing for the coming kingdom. There is no time for the pleasures of marriage. At best, or worst, Paul allowed, "It is better to marry than burn." Scarce tribute to the sacredness of flesh or the gift of the senses: We should be in the world but not of it. Our true citizenship is not here.

Christianity has always been ambivalent about the senses, the flesh, and the wonders of this world. Theologically, it affirmed that a loving God creates body, mind, and soul ex nihilo. No demiurge or devil contaminates mortal flesh or has control over the course of time. The church, *in theory*, rejected any kind of dualism — gnosticism, Manicheanism — that limited God's dominion over time, mind, or matter. But *in practice* the church has been a consistent enemy of carnality. The apocalyptic mood produced two rules of life. Rule 1: In times of emergency the normal enjoyment of the goodness of Creation is curtailed to allow for full dedication to the work necessary to prepare for the coming kingdom of God. Rule 2: All time until Christ returns shall be considered a time of emergency. For two thousand years the church has attempted to maintain this permanent state of emergency.

From A.D. 100 onward, more pragmatic and worldly Christians tried to come to terms with the flawed timetable of apocalypse. When the Lord tarried beyond a generation, it occurred to many Christians that it was necessary to call off the fire drill and live gracefully in the normal mysteries of historical time. Periodically, movements similar to what Matthew Fox has recently designated "Creation-centered theology" break forth within the church. Remembering that "the Earth is the Lord's," Christians celebrate the senses and sing "for the beauty of the earth and the splendor of the skies." But with sickening regularity, the perennial suspicion of the flesh and the Earth returns. Augustine's harsh rejection of the pleasure of sexuality pops up recurrently like Marley's ghost to haunt us. Roman Catholics whose sexual conscience continues to be shaped by a celibate, male clergy (whose first instinct is "Just say no") suffer a deep ambivalence about sex.

In an effort to escape the taint of paganism and protect the transcendence of God, the beliefs of Judaism, Christianity, and Islam have frequently devalued flesh and matter. They thereby prepared the way for the triumph of a secular manner of dealing with the Earth.

Secular Non-sense

The second force that has desensitized our bodies is the emergence of economics as our dominant concern. As Wordsworth said, "The world is too much with us; late and soon, / Getting and spending, we lay waste our powers: / Little we see in Nature that is ours; / We have given our hearts away, a sordid boon!"

According to contemporary ideology, secularism has freed our senses and liberated our sexuality from the tyranny of religious repression. Yet each time I visit Chicago or Bangkok, I have the impression that in the megalopolis — the now and future city — the majority of modern cliff dwellers suffer from an atmosphere in which their senses and their bodies are constantly stressed and exhausted by unpleasant stimuli. Garbage, litter, and garish advertising assault the eye. Traffic, construction, boom boxes, and street noise bombard the ear. Smog and pollution offend the nose. The mile upon mile of dreary boarded-up and falling-down buildings in central Detroit are nearly indistinguishable from the shambles of war-torn Beirut.

The rapid pace (stress and excitement) of city life, sustained with the help of chemical stimulants and depressants, destroys the leisure we need for wonder and appreciation. Continual assault dulls our senses and causes us to withdraw into our isolated private worlds in much the same way as sensory deprivation does. Prisoners kept in dark cells and meditators who voluntarily make use of sensory-deprivation chambers begin to hallucinate.

There are, of course, crannies of loveliness in New York, Los Angeles, Mexico City, São Paulo, Bogotà — parks, museums, architectural monuments, and apartments that have been fashioned into sanctuaries. But urban beauty is increasingly the privilege of the cultural elite. With sufficient money and "good taste," the wealthy can insulate themselves from much of the ugliness and sensory assault. Moving between a penthouse overlooking a park, an elegant restaurant, and a weekend place in the country allows the fortunate few to keep their senses alive in what is otherwise a desensitizing and dispiriting environment.

The more we abandon public spaces to ugliness, the more beauty retreats to the private realm. In direct proportion to the decaying sensory delight of our cities, we decorate our bodies with fashion and hang "art" in our homes. The most sophisticated among us have replaced the celebration of budding dogwood and changing maple leaves with worship of the latest styles.

A backward glance at the drawings on the walls of the Lascaux caves shows that human beings have always had an eye for beauty and the capacity to create beautiful objects. Until recently, art was infused with the spirit of worship — witness the sense of reverence and appreciation that emanates from Van Gogh's sunflowers and Georgia O'Keeffe's orchids. Artistic creation was a celebration of and a dialogue with the beauty found in the ordinary world of the senses, *not a replacement of it*. But today, increasingly, art like religion has become an end in itself rather than an invitation to contemplate beauty and sacredness. As our surroundings grow more sensually degraded, "art" becomes a special thing exhibited in museums or galleries. We seem to have lost the primal wisdom of the Balinese saying, "We have no art, we make everything as beautiful as we can."

The planned obsolescence of consumer culture is a form of capitalistic asceticism, a refusal to cherish things. In an economically driven society, we use and dispose of things rather than adore them. We lack a wonder-ful materialism. Our habit of conspicuous consumption is a case of looking for love in all the wrong places.

THE GIFT OF THE SENSES

How do we "cleanse the doors of perception" so that we may *adore* rather than merely *utilize* things? How can we recover the spiritual dimension of the life of the senses and rediscover the body as the site of revelation? What would it mean to live as if "the word became flesh," as if the eternal logic and intentionality that inform all of Being were present in a wild orchid?

The Latin word *datum*, which means "gift," gives us a first clue. In the beginning is the gift of color, taste, sound, smell, touch. Delight is built into the physiology of the senses. The eye is excited by scarlet, soothed by celadon, calmed by azure, clarified by black and white. We rejoice spontaneously in the lilt of a meadowlark and are put on edge by the shrill cry of a red-tailed hawk. Alice Walker in *The Color Purple* is close to the primal theology of the senses when she has Shug say: "I think it pisses God off if you walk by the color purple in a field somewhere and don't notice it. . . . Any fool living in the world can see it always trying to please us back. . . . It always making little surprises and springing them on us when us least expect. Everything want to be loved. Us sing and dance, make faces and give flower bouquets, trying to be loved. You ever notice that trees do everything to git attention we do, except walk?"

That instinct for gratitude and celebration that religion formalizes as worship from the beginning permeates our sensory contact with the world. A baby's lips naturally rejoice in the nipple. The eye is arrested and sinks into happy contemplation of the sun setting over the darkening sea. The ear gives spontaneous thanks for the sound of falling water. The fingertips praise the smooth stone.

We are born making sense of things. Discrimination and judgment are in the eye before they are in the intellect. The nose and ear judge between good and evil long before the mind or conscience has been tutored in moral categories. We taste the world and find it pleasing to the palate, or we spit it out as sour milk. The scent of lilacs opens the nose; the odor of decaying flesh closes it. A skunk automatically establishes the right distance between itself and us.

One of the great bits of nonsense of the modern mind is the assumption that human beings fabricate all meaning from the intrinsically meaningless raw material that is presented us by the senses. Clearly, the cardinal that flashes into view announces its meaning. Without offering an explanation of its existence, it presents us with one of the basic categories necessary for making sense of the world — the color red.

If you doubt that sense and meaning are connected, try this thought experiment. First, subtract red from the spectrum of color represented in the world. Next, orange, yellow, green, and so on, until nothing remains except nearly indistinguishable shades of gray. What kind of meaning or spiritual delight remains in a world devoid of color?

When we divorce sensuality from spirituality, we create a dis-spirited world. Left to itself, the nose can testify that Secaucus, New Jersey, has been desecrated. A running nose and stinging eyes witness that the wind that carries acid rain and pollution is not the wind of the spirit. The eardrums know that the violent decibels of jet engines and the din of gridlock traffic irritate body and spirit.

The more we desacralize the senses by forgetting to celebrate and be grateful for the gift of beauty, the more we create desecrated environments — the black holes of Calcutta and the slums of the Rust Belt. If, in the name of religion or economics, we try to escape time, matter, and history, we neglect the beautification, enrichment, and stewardship of our land and cities. In the marvelous texts of Tibetan Buddhism, no less than in *The Wall Street Journal*, I look in vain for a poem that celebrates a Briscone pine or invites the faithful to listen to a meadowlark's hymn. In the East, centuries of cultivating the inner landscape of the religious imagination through elaborate rituals, chants, mudras, mantras, yantras, and mandalas have done no more to prevent the deforestation of the outer landscape of Nepal and India than Western capitalism has prevented the clear-cutting of the Cascades forests.

I have come to be suspicious of any religion or form of therapy that focuses exclusively on cultivating the interior life or saving the soul and that does not include a celebration of the senses, an ecological vision, and a concern for social justice. We can aspire to care for and transform this world only if we trust that spirit is incarnate in flesh and dirt. This world *is* our home. We are in the right place. We do not need to escape to heaven or a NASA space colony.

As an antidote to the dullness of the senses, to the drabness of a disembodied way of living, practice the discipline of delight.

As you walk along Main Street, jog in the park, or eat dinner with your family, think of yourself as an artist of the found object, a collector of spontaneously arising incidents of beauty. Let no day go by without adding something to the museum of your experience: a chocolate horse-chestnut newly disgorged from its vanilla-cream pod; a single dappled feather fallen from the breast of a common sparrow; the pattern and tempo of water tumbling in a fountain, backlit by the early morning sun; the unexpected ray of hazel light that flashes from your daughter's eye and plays counterpoint to her smile; the contrast of a turbulent thunderhead and the straight line of an airplane trail etched against the still blue sky; the sweet-acrid scent of burning leaves.

Pause frequently and stop the action by imagining that you are surveying the scene before you through the viewfinder of a camera. How would you frame the picture? What would you include and exclude?

Study a single rock. There is a Zen story about a novice climber who apprenticed himself to the greatest mountain climber in the world. He expected to be instructed in all of the esoteric techniques that the master was reputed to have perfected. Instead, the master selected a small rock from the garden, gave it to him, and locked him in a room for a year. Having nothing else to occupy him, the novice stared at the rock, played with it, tasted it, felt its every minuscule nook and cranny and smooth surface, studied its variations in color and temperature on moonlit nights and rainy days. When the year ended, the novice had an exquisite knowledge and appreciation of every tiny detail and nuance of the rock. When he was finally released from his solitary vigil, he went into the high mountains and climbed the steepest pitches with great ease, because ledges and fingerholds that had previously seemed narrow and precarious now appeared enormous and welcoming.

THE REENCHANTMENT AND TUNING OF THE BODY

When I was a child, my father would hand me a tuning fork to find the right pitch for beginning a song. I would hit it against the table, and the sound — *twanggggggggggg* — would fill the room and the vibrations would pulse through my body until they tickled my eardrums and my voice found its proper place on the scale.

Originally, we were all enchanted beings. As children, we were natural mystics; whatever was happening without was happening within. I did not run *like* the wind; I *was* the wind running wild through tall grass. Effortlessly, I metamorphosed, became a hawk soaring across a valley, a snake slithering across a rock. Horses talked to me, and I spent many happy afternoons galloping, whinnying, and bucking. Whippoorwills and barn owls sang me to sleep, and many times I woke in the darkness and had to feel for fur on my face to find out if I was a boy dreaming I was a bear or a bear dreaming I was a boy. Before we learned to keep quiet about taboo subjects and to forget our immense knowledge, we were all delightfully and painfully omniscient and clairvoyant. We moved to the rhythms of those around us; our bodies danced our fathers' and mothers' joy and mourned their sadness. Compassion was unavoidable. I remember how I cried when my father's eye was badly scratched and he lay for three days in a dark room. When primitive myths tell us that we once spoke and understood the languages of birds, animals, reptiles, and insects, they remind us that childhood was a time of at-one-ment, of communion of sentient beings when all creatures shared a single body.

Think of the body as an elaborate tuning fork that may reverberate either to cacophony or to harmony, to heavy metal or to the music of the spheres, to the vibrations of jackhammers tearing up a street or to the "Ode to Joy" in Beethoven's Ninth Symphony. We are vibratory beings. Atoms and hearts alike are governed by pulsation. Sickness and health, destruction and creation, are dependent on being in tune or out of tune. Arrhythmia, a pathology of an unsound heart, is a question of bad vibes, missing the beat, marching to the wrong drummer.

Carry the metaphor of the tuning fork a step further. Mystics as well as modern brain theorists like Karl Pribram have put forth the notion that the human mind-body-spirit is a hologram — an elaborate reverberatory nexus through which flows all the vibrations-currents-impulses-information of the universe. In many ways, the metaphor of the hologram is a quasi-scientific restatement of the Christian idea of the *logos*, which is at one and the same time the creative rationale within the mind of God and the essential structure of the human mind. According to the Gospel of John, the *logos* became flesh in Christ. In the Hopi version of this idea the human spine is like a radio tuned to the cosmic vibrations and to the messages and chants of the holy people. Tantric forms of Hinduism and Buddhism consider the body to have an ascending order of chakras or reverberatory centers that may be tuned to different spiritual realities. Tibetan monks have developed chants in every octave that the human voice can sing that are said to repair the "unsound" body and

retune it. Chanting the central mantra *om*, the sacred sound, the quin-
tessence, the seed-syllable of the universe, the magic word, our consciousness returns to its divine origins. In all of these traditions, the
practice of chanting reminds us that we can have a sound-body, sound-
mind, sound-spirit only when we tune ourselves to the symphony of
Being. Take away the vibrations from the strings of a violin, and there is
no musical instrument; take away the harmonic interplay between
protons and electrons, and there is no atom; take away our attunement
to the world beyond the self, and there is no human spirit.

My own explorations in tuning the body have not been primarily
along the lines of an Eastern meditational practice aimed at inducing
the kundalini—serpent power, prana, informing energy of the
universe—to rise up the axis of my spine. I lack the patience to create
the Tantric superstructure of imagination of the subtle body by meditating systematically on the various chakras. My sporadic efforts to
assume the lotus position and remain motionless through endless
hours of meditation produced more pain in the buttocks than enlightenment. As a Western man, I am inclined to more active bodily
disciplines—the Zen of wall-building, orchard-planting, wood-
chopping, mountain-climbing, horseback-riding, and walking.

The quest starts with dis-ease, pathology, the realization that body-
mind-spirit have become alienated. My awareness of the inseparable
union of body and spirit began with the discovery of my own lack of
grace and my disgrace.

I remember the shock of alienation in the ninth grade when I lost a
fight with Ray Snead. In my estimation Ray was a wimp, so I was
doubly humiliated when he rubbed my face in the gravel. My consciousness seemed to regard my body from afar and to be ashamed. I
immediately sent away for a Charles Atlas body-building course and
began to construct some muscles. The results weren't bad. Within a
year I was trim at the waist, had good triceps, biceps, and pectorals, and
was determined that no bully would ever kick sand in my face again.
Thus equipped, I tried—vainly—to learn boxing and judo before I
took up the gentlemanly sport of wrestling.

It didn't dawn on me until my middle thirties, after more body-
building and physical discipline, that I had organized my body around
the mirror, the opponent, and the job. The body I had fabricated

looked good, competed adequately, and functioned efficiently, but it was permanently tensed against the invasion of tenderness. I told it what to do, and for the most part it obeyed like a well-paid sullen butler. It was better at work than play: a good, stylish, serious, productive, disciplined, neurotic, death-defying American body. But just when it got close to the body-image I held in my private Platonic heaven, I became painfully aware that it — and I — had little direct sensuous or kinesthetic awareness and practically no ability to surrender to the soft streaming sensations that accompany the play of intuition, imagination, and graceful sexuality. I did not allow the soft animal of my body to love what it loved.

In my attempt to liberate my body from the captivity into which I had fallen, four guides appeared to help me understand the nature of incarnate spirituality — Rudolf Otto, the cartographer of the holy; Wilhelm Reich, the early psychosomatic theorist; Norman O. Brown, the prophet of Dionysian Christianity; and Ida Rolf, the grande dame of body therapists.

Rudolf Otto, whom I described in Chapter 6, gave me the first theoretical clue that helped me forge a kinesthetic link between the body and the experience of the sacred. The experience of the holy, he said, always involves *trembling*. In those extraordinary moments when we dare to see life in its undomesticated rawness and inexplicable beauty and are stripped of the illusion that we can comprehend and control reality, our bodies are moved by powerful emotions. At once, we tremble in terror before the majesty of life, are struck dumb with wonder, and are inhabited by joy. Thus, Quakers quake, Shakers shake, dervishes whirl, and Haitian spirit-dancers go into ecstatic trances.

Otto's analysis implies that we can only experience the holy if we are able to surrender to e-motion and allow ourselves to be moved. If we become obsessed with remaining in control of ourselves and others, we will armor and desensitize our bodies and will systematically prevent ourselves from being shattered by the experience of the holy. Without bodies that are able to tremble, wonder, and enjoy, we are senseless, feelingless, and dispirited.

Where do you tremble? Where do you allow yourself to lose control? Where do you allow yourself to be inhabited, taken over by a life-force larger than your ego? Have you grown rigid? Do you prefer the status quo to the life of the spirit? If your relationship to your body is the visible manifestation of your relation to your invisible spirit, what does this say about you? Do you ignore or attend to your body-spirit? Punish or cherish it? Treat it as a work-animal or as a friend?

Wilhelm Reich's psychology gave me the second clue that helped me understand the somatic component of the dis-spirited life, the way in which the body becomes armored against inspiration and compassion. Reich, a contemporary of Freud, forged an inseparable link between psyche and soma and provided a theory that was to become the basis of modern body-oriented therapies — Rolfing, bioenergetics, Alexander method, Feldenkrais work, and others. Freud had portrayed the ego as a kind of embattled fortress that employed all kinds of defense mechanisms to ward off the impossible demands of the angelic crusaders of the superego and the barbarian hordes of the libido. Its greatest ally in this unequal battle was the insight gained in psychotherapy that made conscious the distorted strategies of the unconscious. It fell to Reich to translate Freud's vision of the embattled psyche into somatic terms.

Reich's great discovery was that every psychological defense mechanism has a physical-muscular corollary. By chronic muscular tension, we create what he called the body-armor or character armor that makes us rigid and closed in body-mind-spirit. For instance, a man beaten as a child forms his body into a permanent stance of cringing or defiance. A woman who was sexually abused as a child tightens and desensitizes the musculature of her pelvis in order to "forget" the original trauma. When we are terrified of the unpredictable chaos of life, we create a totalitarian ego and an uptight body to defend ourselves against what we fear. Anxiety tightens and narrows the chest and belly and constricts the flow of breath, so that spontaneity and surrender to inspiration become impossible. A warrior or competitor with a paranoid worldview forms both the mind and the body into a weapon. Hard-headed categories — us or them, good or bad, white hats or black hats — and body-armor that desensitizes our feeling are two sides of the same coin. Reich convinced me that if I wanted to be more open and compassionate, my body-armor would have to soften. To journey down into the underworld of the unconscious and explore the divine and demonic spirits that dwell there, I would have to disarm the chronic muscular tension and tight intellectual style that isolated me in a self-protective world of ideas.

In 1967, while I was still a seminary professor, I encountered two books that became events in my life. They provided me with elegant theories out of which I constructed the maps for my journey for a decade. In Norman O. Brown's two books *Life Against Death* and *Love's Body*, I found a vision of what the body would be like if it were inspired, resurrected, reenchanted. *Love's Body* remains, to my mind, our single most important book for creating a uniquely modern Western incarnational spirituality.

By close analysis and outrageous word-play, Brown shows that we have destroyed the erotic capacity of the body as a whole and designated the genitals as the sole remaining site of ecstatic pleasure. By committing our time, our energy, and our imagination to a life of warfare and compulsive work, by organizing our lives around abstractions, by sacrificing enjoyment of the here and now to pile up surplus possessions, by constantly postponing gratification until the work is finished, we desensitize our bodies. Our ears become so stuffed with noise, chatter, advertisement, and purposeful talk that we don't listen to sighs and whispers of the changing winds. Our noses become so clogged by pollution that the deep emotional centers of the limbic brain that are directly stimulated by odors lie dormant, and we can neither smell nor remember roses. Our lungs, constricted by shallow rapid breathing, become incapable of yielding gracefully to the breath of life. Having numbed the body-mind-imagination, we proceed to create the myth of romance and expect genital sexuality to provide us with all erotic and ecstatic pleasure. Burdened with this impossible expectation, genital sexuality inevitably disappoints us. The single Technicolor experience of sex is not sufficient to make up for the deprivation of dwelling in the monotone, corpotechnic world of efficiency, competition, and economic reward.

Brown makes the radical suggestion that we need to reorganize the psyche and resurrect the body by giving our primary loyalty to pleasure rather than to what we have erroneously considered "reality" — the world we construct from artificial scarcity, anxiety, postponed gratification, and obsessive work. Our senses need to be liberated from our obsession with getting and owning. A lover's body, a fully inspired body, would no longer be organized around defense mechanisms or character armor but would be open, vulnerable, and erotically connected to the encompassing world.

"To return the word to the flesh. To make knowledge carnal again; not by deduction, but immediate by perception or sense at once; the bodily senses. The reality of the body is not given. . . . It is to be built not with hands but by the spirit. It is the poetic body; the made body; Man makes Himself, his own body, in the symbolic freedom of the imagination. The Eternal Body of Man is the Imagination, that is, God himself, the Divine Body, Jesus: we are his Members. To find the kingdom in one's own body, and to find one's own body in the outside world. The body to be realized is the body of the cosmic man, the body of the universe, as one perfect man. . . . The body that is identical with environment. . . . In conscious symbolism the alienated spirit returns to its human creator; 'all the gods are in our body.' Redemption is reformation of the creator spirit in man; redemption is deification; we make a new heaven and a new earth."[1]

Like many visionaries, Norman O. Brown is of little help when it comes to suggesting a path that might lead from the actual to the ideal. His diagnosis of our dis-ease is clear — our bodies and spirits are alienated. His vision of the fully inspirited body is powerful and inviting. But what medicine, what therapy, what discipline, what means of grace are available for our healing? Nobody knew what Brown was recommending, and he was not forthcoming about any of the practical implications of his theory. Should we blow our minds with psychedelic drugs? Should we practice "polymorphous perversity" by reverting to indiscriminate sensuality? Should we read poetry and cultivate the erotic imagination? Should we, as the Gestalt therapist Fritz Perls advised, "lose our minds and come to our senses"? Should we encourage sexual permissiveness and public orgies?

Like many searchers in the 1960s, I was fired up by the vision of resurrecting the body but was frustrated by the lack of an embodying spiritual practice. The standard-brand Protestant churches offered little for the body other than the calisthenics of the Episcopal service, with its constant kneeling and rising, the experiment of setting the creed to guitar music, and an occasional dance choir. The hymns might have moved the brain to emote and the limbs to move, but only in the black and Pentecostalist churches were they sung with swing and enthusiasm. I experimented with Eastern body disciplines — yoga, tai chi, and aikido — with limited success because of my unwillingness to accept the traditional authoritarian relationship between guru and disciple.

It was almost by accident that I stumbled onto a partial remedy. In my role as roving reporter for *Psychology Today*, I investigated and submitted myself as a guinea pig to Structural Integration, or Rolfing.

When I laid my almost-bare body on a bed at Esalen Institute, I knew the ten hours of processing (a terrible word) would involve manipulation of the connective tissue of all the major muscle groups in my body. But I sought that latter-day grail — growth — and was willing to submit my tender but sinfully distorted fascial tissue to Ida Rolf's knowing fingers, fists, and elbows. I knew that redemption is never painless, but I was unprepared for the pain and panic when "the work" began on my chest. It hurt like hell. Later, I understood that the chronic tension in my chest muscles had formed a defensive armor that was emotionally, physically, and spiritually restricting.

But at the time, uninformed and unheroic, I moaned, cursed, and wondered what demythologized quest for salvation led me to submit to such painful folly. After the trauma of the first hour, however, slight but unmistakable changes appeared in my posture and stance in life. My feet made more substantial contact with the ground; my leg muscles seemed to be freshly lubricated; there were ball bearings in my joints. Encouraged by this freer movement and heightened kinesthetic sensitivity, I lent my total consent to what felt like a rehearsal for a crucifixion.

As the Rolfing continued, it became clear that I was the cause of most of my pain. My long habit of anxious anticipation of I-knew-not-what catastrophes and a vaguely paranoid suspicion of others had made my muscles chronically tense and rigid. Under Ida's healing hands, I experienced the gradual loss of my character armor. As I learned to relax and allow myself to be softer, much of my chronic tension and pain ceased.

My chest, however, would not yield its defenses or its treasures. Every time the Rolfing hand approached, I went into panic and felt unbearable pain. It was not until the seventh hour of my ordeal that the fortress fell. As Ida bore down on a muscle in my shoulder, I was suddenly flooded with painful memories of childhood fights with my older brother. I became a child again, wept uncontrollably, and brokenheartedly asked my beloved minor god and brother, "Lawrence, why are you hurting me?" The release of this memory, and the grief it occasioned, released the panic-tension-pain in my chest. At the end of the hour, I was able, for the first time in my memory, to fill my lungs in one smooth movement. Inspiring change.

With my release from this and other long-held psychosomatic-spiritual defense systems, I experienced a new openness, ease, and expansiveness. My body became looser, as did my mind. I found myself warming to opinions, people, and events that would previously have raised my hackles. There were other changes. I stood taller and straighter. (Yes, Mother, it does feel better.) The daily pain of an old wrestling injury was gone. Most important, I gained a direct sensuous and kinesthetic awareness of my total body.

As I became more conscious of my body, I felt a heaviness that at first I mistook for depression. A fully sensuous lifestyle involves knowing the essentially tragic character of the human condition — that is, disillusionment. As I identify with my body, I see the insignificance of all those substitute monuments to immortality — hoarded wealth, opulent machines, political empires, youthful facades — that we death-defying Prometheans create. Each is an evasion of the primal sorrow that all we love and enjoy is terribly and wonderfully fleeting and vulnerable. All flesh does decay, and until that knowledge comes to root in our interior, there can be no dancing. It was no accident that the Greeks, who fused Eros and Thanatos long before Freud, were ardent devotees of the flesh and fierce enemies of death. Reinhabiting the body, becoming carnal, is both a joyful homecoming and a heavy trip downward into the humus, the ground and end of human existence, the first and last truth of the flesh.

"Small changes," you may say. "Not world-shaking. A slight increase in the ability to sense, feel, and perceive doesn't solve the problem of evil or house the homeless." True. But for a single individual, the transformation that takes place when numbness is replaced by a capacity to feel a panoply of emotions is momentous. Spiritual awakening changes the entire way in which a person is embodied in the world. The inspirited or resurrected body begins to resemble a tuning fork more than a guarded fortress. Freed from the prison of my body-ego, I am able to touch, taste, smell, hear, and see a reenchanted world. With the doors of perception cleansed, eternity may be seen in a grain of sand, and all the history of grief "in an empty doorway and a maple leaf."

HEALING TOUCH: THE LAYING ON OF HANDS

To resurrect the body, we must put out our feelers, get back in touch with the world.

It's no wonder things don't make sense. We have little tacit knowledge of one another. Our important institutions — schools, hospitals, the military, business — share a common rule: Thou shalt not touch. Most of us were brought up to keep our distance from the world and each other: Don't touch. Keep your hands to yourself. Western men are especially constrained by homophobia and limit touch to a sterile handshake or to giving or taking a "hit" in body-contact sports. Friends do not stroll hand in hand. We are a tactophobic culture, accustomed to "reach out and touch somebody" by phone but inhibited about the communion of flesh. Marshall McLuhan to the contrary, we are increasingly a high-tech, low-touch culture.

Mainstream religion in America is largely an out-of-body experience. A few Baptists still practice foot-washing, but none follow Saint Paul's admonition to "greet one another with a holy kiss." In church, no carnal knowledge is permitted, no hugging, dancing, or laying on of hands.

I can almost hear the chorus of objections: "Aren't you confusing sex and spirituality? What are you talking about, some kind of New Age 'hugging' ritual? I don't think fondling strangers is going to help me find my soul."

It is difficult to see how we can recover palpable relationships to one another when we have so sexualized the sense of touch that we are uncomfortable with bodily contact. Touch itself has become suspect. In the present climate of near-frantic awareness of sexual abuse, it has become difficult to dissociate touch from the notion of caressing and fondling. Teachers are afraid to touch students for fear of being charged with sexual abuse. Military officers and enlisted men are terrified that gays will subvert military discipline by touching. Parents routinely exile their babies from the common bed and are growing wary even of cuddling their children for fear of committing psychological incest.

Nevertheless, to heal our soul-body we must touch one another. Monkeys raised in isolation from their mothers and deprived of touch become depressed and hostile. Untouched infants languish, even when all their other physical needs are satisfied. Untouched men and women fortify their bodies and minds to endure loneliness. In one experiment, in which checkout clerks were instructed to give a glancing touch to every second customer when returning their change, psychologists discovered that those who were touched felt significantly better about the store in which they had just shopped. Throughout the pretechnological world, touching — or as the New Testament says, "the laying on of hands" — has been an important part of spiritual healing. Recently, in Brazil I attended a service in the Umbanda Church in which the elders — men and women — went into a trance and purified members of the congregation by running their hands over the entire length of the body.

During a semester I spent teaching at University of Florida Medical School, I conducted an exercise in which I had students divide into dyads and experiment with three types of touch. First: Take your partner's hand and examine it clinically. Second: Touch your partner's hand in a seductive or sexually suggestive manner. Third: Touch, caress, or massage your partner's hand in a way that is not sexual but that intends both to give and to receive a modicum of sensory pleasure. I then posed questions: "What is medical touch? What kind of touch sickens? What kind of touch heals?" Finally, I asked them to consider the hypothesis that if they touched patients only in a clinical manner, they further sickened them by treating their bodies as objects; if they touched them in a sexual manner, they sickened them because it was an invasive and inappropriate intimacy; and the healing touch should always intend not only to garner clinical information but to give and receive some sensory — but not sexual — pleasure. Needless to say, the discussion about the experiment went on for days.

To be in touch with one another, it is not enough to gather objective knowledge, to remain at a distance, or to limit intimacy to sexual contact. "To let the soft animal of your body love what it loves," you must recover the pleasure of innocent touch. Since we are incarnate spirits, the grace that allows us to trust the mystery that surrounds us must come through our senses. Our souls are palpable. Please touch.

BREATHE THROUGH ME, BREATH OF GOD

The most immediate way to experience the body as the temple of holy spirit, to feel flesh being inspired, is to pay attention to the simple and profound act of breathing. Let's return to the beginning of this book for just a moment. The very notion of spirit arose from the experience of breathing. The breath that moves through us is the immanence of the prime mover, the holy spirit animating us moment by moment.

"To reconcile body and spirit would be to recover the breath-soul which is the life-soul instead of the ghost-soul or shadow; breath-consciousness instead of brain-consciousness; body-consciousness instead of head-consciousness. The word made flesh is a living word, not a scripture but a breathing."[2] The testimony of all who have practiced meditation in the Hindu, Buddhist, and Sufi traditions and in Christian mysticism is that the dimension of spirit is as close to us and as immediately available as the act and nonact of breathing. Breathing is at once ordinary and revelatory, a natural and supernatural experience.

The oldest text we have on meditation — Patanjali's Yoga Sutras, written years before the Christian era — spells out the fundamentals of the spiritual discipline of breathing, or *pranayama*, as it is called. Patanjali noted that there is a direct relation between respiration and mental states. Unrhythmic or constricted breath creates mental illusion. By paying attention to the cadence of breathing, we allow respiration to become automatic, which in turn expands the focal length of the mind.

It sounds funny to talk about "discovering breathing" since we have all done it since the moment of birth. But breathing is like dreaming. It yields its spiritual treasure only when we practice the unnatural discipline of bringing into consciousness what has normally remained unconscious. I was well into midlife before I learned the connection between my constricted chest, constricted emotions, constricted breathing, constricted spontaneity, and constricted spirit. Just as psychotherapy helped me recover the unconscious motives that had shaped and restricted my life, the practice of becoming aware of my breath showed me how shallow inspiration inhibited my ability to surrender to my spiritual and sexual passions.

The beauty of experimenting with intentional breathing is that it requires no belief, no faith, no dogma, no authority. Ordinarily, the notion of technique is alien to the spiritual life. The spirit, like the wind, blows where it will. No spiritual technology produces grace. We can go through the motions of religion for a lifetime and still have a hard heart and a paranoid mind. The discipline of paying attention to breath probably comes as near as we can get in the spiritual life to a genuine technique — a prescribed procedure that yields an assured result. If there is a formula for an epiphany in the flesh it is: Follow the movement of your breathing, and it will take you to the prime mover. Breath is the simplest vehicle of transcendence.

Try it. Sit quietly, and pay attention to your breathing. Nothing else. At first you will find your mind wanders, and you will be unable to concentrate on following the flow of breath. Bring your attention back to your breath. When you are able to hold your attention there for a while, you will become aware that you are exerting a lot of effort. Breathing seems to take a lot of *willpower*. It is work. Gradually you will notice that the rhythm of your breathing lengthens, grows slow, and your body softens and begins to *allow* the breath to flow. After a long while you will feel yourself *being breathed*. As you surrender to the movement, figure and ground reverse, the gestalt changes. Who you are changes. Where once you were acting, now you seem moved by a power beyond yourself. Your breath tells you that you are of the same substance as the spirit that moves everything.

The central metaphors of the spiritual-mystical tradition reflect this pivotal experience, in which the ego is taken up within and encompassed by something larger than itself. In the Hindu tradition, the human spirit, the Atman, is discovered to be a part of the Absolute Spirit, the Brahman. In Buddhism the illusion of self dissolves, and the void is filled with the ecstatic knowledge that there is no difference between my mind and Buddha-mind. Christian mystics testify to the experience of finding the point of union between the human and the divine spirit. But orthodox Christianity holds to the idea that there is an absolute qualitative distinction between creatures and God, between time and eternity; therefore the Holy Spirit is not a substance that God and Man share but a special grace that God decides to bestow on some. The closest we get in orthodox Christianity to the perennial mystical notion of the identity of breath and spirit is reflected in the line from the hymn: "Breathe *on* me, breath of God, fill me with life anew." The transcendent Creator animates us with His Holy Spirit and withdraws, leaving us with autonomous breath. He does not breathe *through* or *with* us but *on* us.

From Breathing 101 — "The Elementary Experience of Transcendence" — we proceed to the more advanced course, Breathing 202 — "Inspiration and Compassion." Add imagination to inspiration, and you have the formula for going beyond mystical to moral experience, for developing compassion.

In the varieties of Buddhism in which meditation is central, the rhythm of inspiration and expiration is used to expand the boundaries of the self and the circle of care. As I inhale, I try to be aware of and thankful for the universal energy, *prana*, or spirit filling my lungs, energizing and animating every cell of my body. I take the world into myself, imagining the beauty of a field of wheat blowing in the wind and the suffering of millions in Bosnia or the Sudan. As I exhale, I send out my gratitude, my energy and compassion to all suffering beings. Inspiring, I accept the gift of life. Expiring, I yield, cease grasping, give my care back into the world. Allowing and surrendering, I experience something deeper than my ego moving me — the prime mover, the Buddha-mind, the Brahman, the Spirit of God. As breathing becomes a liturgy, I am reminded moment by moment that the essence of my Being is the practice of gratitude and compassion. I am alive only in the degree that I am moved by the tidal rhythm of receiving and giving. I am a gossamer curtain hanging in a window separating time and eternity, blowing back and forth in the everlasting breeze.

STILLNESS AND TRANSCENDENCE

Just as reframing the ordinary act of breathing leads to a change in our sense of self, the simple act of sitting quietly and observing our passing thoughts and feelings creates a radical shift in identity, an experience of transcending the ego.

I first discovered stillness in the middle of the whirlwind.

In 1972, I was living alone in an apartment on Telegraph Hill in San Francisco, divorced after seventeen years of marriage and at the end of a love affair. My children were living a thousand miles away. My days were filled with emptiness and yearning, punctuated by trips to the Trieste for espresso and stimulation. When night came to the city, hungry ghosts and angry furies came out of the woodwork and wandered around my sparse bachelor apartment in search of my soul. They whispered, "The best of your life is past. You have made too many mistakes, hurt too many people. You can't start again." They taunted me with memories of my failures. Like prosecuting attorneys, they investigated the hidden closet of my days to discover incidents that would prove I was Guilty! Guilty of cruelty, carelessness, egotism, manipulation. They snickered and gossiped in low voices about the fatal flaws in my character, my hidden weakness, my multitudinous fears. Finally, when I had endured as much of their maddening abuse as I could stand, I left the apartment and began a long evening of wandering through the city. I had no destination, only the determination to keep moving until I was exhausted and could come home and fall asleep in a hurry.

I don't remember how many nights I ran from madness and pain. I do remember the moment at about two A.M. near Pier 32 when I finally had had enough and resolved that I would stop running. I walked home, sat in a chair facing the giant pyramid of the Transamerica building that was in the middle of my viewscape, and announced to myself and to whatever demons were lingering in the vicinity, "Here I sit, and here I will sit whenever the chaos swirls around me." No demons appeared.

The next evening, as demon hour approached (about the time my children would be sitting down to dinner without me a world away, and my ex-lover dining across town with her new love), I awaited the onslaught. Sure enough, with twilight they came. But this evening, I was prepared for them. I sat on my throne in the middle of my devastated kingdom and remained motionless. As they circled around and hurled their habitual barbs and accusations, I forced myself to breathe ever more slowly and examine them with clinical objectivity.

Listening carefully to the Guiltmonger, I could hear echoes of Saint Paul, John Calvin, and Dad and Mother in the voice that said, "You have done what you ought not to have done, and left undone what you ought to have done." Facing the Guiltmonger head-on, I demanded a bill of particulars. With what crimes am I charged? "With divorce, abandonment of your children, quitting your job, irresponsible economic conduct, infidelity, and arrogance," he replied. Armed with the shotgun list of charges, I began to sort out the residue of feelings of infantile guilt and shame from mature guilt. Gradually, I separated the betrayals and injuries to myself and others for which I bore responsibility from the wounds I had not caused.

One after another, I named and examined the indiscriminate emotions that were assaulting me. Nightly I invited the dark spirits to visit me, and in the classroom of my own psyche, I began to study the phenomena of anger, grief, guilt, shame, despair, impotence, and blame. I watched the interplay of emotion and self-image, the oscillation of arrogance and feelings of self-loathing. I could see that when I felt superior and judgmental one moment, I would feel inferior and judged the next. I examined how repressed grief and anger were transformed into melancholy, depression, and despair. As I gradually became comfortable with sadness and repentance, I learned the truth of the ancient promise "Blessed are those who mourn, for they will be comforted."

As a host of spiritual explorers from all ages have testified, a marvelous change in identity happens from the simple act of sitting quietly in the presence of the chaos of disorganized thoughts, feelings, and rhythms of heart and breath. Watching the whirlwind that occupied the center of my sense of self, I gradually changed from being the dis-eased one to being the compassionate-objective observer who could transcend the chaos and remain calm. In the middle of that battleground that is my personality — swept with confused alarms of struggle and flight where the ignorant armies of the superego, ego, and id clashed by night — I discovered a peaceful kingdom. I am the sane one in the madhouse of my personality. I am the subject who has the ability to transcend the predicates and accidents of my psyche. The more I *experience and then disidentify from* the wounds and brokenness of my historical condition, the more I gain an identity that is not at the mercy of passing thoughts or feelings. I am that being who has the capacity to transcend my mental-emotional-bodily conditioning. I am the one who can escape the imprisonment of my ancient character armor. I am the one who is not determined by yesterday.

The correct names for this capacity for self-transcendence are — freedom, spirit, and soul.

The first glimmerings of awareness that the self is spirit may come in the experience of discovering a silent and untroubled point within the chaos of the personality. But the ongoing adventure is the life-long exploration of the many modes of self-transcendence. I expect always to be discovering that I am larger than my previous ideas, self-images, and feelings. I overflow my personality. Who am I? What is my ultimate identity? What are the ultimate boundaries of this being I call myself? I don't know.

MOVING AND BEING MOVED:
WALKING MEDITATION

In the quest to become incarnate — fully carnal spirits — we run smack into a paradox. At one and the same time we must completely identify and disidentify with our bodies. In breathing, I become aware that my most intimate act is also a being-acted-upon; "my" body is animated by something "beyond" itself. Sitting quietly and attending to passing thoughts and sensations, I discover that "I" become the observer who is able to transcend my body. The same paradox applies to the practice of conscious awareness of moving and being moved.

The very idea of moving meditation, sacred dancing, and consecrated wrestling seems strange to most modern Westerners. Western religious life is sedentary, and only in Black and "lower-class" churches is there dancing and soul-music. Presbyterians, to say nothing of Episcopalians, don't shake their asses or "get down and get dirty," and Methodists act as if they, like the God of their Official Discipline, should be "without body, parts or passions."

By contrast, as Arthur Darby Nock, my professor of comparative religions at Harvard, always reminded us: "Primitive religion is not *believed*. It is *danced*." Most Eastern religions have developed martial arts — jujitsu, kung fu, aikido, tai chi — that keep the body-spirit lithe and teach the faithful to resist evil in a nonviolent manner.

From time to time, I have practiced formal sitting meditation and have dabbled in martial arts. But my most fruitful moving meditation has always been the long walk.

Walking is an essential discipline of thought and spirit. My soul is a traveler afoot in the world. Like Aristotle (whose school was called Peripatetic, after the covered walkway along which he strolled while teaching), I cannot think clearly if I remain too long sedentary. I believe Nietzsche only slightly overstated the case when, coming across a passage in which Flaubert wrote, "One can only think and write when one is seated," he replied, "There I have caught you, you nihilist! The sedentary life is the very sin against the Holy Spirit. Only thoughts reached by walking have value." I also suspect Immanuel Kant might have been able to follow *The Critique of Pure Reason* with an *Ode to Ecstasy*, had he deviated from his habit of taking only a single walk along the same path at the same time each day.

For me, sitting meditation, like repentance, is *work* that requires a sizable amount of concentration, soul-searching, and willpower. Walking, by contrast, is pure *grace*, an effortless art that produces surprising moments of spontaneous self-transcendence.

When I walk, my mind leaps ahead, skips steps, and presents me with images and ideas out of nowhere. With surprising regularity the thoughts that come to me when I am in a long hike in the hills contain the breakthrough insights I have not been able to reach after weeks of hard intellectual or emotional work. The solutions to my problems always arrive from elsewhere.

Walking re-minds me that my Being is becoming. I'm always going, never arriving. I am no static substance. I have no identity that will not be lost and found and lost again. We once thought that matter was solid and static; we now know "it" to be moving patterns. Substance is energy. Permanent change is here to stay. I must learn to be at home on the road.

Often, when I hit my stride, I experience a kind of kinesthetic grace, in which the line between moving and being moved is erased. Once when I was running with two friends on the slopes of Mount Tamalpais, in late afternoon, we stopped on a rocky beach by Pirates Cove and sat and talked for a long time. The more intimate our conversation became, the closer we moved to each other until we were hunkered down with our faces in a tight circle. When we started to run toward home, we crested the hill and bumped into the setting sun. All three of us looked at each other, and in an instant our individuality dissolved. It was as if the hand of God had slipped into a glove on which each of us was a finger-puppet. Our separate and distinct personalities were enveloped by a larger energy, will, life-force. I felt-knew for a moment that my whole life and the lives of my friends were moved by a force larger than any of us. Later the three of us talked about it, and all of us had a similar epiphany. An ordinary moment had suddenly become transparent, sacramental, symbolic.

The acceptance of one's destiny is like finding the right, the easy, the graceful pace in one's life. Every runner or walker knows the experience of hitting an effortless stride. At such times I sink into the happenings of my life like a stone in water. Surrendering to the inevitable, I drift down, down, down, until I rest at ease on the bottom. I remember the old Stoic hymn, "Guide me, O Zeus, and thou Destiny. I shall follow without hesitation; but even if I am disobedient and do not wish to, I shall follow no less surely." I yield to something larger than my willpower that is moving at the center of my life. As my Aunt Claire used to say, "I finally handed in my resignation as ruler of the universe and was surprised to find that it was accepted immediately."

The human body was formed by hunting and gathering. We are not meant to be sedentary animals. Our body, mind, and spirit become perverse when we cease to move. E-motion, especially compassion, involves the capacity to be moved. Character armor that rigidifies the body inhibits our ability to respond and be moved. Grace is the enemy of stasis and vice versa. Our bodies must be lithe and tuned to yield to the prime mover, energy, *prana*, spirit.

I think it is likely that much of the crisis of the modern mind and spirit comes from the sedentary habits of modern intellectuals. Schools teach us to take life sitting down. Professors and professional thinkers and managers are, for the most part, urban, institutionalized people who work indoors under artificial lights, seated at desks or conference tables, in the company of machines. Perhaps the world seen from this perspective is severely distorted and leads us ever deeper into a labyrinth of self-absorption and illusion. We are becoming more and more addicted to the kind of deracinated, abstract thinking and activity that are the roots of our dis-ease.

In what postures, places, and moods and in the presence of what community can we think most accurately, comprehensively, and hopefully about the human condition?

The simple act of going out of doors is necessary to dis-illusion the sedentary, sheltered mind. The posture of wonder destroys narcissism and hubris. A rock, a cloud, a tree may help us remember who we are — penultimately dwellers within the house of culture, but ultimately citizens of the cosmos. The human spirit must always find its final home within the natural order of spontaneously arising things. Apartment dwellers no less than farmers have their roots in the Earth. The humus enters into the definition of our species. Perhaps the best liturgy to help us re-member our spiritual identity is to take the time to take a stroll on the wild side.

Year by year, as I hit my pace, move in harmony with my body-time, I seem to sink deeper into something that feels like my destiny.

Much of the turmoil of my life has come from struggling to actualize some fantasy or realize an ideal of self that is unfitting. I would like to be happy-go-lucky, leisurely, of lighter spirit. I fool myself into wishing I were somebody totally different from who I actually am. I am unhappy because I am burdened by the demon of philosophy, cursed always to be asking "why," an obsessive worker at the meaning game.

But then in an instant, my perspectives shift, and I accept what before was problematic. I view my history, my parents, my body type, my strange appetite for asking questions, and my unsettled and unsettling mind as my destiny. What was a wound is transformed into a gift. In that moment I know that my ultimate freedom lies in surrendering to this strange being who bears the name Sam Keen. Even though I have exercised my willpower and have fabricated some of the details of my life, I am no self-made man. At a level deeper than my power of self-creation, I am called on to respond to that which I can only inexactly call my essence or my vocation. My destiny unrolls, allowing me to see in the sixth decade of my life the moving force of the "divine DNA" that has been informing my life since the beginning.

I am always dancing with the other, trying to move to the rhythm of the prime mover. As the old cowboy said when he was asked how to ride a horse, "Riding is just like dancing, except you let the horse lead." The same goes for life.

D. H. Lawrence captured the feeling of kinesthetic grace and surrender to destiny in his poem "Song of a Man Who Has Come Through."

Not I, not I, but the wind that blows through me!
A fine wind is blowing the new direction of Time.
If only I let it bear me, carry me, if only it carry me!
If only I am sensitive, subtle, oh, delicate, a winged gift!
If only, most lovely of all, I yield myself and am borrowed
By the fine, fine wind that takes its course through the chaos of the
    world.

SACRAMENTAL SENSUALITY

To recover the spiritual dimension of the life of the senses, we need to cultivate the discipline of en-joy-ment.

To turn sensuality into a sacrament, we must first slow down. Speed is the enemy of the spirit. Take *your* time. Appreciate and celebrate the gift of color and form, taste and texture. It takes time to savor the moment.

Inscribe on your heart the maxim that once appeared on every railroad crossing: "Stop, look, and listen." Make a habit of meditative listening, looking, touching.

Re-mind yourself. Epiphanies are as common as forget-me-nots. The eternal is curled up in the heart of the here and now. The holy may appear in the flaming beauty of maple leaves falling, or in the ecstatic meeting of flesh and flesh, or in the haunted face of a Somalian mother who holds her starving child, or in the awesome patterns that unite quarks and quasars. Be alert.

Create a sanctuary — a room in your house, a garden, a place in the wild — in which you are surrounded by ritual objects that re-mind you to appreciate and give thanks for the beauty of the Earth. Elegantly shaped driftwood, an exquisite statue, cobalt glass, a collection of sea shells. One man I know has a portable altar — a small silver box full of semiprecious gems. From time to time when he is in need of re-minding himself to live appreciatively, he takes out a gem, holds it up to the sunlight, and is bathed in a stream of amethyst or topaz. Another friend keeps a collection of small bottles of exotic perfumed oils at his office to revivify his love of aroma.

Sometimes all it takes to transform a mundane afternoon into a holiday — a holy day — is a small ritual, a sacramental taste of bread and wine, a moment of thanksgiving for a ray of light falling through a lace curtain.

CHAPTER 8

Carnal Knowledge:
Sex and Spirit

"And the Word became flesh."

The Gospel of John

"Listen friend, this body is his dulcimer,
He draws the strings tight, and out of it comes
the music of the inner universe.
If the strings break and the bridge falls,
then this dulcimer of dust goes back to dust.
Kabir says: The Holy One is the only one who can
draw music from it."

ROBERT BLY,
The Kabir Book

PRIESTS AND PORNOGRAPHERS: REPRESSION AND OBSESSION

I have a haunting photograph of a woman in black lace sitting on an altar under an imposing crucifix. A famous photographer (who shall remain nameless to protect the guilty) was recently filming a story in a great cathedral and was accompanied by a lady friend. After the filming, when the cathedral was empty, the lady in question explained that she had been raised in a sexually repressive church and had always wanted to affirm the goodness of her sexuality by posing and being photographed in a sexually evocative manner in a church. Without hesitation, she disrobed, sat on the altar in her black lace lingerie, and looked up at the crucifix as if to say to the tortured body of Christ, "There is glory also in the sacred pleasure of sex."

As sex rears its marvelous-awful head, we reach the opalescent heart of confusion. No human activity is so surrounded with glory and baseness, so full of divine promise and demonic power. It may be praised in gossamer lyrics or reduced to pornographic grunts. It may be the ultimate sacrament, the spiritual union of man and woman, god and goddess, and yang and yin, or it may be the degraded humping of anonymous bodies. It may be a path that leads to beatific union or to pandemonium. Whatever else we may say about sexuality, we must begin by acknowledging that it is surrounded by a cloud of obsessions, a thorn thicket of guilt, a swamp of shame, a double wall of dogma and taboo, and seven veils of romantic illusion. We approach it knowing we are at best one-eyed and at worst blind and must grope our way carefully through the haze.

In discussing sex, we could deal with broad issues of sexuality: how we gain and experience our gender roles; the social construction of desire; the politics of the body, family, contraception, and abortion; the use of sexual symbolism in religion. But I intend to focus on what has become the most problematic aspect of the spiritual-sexual relationship — erotic behavior that involves the potential exchange of bodily fluids. That the spiritual life involves the opening of our hearts and minds to one another in compassion is universally accepted. The difficult question is: In what ways does it involve the opening of our bodies to one another? *Agape* is recommended; but what about *eros*?

The best place to start our story is by setting the historical context that continues to shape our attitudes about sex. The myth of Adam and Eve and the forbidden fruit tells us more about what we do and don't do in bed than the most recent sex survey by *Playboy* or *Cosmopolitan*.

The text of Genesis does not say the fruit was an apple or that the apple was the first euphemism for sex. But the popular imagination has reshaped the original story to read something like this: God placed a naked man and woman in the woods with all the trimmings necessary for a romantic picnic, then commanded them to resist temptation.

"You may," the Lord said, "sample the innocent delights of blackberries and skinny-dipping, but no apples. No carnal knowledge. No sex." Adam evidently didn't know about sex until God prohibited it and Eve showed him her apple and urged him to take a small bite. He did, and she did, and afterward they looked at each other knowingly, flushed with pleasure but no longer innocent. And God, who had just been waiting for them to yield to temptation (being omniscient, He understood that the appeal of knowledge is irresistible), followed them down the garden path and handed them their sentence. For the crime of dalliance and disobedience, they would be evicted from the garden; Adam would be sentenced to labor in the sweatshop of history, and Eve to suffer in the maternity ward.

There is much we could say about the misogyny and antisexual bias that surrounds the Eden story. Historically, it reflects the transition between matricentric and patriarchal cultures, when the Goddess was being replaced by God the Father. Jewish monotheism was emerging triumphant out of a struggle with the ancient agricultural goddesses of Canaan. The snake, the symbol of the Goddess, was transformed into a symbol for evil; and sex, a central part of the symbolism and ritual of agricultural goddesses, was transvalued and placed under a dark cloud of suspicion.

Theologically, the Judeo-Christian tradition has consistently viewed woman, nature, and the sensual life of the body as of lesser importance and dignity than man, history, and the life of the mind. It has remained ambivalent about any positive link between sexuality and spirituality. *Agape,* the most godly form of love, involves no exchange of bodily fluids and is divorced from desire. God is, of course, considered the Creator of all. And yes, the body is part of the created goodness — especially from the waist up. But sex? In ecclesiastical practice, sex is sanctified only if it is done by legally married heterosexual couples, with the lights off, after a shower. All very orderly and clean. Any other expression of sexuality, from masturbation to homosexuality, is evidence that one has fallen under the dominion of the malevolent trinity of the world, the flesh, and the Devil. Even at this late date, the major Christian denominations cannot speak a clear "yes" to any form of sexuality that might have shocked Queen Victoria.

Notice two predictable twists of psycho-logic that result from what has been the dominant Judeo-Christian attitude toward sex. Inevitably, forbidden fruit is considered the sweetest precisely because it is forbidden. Had God forbidden bitter lemons, we would all lust after lemonade. Under the steady repressive hand of Western religion, we have become obsessed by sex and especially tempted by what is taboo, clandestine, illegal, dirty, and sacrilegious. The more our sexual attitudes and ethics are governed by the repressive piety of men in black cassocks, the more we clothe sex in black lace and black leather. Patriarchal puritanism is the breeding ground for pornography, sexual violence, and hypocrisy.

The sex-is-sin school of thought creates its opposite, the sex-is-salvation school of thought. A reaction against the prudishness of his early Methodism marked Hugh Hefner with the obsessive need to turn men into playboys and reduce women to tits and ass. The predictable reply to "Don't" is "Do it now." Sexual repression created the sexual revolution. The promise that the right kind of sex contains the magic formula for happiness began with Wilhelm Reich's gospel of the complete body orgasm, was accelerated by the invention of the Pill, and was popularized by *Playboy*'s and *Cosmopolitan*'s earnest advocacy of fun, games, and recreational sex. It reached its climax during the Woodstock generation's summer of love, when the psychedelic imagination was captivated by the fantasy that if we would only free our libidos, make love not war, and follow the pleasure principle, we might return to frolic in the Garden and be forever young, forever sexy, forever innocent.

At the present moment, the mood about sex is pensive. Herpes and AIDS — which the moralistic minority judge to be punishments visited on homosexuals, bisexuals, and polysexuals for disobeying God's law requiring monogamous sex — have put a stop to much casual sex and have made monogamy and safe sex look better than ever before. Feminism and the men's movement have brought to the surface a long-festering discomfort with our traditional sex roles and identities and are sparking new battles in the erogenous zones. The growing awareness that our individualistic society has radically eroded communal and family values is raising the question of how we can move away from the destructive repression and obsession with sex and recover its sacramental depth.

EATING FORBIDDEN FRUIT

It is easy enough to trace historical and cultural connections between sex and spirit, to compare and contrast the Christian and the Tantric traditions, to analyze, explain, and recommend. But when I drop into the first person singular, I begin to stutter, blush, and wonder whether I should remain silent. I am uncertain whether I can speak about my experience of the ambivalent relationship between sex and spirit without betraying trusts, breaking the canons of good taste, and risking exhibitionism. But I am equally certain that the conspiracy of silence we have woven around these private mysteries has contributed to our ongoing desecration of the flesh.

Once, on a bitter cold day in February in Minneapolis, I overheard someone say: "A Minnesota winter is so cold that exhibitionists just describe themselves." The difference between an existential discussion of sexuality and exhibitionism is a matter of keeping a proper artistic distance. I am convinced that a close examination of my intimate experience provides my best point of entry into the currents that shape the history of my time. But my story is helpful only if it is also a common story. It is with the conviction that millions of men and women have found it necessary to escape from garden-prisons that differ from my own only in detail that I describe my struggle, breakout, and recovery from the erotic-spiritual dis-ease we inherited from the Judeo-Christian-industrial traditions. I proceed with caution, trying to walk a narrow line between revelation and reserve.

My sexual persona was formed in the smoggy atmosphere of shame and guilt under the influence of my quite normal and loving mother and father, who as far as I know, had a rather happy erotic life together. I did not come from a dysfunctional family.

My earliest memory of what I did not yet know was sex was in my fourth year. On a warm Florida afternoon, Mother put me in the crib on the back porch with orders to take a nap. So that I would not be distracted, she removed all toys from easy reach. As endless minutes stretched into a sleepless eternity punctuated only by the drone of an occasional fly, I searched for some way to brighten my exile. Lo and behold, I discovered a marvelous snakelike toy equipped with a sensory interactive device that caused it to change shapes. The more I played with it, the better I felt and the larger it became. And best of all, it was attached to me. How I had overlooked such an object until this time, I could not imagine. I was totally engaged in exploring the multiple potentialities of my new toy when I sensed *the eyes* upon me and heard Mother's voice from distant Sinai, "Sammy, nice boys don't do that."

Primal confusion clouded my bodymind: "I want" and "You should," desire and duty, were at war with each other. The Mother Goddess announced that her face would shine upon me only if I was "nice," which meant not playing with my newly discovered erotic toy. But in the depth of my being, exploring this randy marvel felt like goodness incarnate. Caught in the spotlight of Her eyes, everything shifted and I became ashamed of what a moment before had been a source of growing pleasure and swelling pride. Right and wrong suddenly switched places as I was instructed that the good feelings in my penis were to be considered bad.

Exposed, bathed in the light of shame, I divided my self, Janus-like, into two persons to cope with the dilemma. I shaped one face into a "nice" mask and learned to perform in ways that would win the approval of the Mother Goddess and all the women who would subsequently re-present her. My second face turned toward the protective darkness. To avoid the threat of exposure and judgment, I became secretive and clandestine. My sexuality would henceforth be hidden under the cover of darkness. It would be many years before I discovered that the eyes from whom my carnal secrets were most hidden were my own. Gradually the habit of shame keeps us from biting deeply into the apple of self-knowledge.

The prohibitions and commandments of my earthy father concerning sex were more complex than those of my mother. Sex was not a category that loomed large in Mother's mind. Her concern was obedience to the Word of God. Had the Bible decreed that orgies should be held every Saturday night in the basement of the Presbyterian church, she would have happily sent us on the path of excess (which William Blake, a Dionysian Christian, said leads to the palace of wisdom). Dad, however, had a thing about sex. The rule for both boys and girls was "No sex outside marriage!" The rule was not stated in so many words but was communicated by stories about people whose lives had been ruined by looking for love in all the wrong places, like Jimmy Clyde, who was on his way to a brilliant career in music until he married a floozie who ran around with other men and left him with two kids to raise.

Among WASPs in the South in the 1930s, the rule against pre- or extra-marital sex was universally honored, although frequently broken. What made Dad's ferocious advocacy strange was that it was so out of character. His usual approach to his children was to encourage us to follow our enthusiasms. And as I have said earlier, he was extravagantly sensual. In every way except sex, he urged us to develop our interests and savor our uniqueness. But sex in my father's mind, and therefore in the mind of the son in whom he was well pleased, was so volatile and dangerous, it could be contained only within the firm walls of marriage.

At thirteen I suddenly emerged from childhood into the new world of sex in a liquid, ecstatic dream. Throughout my teens there were the usual beach parties, dates, and pledges of undying love to various steady girlfriends. Because of what I then considered my Christian duty, I valiantly resisted temptation and remained technically a virgin, saving the finale for the woman who was to be my forever wife.

One enchanted evening when I was twenty-one, I met Heather, and we were married a year later. At the wedding, my father sang "O perfect love, all human love transcending, / lowly we kneel in love before Thy throne. / That theirs may be the love which knows no ending, / whom Thou forever more dost join in one."

I entered marriage with the unquestioned assumption that my sexuality needed to be tamed by the bonds of commitment. I expected that my raw sexual urges would be domesticated, that lust would be transformed into a true communion of the flesh by honoring and cherishing. I also expected that finally I would be free to express my sexuality without reservation. Intimacy would allow my wife and me to strip off our personas, set our egos aside, lay down the burden of performing, and come together as gnarled and vulnerable selves. Trusting, giving each other the gift of unconditional acceptance, we would be naked and transparent to each other, two persons joined by carnal knowledge becoming one flesh.

In our innocence, we did not know what we did not know—our unconscious selves. We were too young to understand that beneath the calm surface of the ocean of love and goodwill lay hidden shoals and treacherous currents. Beneath good intentions and unexamined virtues the shadow lurks. Neither of us had any early inkling of our hidden agendas, childhood wounds, repressed angers, unrealistic demands, secret dependencies, excessive desires.

It took me years to understand that the dynamics that frustrated Heather's and my hopes for a liberating marriage, and that made my complicity in divorce an inevitable part of the journey we had started together, were set in place long before I arrived on the scene. In a life, as in a drama, certain actions are scripted. The action in Act II is determined by the themes that have been set in motion in Act I.

After fifteen years of marriage, five years after my father died, I acted out my destined rebellious scenario. Trembling with fear and excitement, I broke the specific taboo against illicit sexual knowledge that had kept my psyche and body in hidden bondage to my father's authority. Names and details are of no importance. I "fell in love" with a beautiful young woman who I assumed was far more experienced in the art of dalliance than I and might sweep away all my sexual timidities and repressions.

A film of the affair—the motel by the sea, the interplay of eyes and kisses, the slight glaze of salt on strange skin, the heated bodies on cool sheets—would not have captured the real story. The act of love itself was neither overwhelmingly passionate nor elegant. The ground did not move. But deep in the foundations of my self, the long-contained artesian waters burst through the rock, and my spirit began to expand and animate my body and mind. Leaving the motel, with sadness and joy I said good-bye to Mother and Father, to the matrix and rules that had nurtured and constrained me, and set forth into that unknown country that lies to the East of Eden. I knew little about the wilderness into which I was about to enter, only that I had been too tamed and needed to recover my passion for life. I wanted to be swept away, to surrender to something beyond myself.

My late loss of innocence and desire for "a touch of madness" was only one of the rocks on which my hopes for a lifelong marriage ran aground. It is neither seemly nor necessary to tell the complex story;

suffice it to say that our marriage was rich and troubled. It ended after seventeen years in mutual care and pain when our paths separated and we released each other from our vows. Inasmuch as divorce can ever be an act of love, ours was. Across time, distance, and remarriage, the climate between us has remained warm.

BREAKING TABOOS: SOME GUIDELINES

Breaking taboos is dangerous. It cost me a marriage that might have endured and left scars on my children that have taken a decade of work to turn into beauty marks. The moment we cross the boundary of what is permissible to parents and authorities, the shrill voice of our infantile conscience rises up to accuse us indiscriminately of irresponsibility, betrayal, desertion, and sacrifice of family and community to satisfy narcissistic desires. "If you break the taboo restricting sex to marriage, what is to keep you from rape, incest, murder, and stealing? Once you throw out guilt and shame, you land in moral anarchy!"

Some taboos are creative, others destructive; some are sacred, others demonic. Incest is a desecration of a familial bond of trust. Rape is an outrage that no society can tolerate and remain civil. Murder is an act that destroys the foundation of respect for others without which there can be no commonwealth. Only a psychopath would overthrow all taboos, but only a fanatic would deny that certain taboos should be broken in the name of freedom and spiritual necessity.

There are times when parental and social values conflict with our maturely chosen values and when infantile shame and guilt created by the authority of the parental conscience collide with our mature sense of shame and guilt. At those moments when our spiritual development is blocked by moralism, we must dare to act in obedience to the creative good. A voice of spiritual conscience calls us forth into a future that is larger and more compassionate than that demanded by the moralistic and tribal conscience. In the same measure that prophetic protest and civil disobedience are sometimes necessary to make the body-politic more just, the descent into Dionysian chaos is sometimes necessary to release sacred creativity.

There is only one place where all taboos are and should be broken —

in dreams. To develop the widest compassion, I must ultimately know that *nothing human is alien to me.* I am monster and saint, murderer and healer, contaminated and pure. The same lust for power and consequent cruelty that drove Hitler festers in a dark corner of my psyche, adjacent to the impulse toward indiscriminate love that animates Mother Teresa. And the only safe and creative way to achieve the more dangerous and destructive forms of tabooed self-knowledge is in dreams. Imagination allows us to sample in fantasy what is inexpedient or demonic to act out. Dionysus, the god of excess and ecstasy, rules supreme in dreamland, just as Apollo, the god of moderation, reason, and law, holds sway over the majority of our daylight hours. When in dreams I sample my promiscuous lusts, murderous desires, and unbounded capacity for love, I am able to awake from the moralistic illusions that I am infinitely better or worse than other men and women. An amoral imagination provides us with the experience in dreamtime of living "beyond good and evil" that is necessary for the development of compassion. I also am that.

Usually the taboos that we must test in action in order to discover our deepest desires are those that are unconsciously programmed into us by our family myths and the ideology of our culture. To win freedom, one person may need to rebel against the constraints of a Southern Baptist family, another against the dogma of an atheistic family. An alcoholic family in effect creates a taboo against sobriety. A fundamentalist family creates a taboo against doubt.

I recently was made privy to a case of creative taboo-breaking that was the inverse of my own. The man I will call Jack, a notorious womanizer, was raised by sophisticated jet-set parents who were somewhere between liberal and libertine in sexual matters. He had been taught by his father's example and his mother's explicit instructions that it was shameful for him *not* to attempt to seduce any attractive women with whom he came in contact. His mother made a practice of pointing out likely women for his affairs and even followed the more promising ones to the ladies' room to give them her son's phone number. If his seduction succeeded, he was expected to share the details with Mom. As a result of such imperatives and encouragement, Jack slept with so many women that when he unexpectedly met one with a familiar face or name, he could not remember whether he had slept with her. Recently, however, he fell deeply in love and was contemplating marriage. For the first time in his life he wanted to be faithful to one woman. But he was unable to do so because he felt anxious when he ceased his compulsive seductions and edged up to breaking the family taboo against fidelity. When I shared my story with Jack about breaking my family's taboo against infidelity, we looked at each other and laughed, recognizing that we had lived the same story in opposite, mirror-image worlds. The other day I read that Jack had married. I rejoice with him in the strange freedom he must experience in his new-found rebellious fidelity.

HOLY EXCESS: THE WILD AND THE TAME

A half-truth is as dangerous as a full lie, as I found out when I tried to be solely a homesteader, even though I am half gypsy. We may be moved by awe-ful delight and surrender to the sexual-sacred energy that moves beneath our personalities when we are cherished and held secure within the enduring bonds of marriage. The great secret of good marriages is that fidelity is a sacred aphrodisiac.

But it would be a mistake to think that sacred sexuality is always tame, gentle, and personal. John Calvin to the contrary, the spirit does not always move us to conduct our sexual devotions "decently and in order." Sometimes a frenzied wind blows through our orderly days, and wild music calls us to the hills.

In the five years between my marriages (time off for bad behavior), I did only a modest amount of what in California was then called "exploring my sexuality." As a recovering Presbyterian, I remained conservative enough to be satisfied with minor variations of plain vanilla. I shared my body carefully with fewer than a handful of women, most of whom I considered candidates for a new enduring relationship.

There was one notable exception, a two-year affair that was an extended sexual devotion.

In this story anonymity is appropriate, not to protect our privacy but because between us it was bodies that mattered. Who we were or had been or might become wasn't important. I had known her slightly when I was married, but each time we talked she was so fanciful and told so many conflicting stories about her past that I was never certain that she wasn't inventing her personal history on the spur of the moment. Her identity was fluid at best and dangerously diffuse at worst. A dozen years after our affair, her delightful discontinuities degenerated into schizophrenia. When the old black magic first got us in its spell, my identity had been pulverized by divorce and dislocation from my family and profession. We connected in southern California, where the illusion of perpetual youth and endless possibility is an article of faith and where I had gone to begin again.

Let a single occasion conjure the whole.

Her one-room apartment might be a harem room for a small-budget filming of *Scheherazade*. The walls are draped with Indian-print bedspreads that billow out to form a canopy over a king-size mattress on the floor. Tantric paintings of royal couples in athletic postures of love cover what little wall space is not draped. An Oriental rug, deep purple with designs like twining snakes, covers the floor. The smell of sandalwood is in the air.

She lights a new stick of incense and brings two cups of plum wine to the bed. They sit with their thighs in full contact. Both are breathless, and the air is tense with electricity, as if lightning were about to strike. They have made love many times over the last year. Each time it is like this. They talk little and try to restrain themselves as long as possible, as if it were somehow unseemly to yield to their urgency. In slow motion, they place their cups on the floor and kiss gently. He looks into the green darkness of her eyes and sees a reflected image of his eyes. In all the eyes — desire. Wordlessly, they undress. She wears nothing beneath her blouse and long skirt. Only now a sense of haste overtakes them. There is no foreplay, no effort to excite. Already an invisible current is pushing them outward from the shore into the deep water. They force themselves to breathe quietly to slow their velocity. He puts his hand between her legs and finds her fluid and throbbing. She leans back against the pillows, and he enters her with tantalizing slowness, pausing like a diver at every stage of the descent into the underwater cave. The moment he touches the bottom, she erupts into convulsions. He breathes deeply and waits. When her breathing becomes calm, they begin to move together, pausing to let the fluid warmth trickle into every recess of their bodies. Rhythmic waves sweep them along. The incense burns to ashes. After an endless time of surfing on the waves of sensation, they fall together into the ocean of oblivion. Afterward, they lie together, washed clean by their shared passion. Several times in the night their bodies move together until lovemaking and dreams of lovemaking intertwine. Waking, he starts to draw her closer into his arms, only to find that he has been embracing a pillow. His eyes fall on a note that is pinned on the billowing paisley cloud canopy above the bed: "Sweet man, hound dog, butterfly, tiger, prince of lovers. I barely managed to swim out of the pleasure pool this morning in time to catch the submarine to work. Come early this evening. I plan a feast. Love Z."

There were other succulent evenings and afternoons, but they did not add up to forever. The man and woman did not live happily ever after. Finally, the discontinuities between who they were in and out of bed grew too great. The flesh can bear only so much freight. Their meetings remained explosive but grew less frequent until they became as separate as they had always been.

A voice as old as my primal shame tells me that a story so personal, so unashamedly sexual has no place in a discussion of the sacred. Unless, of course, it serves as a horrible example of a dis-graceful or merely secular mode of sexuality. But I cannot help but honor and celebrate an unguent by which I was healed. To my partner in this communion of the flesh, I owe a debt for the gift of graceful wildness. Her adoration of my body gave me back the innocence of passion, the unashamed joy of being a fully carnal spirit.

As disconcerting as it may be to some people, it is necessary to focus on sacred excess because middle-class sensibilities tend to reduce both sexuality and spirituality to something tame and controllable. But unquestionably most religious traditions have included orgiastic practices within their repertoire of sacred occasions. Most cultures have paid their respects to Dionysus by setting aside holy days for Carnival, Mardi Gras, or Fasching, when wine runs free and sexual permissiveness is the order of the day. Hindu scriptures celebrate the illicit antics of Krishna and the milk maidens. I read about, but have forgotten the name of, a tribe that numbered only 362 days in the year; the remaining days were dedicated to festivals in which all the sexual mores were ignored. No one could be held accountable for what happened during these days, because they did not exist.

I remain sufficiently reserved and private to be uncomfortable with the more excessive expressions of sacred sexuality. Unexpectedly, in 1979, on an assignment from *Psychology Today*, I received an offer to visit and write an article about Plato's Retreat, the first legal public sex club that had opened in New York City.

As I considered the offer, the very notion of public sex made my taboos tremble. A chorus of oughts and ought-nots, don'ts and fears, spoke in disorderly haste. A gathering of elders waited on me with shocked faces — parents, gentle friends, distinguished professors — all the guardians of my former days who had pruned my young and budding mind into a wholesome arbor, useful, fruitful, shade-giving. Dr. Conning of the Covenant Church shook his head silently from side to side at the very idea of what I, once a candidate before the presbytery, was proposing to do. How could I even consider such an indecent thing! My dialogue with the good Fathers was suddenly interrupted when a hairy-legged satyr rode into the parlor from his cave deep in the unexplored regions of my psyche. He looked straight at me and asked: "How could you possibly pass up this voyeuristic opportunity? I promise you will see nothing you have not dreamed about, and you can consider how demonic or divine impersonal sex is from a safe aesthetic distance." Suddenly, I felt a strange shame for all the years I had kept the hairy beast chained in my unconscious. So when he winked, I winked back and caught a taxi to West Seventy-fourth Street.

The manager, a fiftyish woman with a brusque manner and an immobile face that bespoke either boredom or unflappable sophistication, examined my press card and explained Rule Number One. As a journalist, I was free to observe but not to participate; I was to remain clothed and refrain from fraternizing with the natives. My guided tour of the temple of love began in the outer precincts — the bar, the swimming pool, the Jacuzzi, the dance floor — where foreplay might take place, wended its way through side rooms like small chapels in a cathedral where couples might make love in private, and culminated in the central mattress room, where the serious rites of Aphrodite were practiced.

The mattress room featured a wall-to-wall combination of super-size mattresses and tumbling mats. Mirrors on the ceiling and along two walls allowed the actors to admire their performance and see themselves as others saw them. A guard was stationed by the door to enforce the rules, which were posted in bold type: No clothes allowed. Only male and female pairs were to enter (Noah's ark). Once inside, couples might split and recombine in any of the sexual logarithms, limited only by the number of orifices and the flexibility of the involved bodies. Homosexual couples were forbidden. (Nothing queer at Plato's place. Too bad for Socrates and Sappho!) On the mat, some thirty people were splayed in a moving triptych of dyads, trios, and foursomes and were interwoven in daisy chains of assorted breasts, thighs, backs, arms, heads, and genitals.

As I stood at the door of the mattress room my eyes began to glaze and I seemed to be watching a film — a Fellini orgy in *La Dolce Vita*. I had stepped behind the green door, and the people in front of me were familiar actors — Marilyn Chambers and Harry Reems. They weren't real. My brain was postmodern, educated enough by films and music videos to be relaxed with anything that was "just a movie." The spectator, like a consumer of pornography, watches a village being bombed, a rebel being executed, a riot, a beating, an orgy, from the safety of noninvolvement.

Meanwhile, my real focus was inward. Just behind my retinas, a different film festival — "Taboos and Archetypes of Sin" — was in progress, featuring such classics as:

Sodom and Gomorrah. The God of Israel illustrates the consequences of moral depravity by visiting fire and brimstone on men and women lost in sense-lust.

The Condemnation of Aphrodite (alias Ishtar, Astarte, and Playmate of the Month). Again featuring Yahweh destroying those who worship the generative power of sex, participate in sacramental intercourse, and neglect the worship of the True God.

The Fall of Rome. Starring Caligula and a cast of thousands, a morality play in which the nongod of secular history first makes sensate those it wishes to destroy.

The Destruction of Betty Grace. An innocent Southern girl falls in love and is led into sin by an unscrupulous man interested only in sex. She gets pregnant, is abandoned, has an abortion, and dies. (A cautionary tale told by my father.)

Tasting Forbidden Pleasures. A philosopher under the influence of the psychedelic 1960s and the Esalen ethic of experimentation plays fast and loose with love. The results, first comical, twist into a dark scenario, ending in divorce.

With disciplined intent, I shut off my private movies, suspended my subjective feelings, and returned to objective observation to record the facts as they might be seen by a neutral eye. The natives of the mattress room were very active. The majority of couples who entered the room remained with each other. Some watched, fondled each other, and left without attempting intercourse. Four couples in the middle of the mat engaged in lengthy exercises in the missionary position, their mechanical repetitions producing a maximum amount of stimulation and a minimum amount of abandon.

Most attention was paid to the obvious erogenous zones. There was little involvement with (or should I say "homage given"?) the great plains of the belly, the towers of the legs, the column of the neck. No exploration of the web between toes and fingers. No tracing the switchbacks in the ear or the broken pathways that destiny has etched on the palm. Most of the subjects exhibited an almost obsessive haste to establish the genital connection. Little prolonged kissing or embracing. No minuets between eyes. The slow dance of courtship and the adornments of modesty were not part of this erotic world. The atmosphere was reminiscent not of a gourmet restaurant where each morsel is savored, but of Denny's — fast food and a standardized menu.

The evidence of ecstatic self-loss was slight. Little moaning. Few loud cries. No laughter. No yelling out of control. Little involuntary trembling. No boisterous bellows of satisfaction. Only two couples I observed made love with anything that appeared to be a mounting sense of excitement and self-transcendence.

Bare observation at Plato's produced little to stimulate the mind.

Facts alone are sterile. To be interesting they must be caressed, teased, and joined together in a suggestive hypothesis.

As I watched the interactions of bodies, my mind again wandered — or rather, it went synapsing into metaphor, without which the mind is dark and the eye blind. To move from observation to understanding, we have to ask: How is a falling apple like the moon? How is a mind like a hologram? How is an orgy like a . . .? My "subjects" became, metaphorically, a mixed litter of puppies playing on a mat; genital engineers studying the rules of sexual energy; bargain-seekers at an erotic fire sale; ghosts injected with novocaine trying with cool desperation to recover a feeling of the human condition; disembodied genitals in search of romance.

Was there, beneath the casual sex, a deeper human quest? Was this place of fornication (from the Latin meaning underground, arched vault) Plato's cave of illusion? At the beginning of the evening, I had been willing to accept the simplest explanation: Plato's Retreat was a sanctuary where people might explore sensation divorced from feeling. But something wasn't right about this preliminary hypothesis. The data didn't fit the metaphor. If this was a school for the education of the senses, I should have seen more polymorphous perversity. The true artist of the senses overcomes the tyranny of the genital obsession. In the mattress room, the rhythms were too rapid and aggressive to be sensitive. Most of what I saw belonged to the hard-driving locomotive theory of sex.

One obvious fact suggested a different hypothesis. People came to Plato's more to see and be seen than to experiment with sensuality. Why? One couple explained it to me; she said, "Most of us spend a lot of years wondering if we are okay, if we are like other people, especially about sex. Here you can see what other people actually do, and that takes a big load off your imagination." He put in, "I don't think it's just seeing other people. It's also letting them see you. It's kind of a public display or confession of your sexuality." She: "There are times when I want to yell, 'Look, Ma! Look, Dad! I'm doing all those dirty, nasty things you told me not to, and I love every minute of it! I started out with every sex hangup you can imagine, and part of me is still a little girl trying to make sure my life is my own and I have a right to pleasure and love in spite of not being too pretty or too nice." Perhaps orgy is a theater of sexual liberation in which repressed parts of ourselves are brought to light and acted out before the primal audience of the forbidding eyes — parents, authorities, the watching institutions. In the theater of our minds, we force them to accept us in the very act of doing what they forbade. Thus we transcend the prison of the past. The performance is symbolic; it may be therapeutic.

As the evening wore on, the revelation I had expected did not arrive. Some veils of illusion had fallen, but I did not see the unmasked face of the god Eros. What lies beneath the blind urgency that drives us to cohabit in the circus and sanctuary of sex? A strange memory and set of associated ideas came to mind. Suddenly I remembered that this was not the first orgy I had attended.

In the early 1960s, I had been with a large group of people who touched and smelled each other, linked arms, laughed, cried, and melted into one body, one mind, one voice. For over an hour we had mystically been one flesh. I remember the tears and the welling-up in my chest as my little ego burst and I was filled with a mingled essence of other beings. The group — ten thousand of us — reached a simultaneous climax as we held each other, swayed together and sang, "We shall overcome / We shall overcome / We shall overcome — someday / And deep in my heart / I do believe / We shall overcome someday." Then Martin Luther King spoke to the civil rights march in Frankfort, Kentucky, and we were a single body-politic. Our common feeling flowed from a single intuition toward a common goal.

"Yes, but that wasn't a real orgy. You are just playing with words." I think not. My body tingled, was shot through with warmth. An electric current ran through my loins, my head, and my heart. On the scale of sensual delights, the Frankfort experience ranks higher than many genital orgasms I have had. And it taught me that there is an instinctual drive in the body and in the body-politic toward communion. We are moved to come together. The "I" is restless until it rests in "We." To be a self is to search for self-transcendence. In one sense, literal orgies are a symbolic-sexual acting-out of the instinct for transcendence and communion. The privates are demonstrating in public their need for a communion that is both fleshy and meta-physical. In orgies, as in trance, ecstatic prayer, or any deep experience of community, we have the chance for a moment to lay the burden of individuality down, to be washed clean of the persona we hold together with glue, baling wire, and polite roles, and to shed the character we have constructed for a lifetime. Instead of being somebody, we get to be anybody. Flesh touches flesh. All nerve endings are equal. None has press clippings, a title on the door, or a Harvard degree. When we reduce ourselves to flesh, we are, in sex and in death, one body.

Flesh is a parable of spirit.

Now I began to understand what was missing and twisted at Plato's. The prisoners in this New York cave were trapped, self-conscious performers in a hall of mirrors. Here was none of the frenzy of the Dionysian orgy, the fearsome self-loss as individuals trembled on the brink of annihilation and fell into the undifferentiated hands of desire. These players did not know the divine madness reverenced by the Guardians of Plato's Republic. Only those who dare to descend into the darkness beneath personality, where there is no performance because there is no audience, discover the mystical union of all living beings. The true Dionysian orgy was an initiation into the numinous knowledge that in personality we are many, but in essence we are one. Plato's Retreat was fun and games without the risk of transcendence. The fully secularized and trivialized sex of the orgy parlor confined the human spirit to a basement in which there was no window to the stars.

When I emerged from the cave after a long night, I had lost many illusions. In the deepest sense I understood that beneath sexual desire a meta-physical game is being played. In the strictly biological sense, sex may be only a lure to seduce us into keeping the evolutionary game going. But even if we reduce it to this level, it is marvelous to contemplate that in our very DNA, hope still strolls hand in hand with desire. Something in our genes wants the Big Game to continue. But in a more profound philosophical sense, I think Hegel was near to the complex truth when he said, "Truth is the bacchanalian revel where not a soul is sober." I understood that my primal longing was metasexual and could not be satisfied by any number of momentary pleasures of the flesh.

In the dawning morning I spotted a small coffee shop that advertised café au lait and croissants. Minutes later, I was officiating at my private morning ritual. As I poured the dark espresso into the steaming milk and watched New York gather its energies for its daily run at glory, I thought of Socrates' benediction at the end of the *Phaedrus:* "Beloved Pan, and all ye other gods who haunt this place, give me beauty in the inward soul; may the outward and the inward man be as one."

LONGING FOR EVERLASTING ARMS

Why is it that sex and spirit are so interconnected and confusing?

Begin with the experience of longing and anxiety. No matter how much we accomplish or what we possess, something is always missing, incomplete, absent. We can stuff ourselves with every pleasure and still be empty, obsessed by a hunger that cannot be assuaged. The very indistinctness of our existential longing allows us to fill the void with an infinite variety of imagined nostrums for our dis-ease. If only I had more money, security, a Mercedes-Benz, a more loving partner. If only I could acquire the missing "X," my longing would be satiated, my anxiety quieted, and I would be full and at peace. If only she would, he would, they would . . . If only I had . . . If only I could . . .

There are many ways we might analyze human longing and insatiability. Psychologists tend to trace the roots of our dissatisfaction to deficiencies in the family. We were poorly bonded with our mothers, ignored by our absent fathers, sexually abused by our uncles. We are addicted to dysfunctional relationships and unsatisfying habits because we remain adult-children, victims of imperfect parents. Political theorists assume our alienation is caused by too much or too little individualism and commercialism, too rigid or too lax community structure, and unjust forms of social organization. There is more than a little truth in both these forms of analysis. Certainly, kinder and gentler families and economic and political organizations would alleviate many kinds of dissatisfaction.

All spiritual traditions maintain that the longing for some metaphysical fulfillment, like sexual desire, is built into the human condition.

Plato created an elaborate myth of androgyny to explain ontological-sexual longing. Once upon a time, he said, there were three types of human units: a pair of males, a pair of females, and a male-female pair joined back to back. These Siamese pairs were very powerful and could run at great speed by using their four arms and four legs to cartwheel. But since they could never face each other, they were frustrated. Zeus took pity on them and sent a thunderbolt to split them into separate persons. Since that time men and women have been searching for their lost partners. The splitting of the three types of units accounts for the three forms of love — lesbian, homosexual, and heterosexual.

Paul Tillich took the Platonic myth and translated it into modern language. "Love," he said, "is the ontological drive toward the reunion of the separated." To say that love is "ontological" implies that it is not merely "psychological," not a socially conditioned need. Love, the movement from estrangement to communion, is intrinsic, essential, a structural element in human nature. The same consciousness that gives us knowledge and power over nature alienates us from it. The greater our individuation, the greater our separation. Because consciousness allows us to contemplate our lives, we become aware of our alienation and search for some way of becoming reunited with "the ground of our being." Individuality is both our glory and our burden. And longing is the inevitable companion of consciousness.

Our drive for reunion and belonging takes many forms. Tribes, nations, and corporations invite people to become part of a "we" and give up the anxious burden of being a single self. Religion provides a belief-system and a community in which individuals can remember and celebrate the totality to which they belong. "Religion," the philosopher Whitehead said, "is what a man does with his solitariness." In recent times, when both politics and religion have failed to create a sense of belonging, romantic and sexual love have become our favorite paths to self-transcendence. Through love and sex, we seek the connections that community and religion once provided to make our aloneness bearable.

Our sexual and spiritual impulses are driven by the same ontological longing, the same need for belonging. In matters sexual and spiritual, we both desire and resist the same loss and transcendence of self. At one and the same time, we want to be swept away, be relieved of the burden of our aloneness, be rescued from our isolation by our lover, or

God, and yet preserve the integrity of our individual selves. We want to blend, and remain separate, to be lost in the ecstasy of union, and to return home to our familiar egos.

In a parallel fashion, sexuality and spirituality offer the delights and difficulties that come from any surrender of the familiar boundaries of self. Tantric Buddhism maintains that sex and death are especially propitious subjects for meditation because they are the two natural events in which we are automatically stripped of our illusions of substantial selfhood. The same insight is contained in D. H. Lawrence's notion that lovemaking is "a gentle reaching out toward death." Orgasm is a parable. In the moment of ecstasy we finally achieve an end to isolation; the boundaries of self are washed away. And then? No sooner have we disappeared back into our oceanic home than we once again swim rapidly to the separate islands on which we dwell. The loss of self makes the return to self all the sweeter. Every man and woman is perverse, twisted, but the twist is ontological, not neurotic. It belongs to the human condition. The question is: How do we make this twist creative rather than destructive? How can we be alone together?

Since Being-becoming-itself is both one and many, authentic spirituality, like sexual love, is bound to be a never-ending game. Existence, according to the Hindu tradition, is Lela or God-Play. According to Hegel, Being-becoming-itself is Love, or Spirit disporting with itself. But never mind. We don't have to accept any metaphysical or religious vision of Totality or God to realize the more modest truth that human existence, and therefore our sexuality and spirituality, is a game. The name of the game is coming and going; lost and found; emptiness and form; journeying into strange lands and returning home; forgetting and remembering the self.

The love game and the spirit game seem to have the same rules:

It takes two to play, a self and an other. The game is composed of alternating movements that are repeated ad infinitum. Self and other move toward and away from each other. The One becomes Many, and the Many become One, ad infinitum. I and Thou become We, and We become I and Thou.

The game ends if the dance ceases, if the paradox is dissolved, if we eliminate either the movement toward the other or the return to self.

We keep love and spirituality alive only by moving simultaneously in opposite directions. You must have a self in order to experience self-transcendence, and vice versa. You must be ego-centric to be eccentric. Understanding and ecstasy (standing outside of the self) are opposite ends of the same seesaw.

How can we distinguish between spirited and desecrated sexuality? Clearly, the sacral, self-transcending, revelatory experiences of sexual communion are not the exclusive property of legally married hetero-sexual couples. But if we are not merely to reaffirm traditional preju-dices and accept the arbitrary sexual standards of our culture that are often hypocritical, cruel, and destructive of our capacity for joy, how can we decide what constitutes sacred, reverential, and compassionate sexual behavior? The moment we venture beyond sexual moralism, we need some guiding principles to prevent us from landing in nihilism.

Sacred lovemaking brings people together in a way that enhances the singularity of each person and their ability to surrender individu-ality both to the relationship *and to something beyond the relationship.* Sexual union should be a microcosmic act that recapitulates our basic spiritual relation to Being. Inspired sexuality makes the burden of individuality bearable, and increases each person's momentum toward consciousness, compassion, and communion.

A sexual meeting may become an epiphany when two people experi-ence each other and themselves as mysterious, awesome, and fascinat-ing. This happens only when two I's who are Thous to each other become We.

In practical terms this means: I do not turn you into an object. You are not a "piece," a conquest, a body for the fulfillment of my desire. We remain ends, not means, to each other, irreplaceable persons, not mere sense organs, genitals, or interchangeable bodies. We come to each other with respect, recognizing that we are inviolable beings with complex and unique histories. Anything that pulls us apart from the totality of the lives to which we have committed ourselves desecrates us.

I remember a particularly vivid testimony about the sacredness of sex from an unusual source. Several years ago a flashy young woman came to one of my personal mythology seminars. Her undulating walk, skin-tight clothes, and plastic beauty screamed "Hollywood." There was nothing warm or heartful about her. She was a bruised and absent soul striking sexually provocative poses. On the last day of the seminar, she began to tell her story. In a detached voice, she reported that her husband was a producer of pornographic films in which she was the chief actress and that she had become addicted to cocaine and other drugs. After relating these facts, she fell silent. Slowly, tears began to soften the contorted beauty of her masked face, deep sobs shook her body, and a cry came forth from her depths: "He makes me do these things, and it violates everything in me. Sex is sacred to me."

When lovers meet with respect for the mystery of their separateness, they may, in coming together, suddenly experience lovemaking as a sacramental dance, an outward and visible sign of the invisible grace that unites the single self to the communion of Being. Only then does sexuality become a path to wisdom and compassion.

PAEAN TO MARRIAGE: MATED TO MYSTERY

Most of my adult life has been spent in the state of matrimony. I was married to Heather at twenty-three, divorced at forty, and six years later I was married to Jananne. Gradually, I have been disillusioned of the romantic myth and have come to understand that a good marriage is an unfolding spiritual journey. Inhabitants of ashrams and devotees of various gurus claim that their guru shatters their egos, destroys their illusions, and forces them to choose between unconditional love or taking flight. Perhaps they do. For me, it has been marriage and the daily discipline of living in a family, rather than any formal religious practice, that has softened my ego, taught me compassion, and allowed my *eros* and spirit to lie down together.

It is not uncommon for even casual romantic partners to experience a momentary mystical union when egos are shattered in the moment of ecstasy. It is much rarer for two people to devote themselves over the years to the ordeal of cultivating unconditional love and transforming shared sensuality into sacramental sexuality. There is an infinite distance between romantic fun and games and the soul-mating of marriage.

Falling in love, we almost inevitably fall into illusion. Attractive persona meets attractive persona and form a mutual admiration society. You see yourself reflected adoringly in another's eyes and vice versa. Fascinated, we polish our surfaces, perform for our beloved audience. Romance brings out "the best" in us.

Thinking that ecstasy and intimacy can only be increased geometrically by marriage, we decide to take the big step. We recite our promise: "For better, for worse, for richer, for poorer, in sickness, and in health, till death do us part." Because we are all entranced by love, we secretly believe our vow magically guarantees that we *will* be joined for better, for richer, and for health. Sometimes after the honeymoon ends, however, we begin to fall out of love and into reality, and "the worst" that we have previously hidden begins to emerge. With growing disillusionment, we discover we have purchased damaged merchandise. His delightful casualness brings with it a careless inattention to details; he can't balance the checkbook and has only a promiscuous relationship to household order. Her forthright manner and sense of responsibility are linked to a ruthless inflexibility, a tendency to blame, and an inability to hang out in bed on Sunday mornings.

For a time, he and she accommodate and set out surreptitiously to change each other. The early manipulations are usually subtle — suggestions of a better way to do things, hostility expressed under the cover of humor, the imputation of guilt and shame. When changes in the other are not forthcoming, the heavier weapons are brought to bear: withholding, fighting, affairs. Gradually, the light dawns: This marriage is not going to yield perfection. We are not going to fulfill all of each other's needs or desires. The tension is growing. We can't go on like this.

In the crisis, the marriage is either broken or transformed. A choice is made to end the imperfect relationship, to settle for an "arrangement," or to undertake to fulfill the vow of unconditional love.

Marriage as a spiritual ordeal begins when, disillusioned of romance, two ego-bound, flawed individuals co-promise. We promise to end our tentativeness; to stop withdrawing; to remove the conditions we have previously set for bestowing the "reward" of our love; to be ego-enemies and soul-friends; to pursue the solitary journey together.

Marriage either strengthens or destroys the ego. If we remain within the fortress of our habitual patterns and imprison each other in pigeonholes of our own making, then we create a shared solitary confinement, an ego *à deux*. Bad marriages reproduce in miniature all the brutality of warfare. Locked together in ego-warfare, man and woman become hateful intimate enemies whose abusive ways are imprinted on their children and carried into future generations. But if wife and husband disarm in each other's presence, practice kindly disillusionment, grow skilled in forgiveness, then gradually the basic trust that is inseparable from faith and indispensable to the deepest erotic ecstasy grows strong. And the kindness of fathers and mothers is visited on the children to the third and fourth generation.

Within the context of commitment between a man and woman, a spiritual dimension of sexuality is revealed that transcends the pleasure-bond. At its most basic level, sexual intercourse between man and woman is plowing and planting, the sowing of seed, the surrendering of two bodies to the procreation of a child. Our deepest sexual passion is born from our drive to pass on the gift of life we have received.

If two people decide their sexual meeting is to be a coming and going with no promise binding them in communion, the genetic intentionality of their bodies will be absent, the vote of their chromosomes, sperm, ovum, and womb canceled, the urge for immortality that animates their bodies denied, their carnal pleasure divorced from loyalty.

Perhaps the frenzy and despair that surrounds sexuality in this generation result from the way easy contraception has seduced us into ignoring the question of our intentions. Moral confusion results when we disregard the meta-physical dimensions of sex. Gliding beneath every wave of sexual pleasure is the silent question: What will be the consequences of this act? Our assumption that the diaphragm and the Pill liberate sexual pleasure from the intentionality of our bodies is very naive. Thirty years of liberal attitudes have changed the inside of our heads and some of our conduct but not the millennial wisdom of the body. In our consumer society sex, like any commodity, has been divorced from our spiritual longing for continuity between past, present, and future. To have a sense that our lives are purposeful, we need to know that we belong within a drama of creation that began before we were born and will continue after we die. When we separate sex from care and creation, or consuming from conservation, we break the link between the present, the past, and the future, and we cease to belong to anything larger or more lasting than our brief moment in time.

When a child is born, the soul-drama deepens. Suddenly, the unconditional love that husband and wife struggle to achieve arrives by grace and is bestowed on the newcomer. Unless we are blocked by unresolved conflicts and unhealed wounds, we feel spontaneous unconditional love for our children. If the love bond with the child is strong and equal, husband and wife may transfer some of the unconditional love they feel for their child to each other. (If not, green-eyed jealousy joins the family.)

I am often struck by how spontaneously children do for us what formal religious practices are designed to accomplish. Sitting in meditation hour after hour, we are forced to observe the flaws in our character and witness our ego-games; in prayer, we repent of our sins and ask for forgiveness. Parenting forces us to develop these same spiritual virtues. A thousand times as I have watched my child develop, I have been confronted by my faults and forced to repent and forgive. My son loses his temper and shouts; his manner and tone of voice are mine. My daughter doggedly pursues her goals and is inflexible to the point of insensitivity to others; the set of her jaw is mine. Daily, in interacting with my children, I see my ego mirrored in their conduct, I witness my unresolved conflicts played out in their confusion, I see my failures of compassion in their wounds. There is no spiritual discipline more stringent, no more constant source of the honest feedback that is essential to root out ego-centrism, than marriage and family life.

When we approach marriage and family life as a sacrament, we encounter the great mystery that is the heart of both love and faith. As a man and woman come to love each other unconditionally, after shattering habitual roles and abandoning masks, they become at once dearer and more mysterious to each other. Lovers, like true saints, have learned to cherish, trust, and embrace that mysterious other to whom they are joined but may never fully understand. Drinking from the fountain of the mysterious other — the Unknown God, the unfathomable soul, the lover who remains a familiar stranger — passion may be renewed daily. So it is that a morning of consecrated lovemaking, like a

sudden encounter with a single blue flower, can bring us sacred-carnal
knowledge that is too deep for words.

> Dear Jan,
> Yesterday, when we made love, something was missing.
> The walls were not there.
> The reserve was not there.
> There was no trying, no pleasing.
> We were a present to each other,
> There was no giving or receiving,
> no yin or yang,
> no male or female.
> Only the giving up
> of our dreadful willfulness.
> Something moved us,
> leaving vacant the separate spaces we usually defend.
> Mysteriously, your self and my self disappeared.
> Inspired bodies dissolved in graceful fluids.
> Together in sweet no/thing/ness.
> And then, we One became two again.

SEXUAL DEVOTIONS

In spite of Hollywood, Victoria's Secret, Drs. Kinsey, Masters, and
Ruth, a plethora of sex manuals, and the prurient hype of the media, a
majority of us remain unreflective about our sexuality. After three
decades of conducting workshops in which I have been privy to a
thousand intimate stories, I have concluded there is widespread sexual
ignorance, repression, and unhappiness. All too much of our thinking
about sex is magical, mythical, and mad, and our conduct, governed by
either fear or grasping, is frequently either aversive or addictive.

Since spirit and flesh are indivisible, there is no difference between
the devotions necessary to enhance our spirituality and our sexuality.

Begin with a willingness to examine, demystify, and de-myth your
sexual persona. Reconstruct the history of your sexuality. When did you
first become aware of yourself as a sexual being? How did you learn the

meaning of and the appropriate response to your sexual feelings? Was your sexual coming of age celebrated or greeted with denial? What attitudes, values, and feeling did you take on by osmosis from your family? How much have you suffered from a conflict between "I want" and "I should"? Do you expect too much or too little from sex? Do you focus on the romantic-sexual quest rather than undertake the more demanding quest for meaning and vocation?

Play with the notion that your sexual style is the mirror that reflects who you are and are not. What does the mirror show you? If your sexual behavior is a metaphor for your relationship to your spirit, what does it tell you about yourself? If you divorce sex and love, how else have you split yourself? If you avoid thinking about, feeling, or expressing your sexuality, what else do you avoid? How much of your carnal-spiritual life is twisted by fear or addiction? Are there ways in which your sexual behavior is an embarrassment to your spirit, a violation of your deepest values?

What do you desire? In what kind of sexual relationship might your deepest longings be satisfied? Imagine what would be, for you, an in-spirited or soul-ful expression of your sexuality. Give your fantasies free play.

CHAPTER 9

Inspired Earth and Animal Spirits

"This is my Father's world.
The birds their carols rise,
The morning light, the lily white,
Declare their Maker's praise.
This is my Father's world.
He shines in all that's fair;
In the rustling grass I hear Him pass;
He speaks to me everywhere."

The Hymnbook, no. 101

"From the sacred set apart to the holy whole. Hierophanies everywhere; no privileged times or places. Every book a bible; and books in the running brooks. . . . Dionysus calls us outdoors. Out of the temple made with hands."

NORMAN O. BROWN,
Love's Body

"Ecopsychology seeks to recover the child's innately animistic quality of experience."

THEODORE ROSZAK,
The Voice of the Earth

SPIRITSCAPE AND THE MODERN ENVIRONMENT

Before there were cities and high rises, before rapid transportation and instant communication, before indoor malls and television, religion was an outdoor experience. To our ancient forebears, animals were not alien species lower in the ladder of evolution but equal members of a mysterious community. The boundaries between humans and other animals were porous. Animal and human souls might easily intermingle. The Bushmen of South Africa, for instance, assumed that when a hunter died, he became an eland, and vice versa. Rock paintings in which eland heads above the rainbow are combined with human legs beneath show the transformation. On a practical level, stalking and killing a swift antelope with a bow and arrow whose range was no more than seventy-five feet required an intricate knowledge of the mind and habits of the animal. Ceremonial dances in which the hunters wore masks and horns and simulated the movements of the eland and the development of hunting skills intertwined to create a sense that hunter and prey animal were one flesh.

Premodern peoples lived in a spiritscape, not a landscape or environment. For the Pygmies, the rain forest was father and mother that gave food and clothing and shelter. For early agricultural peoples, the Earth was Mother and Goddess. And everywhere there were signs, symbols, omens — sacred presences. It is difficult to think of an animal, insect, reptile, or plant that has not been considered soul-mate and sacred incarnation. In some tribe or another, a frog, a beetle, a bee, a bear, a hawk, a coyote, or a deer was revered as the equivalent of a "Christ" whose body was the transubstantiated flesh of God.

One way to define modernity is to trace the process by which nature has been desacralized and God has moved indoors.

The process gets under way in the Old Testament era. When the wandering tribes who became Hebrews came into Canaan, they found a host of agricultural spirits and godlets — Baals — who insured the continuation of the repeatable cycle of nature on which the crops depended. As a tribal god, Yahweh sanctified the victories of his warrior people and was linked to a series of persons and unrepeatable events in the history of the people — Abraham, Isaac, Moses, the giving of the law, the exodus. At first, the Hebrews anathematized and opposed the agricultural goddess and the Baals. It was forbidden "to bake cakes to the Queen of Heaven." As they succeeded in conquering the land and subjugating its people, however, Yahweh, like a Mafia chieftain, took over the domain of agriculture. But even when God was proclaimed to be Creator and Lord of the Earth in both Judaism and Christianity, the central revelation of His will and purpose was viewed as taking place, primarily through unrepeatable historical events and not the orderly cycles of nature.

But while the biblical tradition was hostile to all the manifestations of Goddess nature worship, it remains rich with metaphors taken from the outdoors: lilies of the valley, lions lying down with lambs, sowing and reaping, mustard seeds, grain falling into the ground, dying and coming to life again, wheat and tares, sheep and goats, animal sacrifice, shepherds, still waters, fishermen tending nets, deserts where large rocks provide the only shade. Gradually, as worship was transferred from sacred groves, springs, and fields into the temple, the religion and metaphors of the people of the land — the heathen — were destroyed. Our Father in Heaven came to be worshipped in synagogues, churches, and cathedrals. His will was to be revealed more in books than in birds and beasts. By the time Christianity became the dominant religion of Europe, salvation depended on obedience to God's commandment and participation in the rites and sacraments of His church rather than remaining in harmony with the cycles of the seasons.

There is no exact moment when a secular sensibility and worldview replaced the sacred participation in nature. Gradually, the church destroyed what it considered the pagan gods, persecuted the "witches" who had knowledge of sacred healing herbs, and killed the great god Pan. The desacralization of nature created a vacuum out of which emerged a new love affair, a new spiritual adventure, that was to capture the hearts and minds of modern peoples — science and technology. Maybe it had already begun when the Greeks invented reason and gained speed when Galileo, Kepler, and Newton placed nature on the rack and forced Her to answer in mathematical formulas and quantifiable terms. Certainly it was well established by the time of the Industrial Revolution, when the steam engine and the telegraph allowed messages to be sent faster than winged Mercury.

The epiphany that is the foundation of the modern world is the discovery of the power of the human mind and will. *With the emergence of science and technology, the sense of sacred agency shifted from Nature to Humankind.* The location of the *mysterium* changed. Philosophers, scientists and engineers did not become irreverent or arrogant; they had a conversion experience in which they experienced their ability to understand and change nature as a holy power and responsibility given by God. For better and for worse, we discovered that the sacred power to become prime movers in history lies within our reach.

With the new revelation that the power to understand and change the macrocosm lies within our microcosmic minds, the site of worship changed once again. Consider the difference between the cathedral-dominated cities of Europe and the polycentric modern city. It is obvious that the holy places — the foci around which the most revered activities pivoted — changed. First, universities, artists' studios, laboratories, and factories replaced churches as the places in which our ultimate concerns were expressed. In our time, another shift is occurring, in which our sense of worth and expectation of fulfillment are increasingly invested in the information networks and mammoth organizations of government and business.

Recently, the conquest of nature has escalated. With the advent of information and communication technology, we envision an era of democratic omniscience in which the entire storehouse of human knowledge will be available to any person with a computer and a modem. Within a few generations the human DNA molecule may be sequenced and mapped, and gene-splicing will allow us to reengineer much of our own genetic structure. With enough data-banks and biotechnology, our capacity to re-create the human body (and spirit?) will be awesome. Clearly, we have gone beyond the innocent nibbling at the apple of knowledge to an audacious vision of our potential omniscience and omnipotence. (One small symbol of the hidden hubris of the modern infomaniacs: I just discovered that *pregnant* is not listed in my Wordfinder dictionary. Presumably, those who use computers have no need of such old-fashioned words.)

It is hard to escape the irony of the apple symbol that Macintosh chose as its logo. I am reminded of a cartoon in which, as Adam is about to take a bite of the apple, a messenger rushes up and yells a warning, "Don't do it!" Here we go again. We are being promised that a larger bite of the apple of knowledge will bring us happiness. We may reasonably conclude from past experience with technological innovation that, like the automobile and the airplane, the new information superhighway will bring both benefits and upheaval. The coming global information network will further force developing nations into the iron maiden of the multinational corporate economy and continue the process of marginalizing indigenous peoples and destroying local cultures. Primitive "Edens" such as Bhutan, New Guinea, and the Amazon cannot long withstand the onslaught of the "superior" forms of abstract knowledge generated by the knowledge industry, linked as they are to a market economy that tempts the naive to trade their birthright for modern trinkets.

Nowadays, among Greens, radical environmentalists, and Luddite romantics, it is popular to recast the myth of the fall so that man's (male, rational, abstract, controlling) reason and technological genius are the snake in the Garden. Supposedly, our alienation is the result of our unseemly pride in seeking control over nature. This shortsighted condemnation of science and technology overlooks the changing history of perceptions of the sacred. The gradual discovery of the power of the human mind and will to understand and alter nature is one of the great chapters in the ongoing story of Spirit.

Think for a moment about the unnecessary disease and suffering that were simply accepted as a part of the human condition before we mounted an assault on malaria, yellow fever, plague, polio, leprosy, tuberculosis, and famine. At their best, science and technology spring from the sacred power to transcend the givenness of nature that is immanent within the human mind and will. It does violence to this genuine reverence to demonize the impulse to seek a measure of control over nature. From the beginning of the investigation of nature, we experienced our capacity to understand and change as an awesome and marvelous divine gift. Reason, science, technology developed out of an epiphany. To have refused the gift of power would have been irreverence. The prodigal sons and daughters of Mother Nature would have remained forever passive-dependent children had we not had the courage to eat the apple and set out on the long journey of the spirit that began on the far side of Eden.

Technology is the spiritual koan of our age, the mind-shattering puzzle to be solved. In what direction do we journey when we can neither return to Eden nor go forward to the alabaster city of perpetual progress?

THE DAY I BECAME MODERN

For me, modernity arrived suddenly in 1943 when I was twelve and my family moved from the southern wombtown of Maryville, Tennessee, to Wilmington, Delaware, headquarters for the modern gods — Hercules, Atlas, and Du Pont.

It was dark when we arrived at 306 Blue Rock Road, so we went to bed amidst the chaos of unpacked boxes, with high expectations for the surprises we would find in the morning.

At sunup, my brother and I ventured forth for our first expedition into our new world. Block after block of neat houses. Square. Orderly. We could find no woods or streams. Nothing wilder than an occasional empty lot. At the corner, the Bellefonte trolley line waited to take us the two miles to school. In the distance we could see the silver ribbon of the Delaware River winding its way toward the ocean, promising, something untamed. But when we finally made our way through the maze of suburban streets, down across the Pennsylvania Railroad tracks, we found the flatlands and marshes around the river strewn with garbage and stinking of industrial waste. Hoping for something more promising, we climbed to the highest point on Penny Hill to survey the landscape of our newfoundland. To the north, the oil refineries of Marcus Hook held high the eternal flame, the petroleum torch that burned off excess gas and spewed noxious fumes into the surrounding air. To the east across the river, a Du Pont plant sent a cloud of unknown particulates high into the air. (Later, we discovered the fallout from the cloud by day and the pillar of fire by night caused the emphysema from which my father died.) To the south sat Wilmington, a city without much heart or soul. Only westward did there seem to be evidence of wilderness and freedom.

By the time we returned home from our explorations, a gray fog had begun to permeate my spirit. Images of pathways through the College

Woods, sunlit Tennessee swimming holes, and fields where meadowlarks sang clashed with the new reality of Wilmington, and I fell into that condition of grief and depression peculiar to displaced persons for which there is no name. I knew our family had moved north because of Dad's business, so I buried my sadness and did not speak of it. But silently there grew in me a sense that I was in exile from my true homeland, and I was filled with nostalgia for a lost, familiar spiritscape into which I fit like a bone into a socket.

P.S. duPont High School was my second shock.

In rural and small-town America, life was organized around intimate groupings of family and clan, small-scale business, church and school. People were known by name and story. The history of a family followed its members for generations. Everybody knew that old man Clark's word was as good as his name, and that no matter what Sid Bennett promised you, it was only liquor talking. Chances were, many mothers and daughters had common stories about Mrs. McClure's sixth-grade English class.

From my first to my last day in P.S. duPont, I was lost in anonymity. After being issued an identity card, I was sent to my new homeroom and assigned a locker along an endless hallway of identical lockers that to this day I dream anxiously of being unable to find. Every hour, bells rang and classes changed, and I found myself among a horde of strangers. Student cliques were formed around fraternities and sororities, with highest status going to football players and cheerleaders. "Brains" were generally social outcasts, and kids who had migrated from small towns or rural areas were "hillbillies." A major effort was devoted to patrolling the halls to make certain that no student was absent without leave from class. During my six years of captivity, I encountered two teachers who retained some enthusiasm, none who knew my story.

In exile, I kept my spirit alive by dreams, friendship, and frequent excursions. West of the city, beyond the last domesticated suburb, I discovered a thick woods with a stream running through it, where I would retreat on weekends and sleep under the open sky. When our family business prospered, we bought a house at Bethany Beach, and wind, waves, uninhabited dunes, and northeasterly storms became an unexpected sanctuary. But through the turbulent years of adolescence,

I waited and retreated into my imagination. Nightly, I lay awake designing the ranch I would someday build in Wyoming and fell asleep dreaming of horses.

On June 16, 1949, the day I was to have graduated from high school, my friend Dick Haines and I loaded our camping gear into my Model A Ford and started west. By the time we reached Kansas, our money had given out, and we hired on to harvest wheat. After a few weeks of twelve-hour days (plus chores), brown, brazen, and two hundred dollars richer, we dashed across the sun-punished plains, climbed the Continental Divide, and landed on a ranch in the lush Gunnison valley of Colorado.

After a few weeks of working as a ranch hand and living out my bucolic dream of horses, cattle, and wide-open spaces, I began to notice an intellectual itch. My senses were delighted with the smell of new-mown hay fields, the flash of rainbow trout in irrigation ditches, coyote music from the surrounding hills. My body went forth with pleasure to the labor of chopping, fencing, and tending animals. But soon I began to long for conversations and ideas that would stretch my mind, and a world vaster and more varied than any I had yet known. Without knowing what I wanted to know or why, I began to crave knowledge. Reversing the direction of my quest, I turned eastward toward education and urban civilization.

Over the next twenty-five years, I settled into the tasks and delights of becoming a modern man. As I mentioned earlier, the path of the mind led me to Harvard and Princeton, and the city became my home and the university my cosmos. It was not until midlife that my path began to circle back toward the place of its beginning.

THE GROUND OF MY BEING

My circling back happened suddenly in the summer of 1976, by accident or grace. Jan and I drove the thousand miles from San Francisco to Methow, Washington, to see my old friend Jim Donaldson, who had given up reforming Los Angeles to raise organic garlic. Jan was all for moving to the country, but it seemed either too early or too late in life for me, although I often had had the fantasy that being a rancher might be more rewarding than rounding up philosophical ideas. We were riding up the creek valleys that flow into the Methow River and Jim was giving us his best rap: "Clean air and water. No place like it left in the USA. The gods that Hölderlin and Heidegger spoke about still dwell in the pristine valley nestled in the crags of the Cascades. And we have a chance of preserving it if we organize against the land developers and the forest service. We need your help." "Yes, Jim," I replied as we turned up McFarland Creek road, "but I am no farmer, and there isn't a coffee house or decent movie theater within a hundred miles. It's too isolated for me." About a mile up the dirt road, we stopped so Jim could show us a small farm. "This is the farm we wanted to buy, but it wasn't for sale," he said as we pulled into the driveway for a visit. Over coffee and cookies, John Edwards broke the news: "We decided four days ago to sell this place and move next door."

The next thing I remember was the vision. I saw myself as an old man sitting in this selfsame kitchen watching the aspens covered with snow and noticing a mink dart up the creek bank. I saw myself growing old happily in this place. The sights so startled me that I asked if I could take a tour of the land.

The farm, thirty-seven acres, consisted of a small, low house, a large barn, and an assortment of greenhouses, chicken coops, and storage sheds set at the lower end of a bowl created by enfolding hills, through which McFarland Creek ambled and sang. There was about an acre of apple orchard, two acres of high mesa, ten acres of creek bottom so thick with vegetation you could only guess at the trajectory of the creek, and fourteen acres of pasture surrounded by near-vertical hills covered with ponderosa pine and spruce. The crystal-clear creek funneled down to turn a now-defunct Pelton wheel. Upstream there were two ranches, and then wilderness all the way to Canada.

As we walked, the farm became an animate thing that confronted me with a question: "Do you ever intend to stop moving from place to place and dedicate yourself to being in place on the land?" The college woods and my adolescent dream of living on the edge of the wilderness rose up before me and demanded a decision: Either reach for the dream, or give it up and commit myself wholeheartedly to urban rhythms and city ways. My calculating mind told me the fantasy was impractical. But I heard the land calling my name.

I returned to San Francisco, juggled my finances, and found I could
scratch together ten thousand dollars for a down payment. I called John
that evening and made an offer that he accepted immediately. "The
farm is yours," he said. "Both Dorothy and I decided that we wanted
you to have it. We will work out a payment schedule you can live with."
Our word sealed the matter. Six months later the papers were signed,
and Jan and I began what became our annual migration to spend the
growing season in the Methow — thirteen miles from the nearest store,
twenty-five miles from a red light or theater, in the very epicenter of a
community of coyotes, deer, bear, and a miscellaneous variety of
wildlife too numerous to catalogue.

WATER AND SPIRITUAL FLUIDITY

I knew the theory. I had read Peter Warshall's plea for "watershed
consciousness," and I agreed with the notion that we are ecologically
immoral if we do not know where the water comes from when we turn
on the faucet and where it goes when we flush the toilet. And I felt in
the marrow of my bones what Henry Beston had discovered during his
sojourn at "the outermost house": "The world to-day is sick to its thin
blood for lack of elemental things, for fire before the hands, for water
welling from the earth, for air, for the dear earth itself underfoot." But I
was not prepared to cope with the crisis that interrupted our first idyllic
breakfast on the farm, when the tap water suddenly turned brown. As I
examined the maze of pipes in the basement, despair and panic hit at
the same moment. Here I was miles from the nearest town with a
busted water system I didn't understand. Not only was I not a plumber,
I wasn't even handy with tools. Thus far in life, I had followed the
normal urban rule: If something breaks, get an expert to fix it.

Fortunately, John was home and responded to my cry with an offer to
initiate me into the mystery of country plumbing. "There is always dirt
in the water during spring runoff," he explained, "so you have to
change the screens in the headbox every couple of days. But that's not
likely the problem now. Probably Jeff's cows have been mucking about
near the intake and have stirred things up."

On the way up to the source, we closed all the valves that brought water into the house and opened the irrigation valves so the dirt would be purged before it had clogged the smaller household pipes. John pointed out the places where the main line regularly broke and needed to be patched with inner tubes, baling wire, and tin. Arriving at the headbox I faced a complex of settling tanks and screened barrels that were designed to filter the creek water before it headed south toward the house. The series of screens had to be cleaned in just the right order, or the accumulated burden of dirt would be swept into the main line and thence into the house, where Jeff's finely sifted cow dung would cause the plumbing to become atherosclerotic, curable only by breaking every joint and cleaning every pipe. I got the idea that I was either going to have to hire a full-time plumber or become one. Neither option appealed to me. For a moment, I thought about drinking bottled water and letting the farm return to its natural state.

But when I stuck my hands into the stream to clean the intake screen, the clear waters flowed through my fingers into the recesses of my mind, and in a flash the mysteries of plumbing were revealed to me. Plumbing is just like writing a paragraph. You start with an overflowing generalization, then funnel it into sentences that break it down into smaller ideas. The trick is to keep things moving smoothly by controlling the volume and velocity of water or ideas. First, you have to find a way to stop the flow — a shut-off valve or a period. If you just want to slow down the motion, a half-turn valve or a comma will do. If you want to split the flow, use a Y connection or an either/or. To spread out a thought so it sprinkles a whole pasture of ideas, it is best to use a colon. A parenthesis (like a reservoir) stores up a meaning that is not immediately usable but will be needed later. Nouns are the large pipes that contain a sufficient head of meaning to drive the basic idea through the smallest artery of the paragraph. Verbs are the running length of smaller pipes that increase the velocity of the water. *Ifs, ands, buts, withs,* and other conjunctions are the various fittings necessary to join ideas of unequal dimension.

Once the logic of plumbing became clear to me, the mechanics followed easily. Within a month the water system was a familiar story. I could tell by the pressure or the size of the particles in the tap water what was happening up the creek. Remote sensing. I learned where to break the pipe to clear the obstructions of sediment and how to make

elegant joints with PVC pipe. Plumbing, as Plato said about philosophy, is a matter of cutting nature at the joints. Near the end of one
frustrating day, I invented an ingenious way to backflush an inaccessible stretch of the drain system, and Eureka! the problem was solved. I
felt as satisfied as if I had successfully explained the categorical imperative to a freshman class. That night I dreamed that my older brother
Lawrence, the mechanical genius of the family under whose shadow I
had fallen, put his arms around me, and I was as tall as he.

Water, air, earth, and fire are at once practical necessities and
alchemical elements — primal psycho-symbolic reality.

On the pragmatic level, water is the name of the game in the rural
West. During my first year in the Methow, I found that the natives talk
about water the way Californians talk about real estate or expanding
one's consciousness. The value of farm or ranch land is determined by
its water right and its proximity to a river or a creek. And water rights, in
turn, are determined by the historical order in which the farms were
settled. The first place to be settled, no matter its position on the creek,
received the first water right, and so on. Luckily, we had stumbled into
a profligate wealth of pure water. Our farm had been settled in 1890
and had a third water right to 167 gallons per minute. Pure water.
McFarland Creek begins as a network of small streams high in the hills,
frequently (like the human spirit) moves half the burden of its flow
underground, bubbles to the surface, and then descends again. A mile
upstream, the creek disappears into a swamp, travels underground
across my neighbor's farm, and reemerges a hundred yards before our
property line. By the time it reaches us, it has been filtered by its
subterranean journey, as clear as a mind that has been refreshed by a
descent into dreamtime.

Daily I cup my hands, drink deep from the creek, give thanks, and
shudder to imagine the coming drought, the dryness of spirit. Drinking
deeply of pure water, I quench my thirst and am thankful for a simple
goodness, and I grieve knowing of the growing desecration of our
wellsprings.

Item: "Conserving Water Urged as a Way to Avoid World Crisis.
Scarcity may affect peace prospects as well as population growth. . . .
Not just drought and global warming, but water wastefulness and

mismanagement are threatening to create a crisis in the 1990's similar to the oil crunch of the 1970's."[1]

I am troubled by the arid character of the modern mind. Something we can only call spirit is drying up as our underground water sources are being contaminated, exhausted, and dry. I suspect our loss of a liquid imagination is related to the pollution of our streams and our urban exile. As embodied creatures, whatever we do to the environment, we do to ourselves. As without, so within. The structure of the human soul mirrors the world in which it dwells. The nature and content of the mind as well as the balance in the relationship of consciousness and unconsciousness is in large measure determined by the environment. The speedier, noisier, and more intense the environment, the more the mind becomes exiled in linear, daylight, pragmatic consciousness. Can our soul be restored, can our cup run over, if we no longer lie down in green pastures or rest beside still waters?

Water has always been associated with meditation and the ability to sink into the deep. Water was the element sacred to the Mother Goddess who governed the moon and moved the tides of the sea and menstruation. She and her sacred serpent presided over the waters that led into the underworld. In Taoism, the way of water is the metaphor for wisdom. And if we need scientific confirmation that water changes the flow of the mind, we find it in the research that shows that a high concentration of negative ions caused by falling water and ocean waves has a calming effect on the psyche.

I suspect that genetically coded within the mind is a remembrance of, and an organic need for, a certain repertoire of experience of the natural world. As we need certain vitamins to sustain bodily health, for spiritual health we need: lonesome vistas where the eye can stretch to the horizon without seeing other human beings; the reassuring sight of something that grows from seed to maturity; the fearful and humbling ferocity of wind and lightning storms; the encouraging light and warmth of the sun; the cleansing flow of water. It seems quite likely to me that the technological compulsion that threatens our survival is a result in large part of our being trapped in rationalistic modes of thought and being exiled from the fluid depths of our intuition and imagination. We are cut off from the moon-governed tides of the sea and the mind, from the primal depths where Leviathan swims and thought curls to form a spiral of ideas that might, poetically, place the pink caverns of a conch shell suggestively near a vagina.

Ah, but here I am trying to analyze and explain a mystery into which I have been initiated by the waters of McFarland Creek. A dozen yards outside my small studio, the creek rushes downhill, falls over a ten-foot moss-covered rock, crashes into a pool, picks itself up, and does the same thing in a second waterfall before it jogs downstream. If the decibels were counted, the double waterfall would probably be in the range of a jet engine cruising at 600 miles per hour. But the sound is strangely soft and porous. It is full of silence into which an imagination accustomed to going down rabbit holes and snake tunnels can disappear and reemerge into a separate reality. I am too rational to believe in fairies and little people, but any time of night or day when I am not trying too hard, I hear voices I am tempted to believe come from water spirits. I can never quite catch their words, but the tune is clear. And sometimes the music lifts a heavy thought into a lyric register, and on rare occasions it comes to grace a sentence I am writing. So if you should come across a sentence herein that unaccountably blows a wind across some hidden Aeolian harp in your spirit, you may assume it is a gift from McFarland Creek.

GROWING THINGS: SACRED CREATIVITY

For the last two decades, first at McFarland Creek and currently at our new farm in Sonoma, I have been intimately involved with the management and enjoyment of growing things. I have planted, tended, and eaten of the fruit of the trees of life: apples, peaches, pears, plums, apricots, and nectarines. I have spent many hours kneeling in the humus, seeding and watching hope come to incarnate fruition in corn and basil.

In no year have we ever grown more than a small portion of the food necessary to feed our family. But the gardens and orchards I have tended have given me, besides delight, vegetables, fruit, and a harvest of rich philosophical metaphors. Fiddling around with growing things teaches one the profound difference between fabricating and cultivating, producing and nurturing. In the organic world, there is no manufacturing, no instant gratification. Apple seedlings mature slowly and must be patiently tended season after season before their fruit may be enjoyed. To garden, I must surrender my will-to-power and learn to respect the inborn rhythm of tomato plants and string beans.

Through composting, pruning, and tending an orchard, I have come to understand the fundamental philosophical mistake and intellectual-spiritual dishonesty involved in using the word *growth* in the realm of economics and politics. Sinister things are baptized when *growth* is kidnapped from its legitimate and literal home in the organic realm and used, unthinkingly, to sanctify economic and political policies. Psychologists, businessmen, and politicians alike justify their endeavors by claiming they are producing growth—personal growth, economic growth, corporate growth. As a nation, we are obsessed with something we call "economic growth." Every politician and CEO assumes that a healthy economy or corporation is one in which the curve of growth rises steadily and perpetually. The gross national product is taken as the single measure of well-being.

If we translate "economic growth" into behavioral terms, however, a disturbing picture emerges. It means more men and women are leaving home every day, working in largely sedentary jobs inside buildings, following routines dictated by impersonal corporations over which they have little control, living in increasingly anonymous and uncivil cities whose infrastructures are breaking down, consuming packaged commodities, and depending on experts to provide them with services, food, entertainment, and health care. The "growth" we obsessively pursue and insist on calling "progress" seems more like the rapid profusion of cancer cells than the orderly dance of soil and seed that leads in the ripeness of time to an ear of corn.

Why are we so obsessed with "growth"? Why the rhetoric, the co-optation and prostitution of this once-sacred word? I suspect it is because a large percentage of modern urban populations (and this by definition includes the most influential intellectuals, propagandists, and word-merchants) know about growth only in a metaphorical way. Because our daily horizon is fabricated from cement and steel and machines in motion, we have lost the tangible sense of meaning and hope that had been part of the experience of planting and gathering.

All growing things have an orderly rhythm, a life-story that has direction and purpose. You can count on the process of birth, maturation, decline, death, and return to the humus. But the ideology of progress notwithstanding, it is not certain that technology is taking us in a healthy direction. So we grant motion, change, and speed the honorific titles of growth or progress. And like all unexamined creeds, this one tries to repress our doubts and uncertainties. In the United States we brag that 3 percent of our population grows the food for the other 97 percent. But this often-quoted statistic may be less a sign of progress than a terrible reminder of how deracinated we have become. The majority of us have traded the life of wage-slaves for the more independent and strenuous life of the land and the village. If I were miraculously elected president, I would instigate a policy to help millions of families who are so inclined to reinhabit the countryside, to reinvigorate village and rural life. We would be a healthier nation if a majority of us were intimately acquainted with the literal meaning of growth and had some rich dirt under our fingernails.

It is not necessary to forsake our cities to honor our kinship with the land. In my seminars, I ask people to draw the ideal environment in which they would find the greatest satisfaction of their spiritual longings. "Where would you live? With whom? What kinds of activities would fill your day?" I ask. I have found that about 95 percent of the people situate themselves in or near mountains, lakes, oceans, forests, and farmland. As the power of the image of the Marlboro Man demonstrates, in our fantasies we belong in the wilds even when we dwell in high rises. We find myriad ways to celebrate earthiness. Each spring, families in New York and Boston apartments religiously plant tomatoes in window boxes and celebrate a juicy harvest in midsummer. Tucked away in cultivated beds in the backyards of manicured suburban homes, vegetables and herbs flourish, tended by fanatical gardeners. Millions whose only contact with produce is at the corner market ritually escape from the cities to backpack in the Rockies or Adirondacks. Perhaps one day in the not-too-distant future governments will create imaginative programs to revitalize rural and village culture and end the lemming migrations that are condemning increasing multitudes to live in megalopolises. Until then, many of us re-member our kinship with the sacred creativity of the land by planting symbolic seeds and taking ritual journeys to high mountains to listen to the wind in the pines.

WEEDING AND KILLING: SACRED DE-STRUCTURING

In tending to the life of the land, I have inevitably been involved in destruction. To grow a decent crop or a decent life, one must become accustomed to death.

I wage yearly warfare against a plague of thistle and weed. No one who has struggled against Barnaby or Star thistle will be tempted to worship pure vitality. I could use less *élan vital* in the pasture. Each spring we pull and burn the stuff but stop short of the official recommended way of destroying it — spraying 2-4-D. Nature needs some medicine for infestations, but chemical warfare seems too harsh a remedy for a seasonal rash. The minimum intervention seems best; acupuncture rather than surgery. Ask the old-timers, and they will tell you that infestations of noxious weeds come and go. Thistle, like most dis-eases, is a coded message that we would be wise to translate rather than cure. It may be telling us that the land has been overgrazed and that its delicate grasses must be preserved, or it will erode and disappear in the whirlwind.

My awareness that the humus by which we humans are defined is also a killing ground grew out of my encounter with Billy.

Until Billy arrived, my acquaintance with goats was largely literary. I knew only that they were sacred to Dionysus and were reputed to have lusty temperaments. So when my neighbor John dropped in one evening and offered to help me catch a mother and son who had been abandoned and were running free on an old mining claim up the creek from our farm, I accepted.

We jumped in the pickup and bumped along a dirt road until we came to a tumble-down cabin where Mama goat poked her head out the door to see what was happening and Billy peered at us from behind her protective presence. We approached diplomatically, bearing gifts of grain, but the natives fled to a nearby thicket. We coaxed, spoke kind words, and proclaimed our innocent intent, but all the goats did was cock their heads and look curious but disbelieving. Finally we realized it was going to take some cunning and force to convert them to the civilized way. I went around one side of the bush and John around the other. The goats, smelling an ambush, split in opposite directions, divided our attention, and trotted back to the shelter of the house. John and I reassured each other that we were smarter than the goats, put our minds to strategy, and ambled casually toward the house until we could rush the front door and trap them inside their fortress. We first wrestled Mama into the truck and left Billy behind, counting on abandonment anxiety to soften him up a bit. While he bellowed curses, I lassoed him and tried vainly to lead him to the truck. Finally I picked him up and carried him, struggling, to join his mother. When I got in the cab of the truck, I smelled like goat—an odor impossible to describe or to mistake. On the way home, we congratulated ourselves for having won the battle. Little did we know.

Mama and Billy took to civilization more easily than we imagined. That is, they learned to expect their daily dole of goat pellets as their God-given entitlement, in addition to the right to consume all growing things within reach. Do not imagine that a mere twelve-acre pasture plus welfare satisfied their basic needs. A fence, to a goat, is of the same order as loose cash to the criminal mind—a matter for liberation. While we were still trying to make the conditions of their "captivity" comfortable, they had figured out thirty-seven ways to escape. Had they merely returned to their remote haunts in the hills, there would have been a rough justice in events. But no. Like sociopaths, they circumvented the fences, frequented the neighbors' gardens, nibbled the bark and branches of young fruit trees, hid during the day in the badlands along the creek, returned toward evening as if nothing had happened, and charmingly demanded their daily bread. It was not long into our tenure as the "owners" of goats that we began to have paranoid fantasies that they had somehow conspired to arrange the whole matter of their capture and incarceration and that they were laughing at us behind our backs.

In due course, yet more joy was added to our lives when Mama grew great with child. Or rather, with twins. Such luck! In her own passive-aggressive style, Mama turned out to be incompetent to give birth by herself, and I, a complete amateur in animal midwifery, had first to help her with the delivery and then to convince her to let the kids nurse. Probably she didn't want to ruin her figure by breast-feeding.

Soon I began to feel like a happy father in an unhappy marriage. I would gladly have divorced Mama and Billy if it hadn't been for the kids. They were pure lyric spirits, wild and warm. They romped and played with each other, bounded onto Mama's back, jumped straight up into the air, and pirouetted on their hind feet with elegance and grace that Baryshnikov would have envied. When we went to visit, they crowded around and nuzzled our outstretched hands. Even Mama seemed mellowed by their winning ways and was content to stay in the pasture by day and the barn by night. We were all rapidly becoming one happy family.

Except for Billy. Billy seemed to have read all the worst books on aggression, territorial imperative, and sibling rivalry. From the beginning he was an ill-tempered brother, concerned only with establishing dominance. Under the guise of educating the young in the ways of the world, he taught his siblings how to butt heads, but he used his authority mostly to bully his charges. As the little ones grew large enough to mount, Billy added buggery to butting and gave them no peace fore or aft. After suffering the chaos of Billy's rude, crude, and unattractive ways long enough, I determined to see harmony returned to the fold at all costs. Since Billy was too old to castrate, it was clear that the time had come to invite him to be the honored guest at a barbecue.

I had never slaughtered or butchered an animal and felt both ignorant and squeamish as the time approached. David came over from Libby Creek Farm and offered to do the dirty work for me. At first I was relieved. But the more I thought about it, the more I became convinced I should do my own killing. I was no vegetarian, so I could not claim any moral objections to the taking of animal life. I just didn't want to be present when it happened. I could eat meat that was neatly packaged in cellophane, but I didn't want to look the condemned animal in the eye. It was therefore with enormous ambivalence that I borrowed a rifle and went to the barn to do the job.

Billy was tied to a post, loudly protesting having been separated from his kind. Trembling as I approached him, I slipped a shell into the chamber and took aim. A wave of nausea crashed through my stomach, my vision blurred, and I was forced to pause, breathe deeply, and wait for the feeling to pass. "My God," I thought, "what if I don't kill him with the first bullet?" Again, I raised the gun and waited until I was certain that his brain was directly in line with the end of the barrel. And then I pulled the trigger. Billy jumped, startled by the sound of the shot, cried out as if he had received a sudden blow, and fell to the floor. "I'm sorry, Billy. I'm sorry," I said. For a minute he kicked violently as if trying to free himself from an unseen enemy, then yielded to the soft spasms of dying. Then it was over. He lay still, and I sat down because I was shaking.

I sat for a long time immobilized by powerful currents of feeling. The feeling nearest the surface was nausea and disgust tinged with fear. I had violated the great taboo — taken a life. Somehow it seemed all right for me to allow animals to be sacrificed to feed me. But how could I retain my image of myself as a gentle man, now that I had knowingly killed? By my action, I had suddenly become one of those (mostly men) who are willing to acknowledge that to be human is to inhabit a world that is, among other things, a killing ground. It is obvious to the mind that life feeds on life, but for the most part my civilized heart had refused the bloody wisdom that we are all killers. Looking at Billy's body, I felt the sacrilege of having destroyed something I could never re-create. For a moment I wished his promiscuous spirit might reanimate his body. I wanted to bring him back to life and tell him it had all been a terrible mistake and return him, unrepentant, to the pasture to molest his siblings. I thought of becoming a vegetarian.

But a far more troubling feeling began to surface. Yes, I was sad, but I was also excited. My body seemed stretched to its capacity, full, and throbbing with a sense of power that was certainly erotic but not genital. Some part of me that I found hard to respect had felt both satisfaction and pleasure in the act of killing. To have the power to kill is to stand for a moment in the presence of the same mystery that created life, not as a victim but as a godlike creature who can control the fate of another living being. Instead of being the small creature cowering before the overwhelming threat of death, I was the one who held the thread of life and death. I wanted to deny the feeling, to turn away from my hubris. The forbidden knowledge threatened to cast me into the company of those I most despised — killers, mercenaries, torturers, and necrophiliacs who create war to satisfy their perverse passion.

I thought about a dream I had had several years before that had not ceased to haunt me. In the dream, I was being led into an underground room by men who were to initiate me. In the smoke-filled room, two of the men fought a brutal battle with fists and knives. As I watched, one stabbed the other to death. Horrified, I ran out to find the police to report the murder. When I awoke, I was flooded with panic and lay for a long time thinking about the dream, identifying with the moral outrage of the person in the dream who was "me." Then it occurred to me that I was all the characters in the dream, and I put myself imaginatively inside the two fighters. As I did, I felt the exhilaration of the fight, the ecstasy of the full-out battle for survival. The dream seemed to take me down into some premoral dimension of my being, where the will-to-live was pure and unfettered by any cultural considerations. And the pure essence of animal fierceness seemed to be a prerequisite for the more gentle virtues. An unaccustomed sense of safety stole over me as I recognized with visceral certainty that should I ever be forced into a situation where I had to fight for my life, I would not be too "civilized" to survive. The dream, far from making me more violent, relieved me of a sizable portion of my primal fear and deepened my trust in my ability to take care of myself.

The sinister wisdom into which Billy's death initiated me came from the same source as the dream. I am, we are, both more animal and more godlike than we are comfortable in recognizing. Our civilized personalities are rooted in a premoral gift of pure sacred power. Touch the raw will-to-live in yourself and the power to take life, and you are as much in the presence of the holy as you are in lovemaking, giving birth, and creating. We know the holy spirit in ourselves only when we enter into the dreadful and marvelous knowledge that we, like the Almighty Source of this borning and killing ground, are both creators and destroyers of life. It is a holy *and inescapable* responsibility to stand at the junction of life and death.

I suspect that one of the unconscious forces driving the exodus from rural life into the cities is the sentimental desire to deny our awesome responsibility for the taking of life. So long as we purchase our food in plastic wrappings in antiseptic supermarkets, we can avoid direct participation in the sacred-tragic-terrible-necessary act of killing.

The current abortion debate is only one example of the moral confusion that results when we refuse to recognize and claim the terrible-sacred human responsibility for the creation and destruction of life. Neither side is willing to examine the question of the taking of life in the larger context of animals raised and slaughtered for food, officially sanctioned killing in execution and warfare, and death by starvation caused by population explosion.

When we sanitize and rationalize our lives too much, we cease to ponder the great agonal questions that give human life its tragic dignity. Under what conditions is it moral, necessary, and sacred to destroy a life? When is slaughtering animals, aborting babies, executing criminals, and killing in warfare justifiable? How do we deal with the awe-ful responsibility, ambivalence, and guilt of killing? How can we live with hope and compassion in this borning and killing ground that is the Earth?

I have no satisfactory answers to the moral dilemma of killing. I am convinced that recognizing our terrible responsibility to destroy as well as create is better than cultivating the illusion that we are innocent. In that way we are likely to destroy as few living beings as possible — animals, enemies, or unborn children. Last year, traveling in Bhutan, I noticed how Buddhists handle one part of the dilemma. Theoretically, Buddhists don't eat meat because an animal is likely to be a reincarnated person and the cow you butcher may be your great-grandfather. In practice, no one eats the abundant fish that inhabit the streams because it is not worth the karma — the moral contamination — to kill one fish that will only feed one person. But yaks are butchered, the moral justification being that taking the life of one large animal allows many people to be fed.

Dwelling on a piece of land I have come to love, I have developed one simple test for the morality of destruction: Does it lead to a greater variety and a higher quality of life? It pleases me to note that the community of sentient beings hereabouts has expanded. There are more species of trees, birds, and animal life in residence on "our" land now than before we began to make improvements. By cutting an overabundance of bay trees, I have made room for cedar, spruce, birch, bamboo, tallow, and olives as well as a varied orchard. As a result, new varieties of birds and insects have come to dwell with us.

Does this principle help in dealing with abortion and overpopulation or aggression and warfare? Are we justified in using contraception and abortion to prevent the overpopulation that is rapidly reducing the quality of life for masses of human beings and condemning thousands of other species to extinction? I think so. Will armed intervention in genocidal wars in Bosnia, Afghanistan, or the Sudan insure a greater variety and higher quality of life? I doubt it.

ANIMAL SPIRITS

One-third of North America's eighty-six species of frogs and toads are in danger of extinction: "Herpetologists . . . say frogs are the ideal creature to reflect the health of the environment. . . . Amphibians represent the global equivalent of the proverbial canary in a coal mine."[2]

The Dow Jones index continues to rise.

One-half to one-third of earth's species could be extinct in the next thirty years.

The Dow Jones index continues to rise.

Within the perspective of the modern technological-economic myth of progress, all animals except humans are expendable. CEOs of multinational corporations and government economic planners do not meet and conspire to create a "final solution" that involves the extermination of all nonhuman species. It is only in fact, not in theory, that the continuous expansion of business and the creation of worldwide market economies involves the genocide of inhuman species. (Pets and domesticated animals useful for food excepted.)

Once upon a time, among hunting peoples, ceremonial life was addressed largely to creating a covenant with the animals, reconciliation, and veneration. "In the beginning of all things, wisdom and knowledge were with the animals; for Tirawa, the One Above, did not speak directly to man. He sent certain animals to tell men that he showed himself through the beasts, and that from them, and from the stars and the sun and the moon, man should learn. Tirawa spoke to man through his works."[3]

The feeling of the anima-animal connection is essential to pre-modern religion and is still present in children who believe they can talk with cats and horses "before they learn better." An Eskimo myth tells us: "In the very earliest of time, when both people and animals lived on earth, a person could become an animal if he wanted to and an animal could become a human being. Sometimes they were people, sometimes animals and there was no difference. All spoke the same language. That was the time when words were like magic. The human mind had mysterious powers. . . . Nobody can explain this: that's the way it was."4

The traditional spiritual disciplines of prayer, meditation, and mindfulness are useful in cultivating an awareness of the inner life. But an excess of focusing on the self is narcissistic, wearisome, and boring. These days I look in vain among the various schools of psychotherapy, twelve-step programs, churches, guru groups, and Buddhism for any suggestion that modern spiritual life may require a renewal of communion with our animal familiars.

On an average day, if you stop, look, and listen, you will discover phyla of angels bearing messages from the wild. Unless you live on the margins of civilization, you will not encounter a leap of leopards or a pride of lions. But even in Central Park you may come across a covey of quail, a paddling of ducks, or a nest of rabbits. From any of these creatures you may learn the great spiritual lesson that you are not the center and sole reason for the existence of the universe. Any squirrel or English sparrow will testify by its *joie de vivre* that human ego-centrism and species chauvinism are both a mistake and a sin.

On several occasions recently, I have been a recipient of an unmistakable grace. Shortly before dawn a couple of years ago, I was wakened by cat growls in a very low register. "Can't be our house cat," I thought. I went out to look but could find nothing. Next morning, the same thing occurred. The third morning, I crept out of bed, followed the sound of the bass fiddle cat music deep into the woods, and came upon two bobcats sitting at opposite ends of a log, growling a duet to either Mars or Aphrodite. I stood silently, waiting for the drama of either combat or love to begin. A timeless interval later, the concert ended and the singers disappeared silently into the semidarkness. I felt I had been an honored witness at a sacred ritual, blessed by the wild grace of beings whose beauty and mystery were not dependent on humankind. It is said that in ancient Greece in the Eleusinian mysteries, the climax of the ceremony of initiation was the moment when the initiate was shown a single ear of corn. Perhaps epiphanies are always like this: Something as ordinary as an ear of corn, bread and wine, or a bobcat suddenly becomes transparent to the creative source from whom all life, all blessings, flow.

The recognition of the sacredness of any creature or thing brings with it a moral imperative.

Every so often, I catch a glimpse of one of the sacramental cats hunting for mice in the meadow, and I am reminded of my obligation to walk respectfully on this land that I share with so many wild animal spirits. We humans show little enough concern for those of our own species who have been displaced and rendered homeless by heartless economics. For the thousands of other species that we are driving into exile and extinction, we have neither compassion nor repentance.

Our hardness of heart toward our coinhabitants springs from our habit of thinking of animals as strange, alien, and other. With the exception of "pets," we tend to consider animals as wild and therefore dangerous. In the American West, we conducted propaganda campaigns against wolves and mountain lions similar to those we used against Communists. They were a threat to us; therefore our programs of systematic destruction were justified.

When Mark and Delia Owens lived for seven years in the middle of the Kalahari Desert in an area where the animals had never seen human beings, they found that lions, panthers, jackals, and hyenas rapidly moved into their camp and lived side by side with them with neither fear nor hostility.[5] Change the eyes with which you see and the world changes; "wild" animals become familiar spirits. Consider the snake a messenger from the gods, a sacred creature, and you may understand how it is possible for Hopi Indians to dance holding a half-dozen rattlesnakes and never be bitten.

In the last decade one of my best mentors in the art of living has been a horse. I first saw her standing down by the river, head high, hair aflame, backlit by the sun. Delicate and wild. She walked with an aristocratic carriage, nearly prancing. We glanced at each other, and I edged around for a better look, only to find that her eyes had followed

me. All my adolescent fantasies of horses and cowboys were immediately reanimated, and before I knew it, I was the nervous owner of a
three-year-old half-Arab mare — Prana — who had never seen a saddle.

I had not ridden a horse since I was a child, so I turned Prana over for
the winter to Bonnie, a young horsewoman, for some preliminary
training. By springtime, she was broken to the saddle and ready to ride.
Broken is the wrong word. Perhaps not even *tamed*. Let's say she
submitted to the saddle and bridle without protest and permitted
herself to be mounted — but as I was shortly to discover, not to be
controlled.

When I first came calling bearing apples in place of flowers, Bonnie
helped me catch and saddle Prana and pointed me in the direction of
the gate that led beyond the stubble fields of dry-land wheat to the open
hills. So long as we were climbing the slope, we moved together in a
long swaying motion, the steepness of the grade limiting her speed and
gait. But once we reached the first long level stretch, Prana shifted
gears into a high-stepping, bone-jarring trot. My ass began to play
percussion with the saddle, and discomfort rapidly gave way to a rising
crescendo of fear. I was not riding Prana, I was being taken for a ride,
and we both knew it. The red-headed witch had me in her power and
was headed into the wind. Worse was yet to come. Warmed up, she was
now ready for the full pyrotechnics. First, she broke into a canter and
then a full gallop, and as we started down a long ridge leading into a dry
stream bed, she began to fly, touching the ground every hundred yards
or so just to pay her respects to the law of gravity. By this time my
relationship with the saddle was fleeting, strained, and approaching
divorce. With every ounce of authority I could muster, I pulled back on
the reins and yelled woe, woe, woe (is me). Strictly to humor me, as the
executioner with mock civility grants the condemned man a last meal,
she complied with my request and reduced her speed to a mildly
breakneck pace. Seizing my advantage, I aimed her up a steep embank-
ment. While she was momentarily slowed by the effort, I explained that
I was going to have to be in control of our relationship until I lost some
of my fear of death and abandonment and gained a firmer seat. I
promised passion and a loose rein in the distant future, but for the
moment I wanted no Dionysian dashes or unpredictable climaxes. At
fifty, I still had an appetite for a bit of madness, but I didn't want the

beast to run away with me. Just to be on the safe side, I dismounted when we reached the top of the hill and walked the lady home.

My next years with Prana were a continuing meditation on the relationship between surrender and control. From the beginning, I understood that Prana was an incarnation of her name (the Hindu word for breath, energy, spirit) and that learning to ride was going to be a rigorous spiritual discipline. My *pranayama* — the yogic practice of concentrating on breath until inspiration and expiration are experienced as the breath of God — was going to involve learning to relax my obsession with maintaining control and surrendering myself in trust to the prime mover. The Zen of riding, like prayer, is a matter of achieving a balance between yielding and responsibility. The goal is for horse and rider to move as one; thy will and mine in harmony; Brahman and Atman united in a single act of inspiration and expiration.

The fundamental rule of the spiritual quest — to establish direct contact with the sacred rather than depend on intermediaries, authorities, dogmas, or institutions — is also the first rule of horsemanship. I soon discovered that when I attempted to ride Prana with a saddle, I could not feel her movements. The only way I could retain intimate contact between the seat of my pants and her back was to ride with a thin bare-back pad. At first it seemed risky and foolish to give up the small measure of control the saddle afforded me. For the best part of a year I rode in the hills in a state of high anxiety, sometimes bouncing along at an uncomfortable fast trot, sometimes hanging on with aching legs as Prana galloped out of control at terrifying speed. But gradually my insecurity gave way to tacit knowledge as man and horse communicated intuitively with the kinesthetic language of muscle and movement, I and Thou in wordless communion. Like lovers, we learned each other's rhythms and body language. As any rider or mystic will understand, the day came when I could sit at a full gallop, balanced at the still point behind the withers, motionless in the dance.

Inevitably, in the beginning of relationships we think of others — neighbors, lovers, or God — as strangers. They are alien, different, foreign, remote. The gulf between us and them seems unbridgeable. Communication becomes possible only when we change our working assumption and consider the other as more like than unlike ourselves. Communion involves the awareness that I and the other are, in some way not yet fully understood, already linked in a community. One day as I was struggling to keep Prana under control, it occurred to me that I might have more success if I thought of her as a high-strung person rather than as an uncontrollable horse, and treated her accordingly. As my hands searched out and began to massage the tight muscles along her neck, to caress her ears and rub her forehead, she sighed greatly, dropped her large head, and leaned against me. Touching her as I would a lover, I felt that continuity between her life and my own whose correct name is *compassion*. From that time, riding ceased to be a struggle for control and became a deepening dance of man and horse, two animal spirits moving with one mind and one body. Almost.

My final lesson in letting go was the hardest. After ten years of a fine partnership, Prana and I still had an irreconcilable difference of opinion about the proper speed for a normal ride. I favored a relaxed pace, she the full-speed-ahead approach. With all the trust and firmness of seat I could muster, I was still uncomfortable with her hell-for-leather philosophy of life. One day a friend with whom I rode said, "The only problem with that horse is that she's all wind, energy, and fire. It isn't fair to ask a cheetah to go for a slow stroll. She has too much spirit for trail riding — she's a natural endurance horse." In an effort to save our marriage, I decided I would give her the opportunity to go the distance her nature craved.

So it was that at five o'clock on an October morning before the sun was up, I was preparing for our first fifty-mile endurance race. In the semidarkness, I kept wondering: "Why am I doing this? I can't ride that far. This is madness. Maybe something will happen, and I won't have to do it." The sun was rising when ninety-four horses assembled at the starting line. Much excitement, and many jumpy horses and riders. Prana was uncharacteristically calm, and I was a mixed mass of anxiety and excitement. I waited for most of the horses to pass and took my place toward the end of the pack. By the end of the first thirteen-mile loop, when we stopped for the first vet check and hot tea, Prana was just warming up. Throughout the late morning she moved smoothly at an extended trot, and before I knew it it was lunchtime and we were at the thirty-five-mile mark.

Moving into the early afternoon we fell into an easy rhythm. My fears of falling, failing, and being out of control evaporated as we moved along narrow trails leading up and down steep hills, through forests of red-wood, pine, and manzanita, and out onto the bare golden hills of a California autumn. For hours I rode in a state of self-forgetfulness, caught in the flow of the race. Prana and I finally became a single moving entity — manhorse or horseman, I don't know which. Time, self-consciousness, and anxiety melted, and suddenly we were at the finish line. We had done it. What had started as an ordeal ended in joy.

The triumph of the day was tinged with ambivalence. We had gone the distance. I had transcended my *idea* of my own limits and experienced the ecstasy that comes in those moments of self-forgetfulness when we overflow ourselves. But Prana had finished the race with energy and speed still in reserve. Clearly, her rhythms and mine were not to be harmonized.

We parted on the best of terms. A few months after the race, I gave her to a young friend who is an accomplished endurance rider. We frequently ride together. Both are entered this year in the Tevis Cup — the ultimate endurance race. These days I ride a walking horse and rejoice in a slower pace.

Reading over what I have written in this section, I can hear a chorus of objections from practical people: "Streams, apple trees, goats, bobcats, horses — what has all this to do with spirituality? You have the luxury of living in a rural area, on a farm. Living in an intimate relationship to growing things and animals is not a necessary element in the spiritual life of modern urban people. What you advocate isn't practical for city dwellers."

No, it is not necessary to live with bears and horses to reconnect anima and animal. If you are city-bound, a house cat, dog, or pet python can tutor your spirit. Attend to the antiphonal glances, hisses, growls, purring, and petting that pass between you and your cat, and you will recover the bilingual power you had as a child. If you have no wild animals about, make a ritual of visiting a zoo and feeling your way into the alien spirit of an elephant or antelope. Consider how you may be a guardian of your animal familiars and their habitat when you shop for food and clothing. It will not make your life easier. Only more communal.

Praise God for minor epiphanies and communion with animal spirits.

THE ECOLOGICAL COMMONWEALTH

If, as I have argued, a spiritual perspective involves recovery of an awareness of the intimate relation between anima-animal-humus, we run into a problem. The majority of people in the first world are urban, and we have come to consider the urban-industrial-corporate lifestyle as inevitable. Most city-bound people will resist the implication that they are the equivalent of damned souls and that rural dwellers are the new spiritual elite who are privileged to live near the source of grace. Nevertheless, we are forced to ask some troubling questions. How many more generations can survive the worldwide movement of people from the land into the city? What is the spiritual future of a world where the horizons of a majority of people are shaped by polluted, violent, and alienating environments? What is the probability that our escalating tendency toward urbanization and our fascination with technology, corporate growth, and a worldwide consumer economy will result in an ecologically viable environment, an increase in contented peoples and compassionate communities? I submit that any realistic forecast that extrapolates these current tendencies into the future is likely to predict widespread disaster.

It is difficult to imagine the social, economic, and political changes that will be necessary to re-create our cities and rural areas so that the majority of people can retain some vital connection *and identity with* the jeweled web of nonhuman life. But it is even more difficult to imagine how a spirited human life could remain possible in a landscape in which most other species have been destroyed or exiled to live in zoos or theme parks. When our knowledge of apples is limited to what we buy in the supermarket and our experience of animals to what we observe on Walt Disney, Wild America, or Sea World, we will have finally established our dominion over the earth and destroyed our intimate connection with the web of life. We will then retreat into our inner worlds to search for "self-esteem," a soul, or "spiritual center." But what we find will be profound loneliness. With our animal familiars extinct, we too will become homeless in what was once a cosmos.

Strangely, we have a new vision that will allow human beings to thrive, but we don't know how to put it into practice. The emerging myth of the twenty-first century that is at the heart of the spiritual renaissance of our time is the notion of ecology. Currently, ecology is a modest, emerging science of the interrelationship of living systems. But it is also a Trojan horse that is slowly being taken within the walls of the secular-technological-economic establishment, which is unaware that it contains a revolutionary force. Today, ecology mounts episodic defenses of threatened species of snail darters and spotted owls and demands the preservation of wetlands. Tomorrow, it will unfold a full vision, a reorientation of our psychology, economics, and politics and a plan to redesign cities and wilderness to allow us to live in harmony with other sentient beings. In time, from the cocoon of ecology there will emerge ecopsychology, ecospirituality, eco-nomics, and ecopolitics.

As the emerging science of the sacred, ecology requires spiritual disciplines very different from those that flowed from the theology of the Middle Ages, the Reformation, and the Industrial Revolution. In our time, authentic spirituality needs to be rooted in the *ecological imperative: Live in such a way that all future generations can enjoy as much or more biodiversity as we have enjoyed.* All else is self-serving delusion. Any form of spirituality that focuses exclusively on individual well-being and prosperity *is the dis-ease* for which it pretends to be the cure. Traditional religion agreed in identifying self-centeredness, greed, and delusion as the essence of hubris, sin, or maya. From the emerging ecospiritual perspective, *The Wall Street Journal* (the wisdom of this world) is foolishness. What could be more myopic and deluded than the belief that a worldwide marketplace economics can preserve the sacred bond that unites human and nonhuman life?

The words *spirit* and *ecology* both imply a vision that affirms that the whole is prior to the parts and therefore that all species of life are linked in a great chain of being. Within this vision humans, aphids, grasshoppers, earthworms, field mice, hawks, and coyotes are a commonwealth involving mutual rights and responsibilities rather than a miscellaneous collection of material resources for potential human exploitation. The interlocking varieties of intelligence that make up an ecosystem are choreographed moments in a single dance.

Somehow, we must phase out the central Western myth that we can conquer and control all "alien" forms of life and learn to fit gracefully into our limited human niche. Our urban mentality notwithstanding, we must place our enthusiasm for fabrication and consumption within the context of respect for the created world. Our cities will remain humane only if they are surrounded by green belts, sown fields, and wilderness. For modern men and women no less than for ancient hunters, gatherers, and farmers, the cultivation of a healthy spirit is inseparable from identifying with the humus. Even if we are housed in high-rise apartments on mean streets, the horizon of our spirit remains outdoors in a sanctuary not built with human hands. Our song is only one voice within a harmonious hymn of the universe.

How (or whether) we will make the necessary transition into an ecological era is impossible to predict. Systemic changes involve more novelty and surprises than futurists, government planners, and chaos theorists can even imagine. At the moment, we live in a turbulent intersection between eras. For the time being, like ancient Christians who awaited the coming of a new kingdom, we may keep our hope alive by performing symbolic actions that orient our lives to a new ecosocial order that may not come into being until our children are grown. Practice the new liturgies, perform token gestures — recycle, walk to work, grow a garden, limit consumption, strive for voluntary simplicity. These token gestures are pregnant with a foretaste, a redolence, an earnest of the now and future commonwealth.

ON BEING IN PLACE: DWELLING AND STORYTELLING

In our time, psychotherapy, ecotherapy, and sociotherapy all involve a process of radical remembering. The myth of progress assumes "we can't turn back the clock." The myth of the spirit assumes that the healing of psyche-environment-community involves recovering the lost memory of our individual and species childhood. To elaborate on a theme of Gabriel Marcel, "Hope is a memory of the future." Our hope for a human future involves the resurrection of our ecomemory.

The task of imagining and creating new forms of community in which humans remember and cherish their kinship with the nonhuman world is our new vocation. As my friend Jim Donaldson put it in a letter: "Ecological service is now the holy standard for spiritual authenticity. We can develop the best of spirit intentions, but without strong forms, bold new collective strategies such as ecomonasteries, cooperatives of sustainable energy and agriculture, strong collective political resistance to further destruction of totem species like the salmon, we will still have an anthropomorphic spirit life. Often I think that, these days, a person who is not committed to ecological service is a real monster." We have to reinvent ecocommunity — green cities, villages where people live and work, and rural centers of culture. No simple solutions will suffice. My insight into how we approach this enormous vocation is limited to a rule of thumb that I have gleaned from experience: A place becomes a dwelling for my body and spirit only when I settle down long enough to cherish and cultivate my relationship to it.

I can no more love cities or the Earth in general than I can love women in general by seeking to have intercourse with all women. The college woods and the Cascade Mountains have taught me to cherish the timbre of the wind moving through pine, hickory, and oak and to be watchful for the appearance of thrush and fox. Lately, I have gained an intimate knowledge of the seasonal patterns of pasture grass and the life-cycles of peach trees, and I have become acquainted with the ways of successive generations of acorn woodpeckers by dwelling on and tending a piece of land. Ever so gradually, I have been drawn into the knowledge of my kinship with these others who share this domain.

Today, science is searching for a theory of everything, a single principle that will unite our knowledge of the physical universe. In the realm of the human spirit the strong force that binds us together in a single communion is *the story*. The ground of compassion and community is the shared story. The identity of an individual is forged by the process of creating an autobiography; a marriage is made by the interweaving of two life-stories; a community that is founded on a common history. In the same way an intimate relationship with a city or with the land and animal spirits is created by dwelling in a place long enough for everything in the environment to become infused with stories. A place becomes the sacred ground of my being only when I have tended and enjoyed it long enough for each spot and inhabitant to have a rich history of associations and stories.

In *Ceremony*, Leslie Silko tells the story of a young American Indian whose experience as a prisoner of war nearly destroyed his will to live. In a quest for healing, he began to explore the old myths and the sacred places of his people. In a memorable scene, he found himself beside a pool where he watched spiders, frogs, and dragonflies and remembered the stories he had been told as a boy.

"The spider came out first. She drank from the edge of the pool, careful to keep the delicate eggs sacs on her abdomen out of the water. . . . He remembered stories about her. . . . She alone had known how to outsmart the malicious mountain Ka't'sina who imprisoned the rain clouds in the northwest room of his magical house. . . . Dragon-flies came and hovered over the pool. They were all colors of blue — powdery sky blue, dark night blue, shimmering with almost black iridescent light, and mountain blue. There were stories about dragon-flies too. He turned. Everywhere he looked, he saw a world made of stories, the long ago, time immemorial stories."

I think the era is ending when we can afford to be migrants, moving every five years, never belonging anywhere, always on the go. Certainly for me, after an American lifetime on the road — living in ten states, nineteen cities or towns, and moving more times than I can count — it is time to come to ground. Five years ago, we bought sixty acres of unimproved land near Sonoma, California. What was then real estate, bought and owned, has gradually become a hearth, sacred ground — a storied place.

Walk with me.

When we came here, there was only a rough dirt road and a ford over the creek. During the long months when we were fighting with the county authorities to get permission to buy the land, we came on weekends, camped, and carried stones to build these two bridges you see. Once a storm washed them out, so we brought in concrete culverts and started over.

Agua caliente flows year-round — only a trickle in midsummer — but isn't a good source for drinking water: too many unknowns. We don't know how much pesticide drains into the watershed from the vineyards that are above us or what animals bearing giardia may drink from it. One parched August afternoon I was exploring the creek, and I saw a colony of luminous emerald ferns growing high on the bank next to a large boulder. Searching for evidence of a hidden spring, I cleared the matted foliage from around the roots and found a seep. Digging deeper with my bare hands and a sharp rock, I made a miniature holding-pond and sat down to watch and wait. Within a minute the gallon-deep reservoir was filled with muddy water. Three minutes later the lake cleared, and I could see by a faint cloud of disturbed muddy water that fresh water was flowing into the pool from a source higher up beneath the boulder. Excited, I dug deeper, excavating the moist loam from under the rock. More water. By the time I had enlarged the reservoir and observed the flow of water enough to be reasonably certain I had discovered an underground spring, darkness was setting in, and I was forced to return to the tent that was our temporary home. The next day, and the next, and the next, I returned with axe and saw, stripped off my clothes, knelt in the growing bed of mud, and dug up under the rock. I followed the seep to a rivulet, the rivulet to a fingerling, the fingerling to a six-gallon-a-minute spring of crystal-clear water that comes from so deep in the earth, it is unaffected by rain or drought. Drink, taste the sweetness, satisfy your thirst.

I planted this orchard three years ago — two of every variety of fruit tree — and this summer we got our first cherries, apples, almonds, and peaches. You will notice it is fenced. At first we had only an electric fence, and the two yearling deer that live in the hollow would come up to the fence, touch it with their noses, and retreat. But this year they were emboldened by two more youngsters whose taste for apple bark would not be frustrated, and they took to jumping the electric fence. So I had to build a higher one.

The site on which we chose to build our house is exactly where the old Norrbom homestead stood a hundred years ago. If you look carefully, you can still see the old stone oven set into the side of the hill. This place has been inhabited for a long time. When we were digging the foundation, we found a perfect arrowhead, a gift from one of the tribes that once lived here. I could tell a hundred stories about the building of the house, stories about the coming of age of my son Gifford, who was the chief builder, about the healing of a marriage that took place as Jan and I worked together, about epic struggles with county authorities, about the pileated woodpecker that nested in the dead maple tree and watched us build. But there isn't time for that.

It is enough to say that over time, the land, the plants, the animal spirits, the persons who dwell here, and the stories we have come to tell have become a part of a seamless web. I and they intermingle; we are one flesh. I have become incarnate by husbanding. So much a long communion makes us what we are that person and land intertwine to become one body. A place becomes a sacred dwelling only when it is filled with care and stories.

CHAPTER 10

The Public Spirit: Creating a Compassionate Community

"Earth shall be fair, and all her people one:
Nor till that hour shall God's whole will be done.
Now, even now, once more from earth to sky,
Peals forth in joy man's old, undaunted cry—
'Earth shall be fair, and all her folk be one!' "

The Hymnbook, no. 490

"Seek the welfare of the city where I have sent you into exile, and pray to the Lord on its behalf, for in its welfare you will find your welfare."

JEREMIAH 29:7

"We expect a theophany of which we know nothing but the place, and the place is called community."

MARTIN BUBER,
Between Man and Man

"The great challenge of our time is to reunite spirituality and politics."

SANDOR MCNAB

We have come a long way together on the journey that began when we faced our existential situation as solitary men or women filled with doubts, questions, and undefined longings and took leave of the familiar community to explore the intimate realm of our autobiographical experience. We have scaled the mountains of the mind, luxuriated in the sacred dimensions of sensuality and sexuality, and rediscovered our place within the earth household.

Many cartographers indicate that the map for the spiritual journey ends here, and most guides do not venture beyond this point. Unfortunately, most of what is written these days suggests that spiritual practice is a matter of cultivating a private garden of inner experiences — mystical experiences, out-of-body experiences, near-death experiences, peak experiences, former lifetime experiences, enlightenment experiences, prosperity, self-esteem, ego-strength — or of improving our relationships with our intimates. Most psychotherapists and self-proclaimed spiritual gurus advocate a retreat into privatism to cultivate our own garden. It is one of the great failures of our system of compartmentalized professionalism that those responsible for healing the psyche and spirit are to such a large extent apolitical in both theory and practice.

The final test of the spirit is not to be found on the mountain heights or in the depths of the solitary journey. Individual men and women in all times and ages have accomplished this. The great challenge is to learn how all kinds and conditions of human beings can dwell together peacefully in the valley of the shadow of history.

Notwithstanding the shortsightedness of our modern spiritual cartographers and guides, most of the maps left by the great classical explorers indicate that, just past the midpoint of the journey, the road takes a 180-degree turn — away from the self and toward the community, away from the cultivation of the private realm and toward compassionate action in the public realm. Once re-membered and re-collected, the self must be forgotten and a new search undertaken for a communal home that lies somewhere beyond the horizon.

To state the matter in a less metaphorical way, the development of a spiritual perspective involves two steps. First, I must aggressively affirm and explore my unique individuality. Second, I must continually resist the nearly inevitable illusion of ego-centricity and explore the ways in which I rise out of, and take my life from, an encompassing sea. In the spirit dance, we continually go back and forth from "I" to "we," from subjectivity to intersubjectivity, from solitude to communion.

EXILE AND THE LONGING FOR COMMUNITY

Like a necromancer, I can diagnose the modern condition of rootlessness and longing for community by examining the entrails of my own soul. I'm a good twentieth-century man. I have carved my individuality out of the rough marble that was given me, tasted freedom within the confines of my genetic and historical destiny. I have a rich inner life, and I pay attention to the winds of the spirit. I live in complex harmony with my wife and take pleasure in grown and growing children. I have intimate friends, a circle of acquaintances, satisfying work, a modicum of fame, financial plenty, land, and horses. I have a privileged, lucky, or graced life. Nevertheless, something is missing. I can't make out the shape of the void or trace an outline of the obscure object of my desire, but I can name it — community.

Like Heraclitus, we modern men and women, stepping into the river of our time, never step twice in the same place. We are always moving on. Ever since we left Europe for the New World and continued westward to the Pacific, we have been a people who believe profoundly in good-byes. We pull up roots and drift on the wind, borne by a blind optimism that we will be transplanted in richer soil. On the average, Americans change their residence every five years or so.

As a result, most of whatever community we enjoy is no longer geographical. My community is a star that exploded and sent fragments into all corners of my solar system. My children and family of origin are spread out over two continents. The friends I reach out regularly to touch with the help of AT&T are scattered in myriad area codes. My professional community extends over a dozen countries where I have worked and beyond that to the boundaries of the literary world.

As the century draws to a close, most of us are refugees living in exile from a spiritual community to which we belong but have never known. We are haunted by an unconscious memory of a time when we lived among our kin and an obscure hope for a homeland that has yet to exist in time or space but that we have glimpsed often in our dreams. Nothing shapes our era, or points the direction of the quest we must undertake, so much as the vacuum.

THE PUBLIC-SPIRITED HERO:
THE OUTWARD JOURNEY

Rub three ideas together: politics-heroism-spirit. If there is ever to be a politics of compassion, it will require a new kind of politician, a new model of heroism, and a new understanding of spirituality. Facets of the same gem.

Here is how Vaclav Havel expressed it: "Sooner or later politics will be faced with the task of finding a new, postmodern face. A politician must become a person again. . . . Soul, individual spirituality, first-hand personal insight into things; the courage to be himself and go the way his conscience points, humility in the face of the mysterious order of Being, confidence in its natural direction and above all, trust in his own subjectivity as his principal link with the subjectivity of the world — these are the qualities that politicians of the future should cultivate."[1]

Today the arena of the spiritual adventure is changing, turning inside out, shifting from psyche to *polis*, from the inner journey to the community.

The history of human evolution can be read as the story of the changing visions of the heroic life. Each age has special challenges that must be met, characteristic agonies, dark forces with which the hero must wrestle. The chains we must break in order to be free differ from generation to generation. Yesterday's daring adventure for the bold becomes today's packaged tour for the timid. What was creative in one age becomes demonic in the next. For instance, in the beginning nation-states bound diverse tribes into a larger community and lessened the warfare between local clans. Now nations are frequently the means of organizing genocide and world wars. Cities originally were sanctu-aries offering freedom from myopic perspectives and the drudgery of the farm. Now they have become enclaves that imprison millions who have no other alternatives than urban ideology and economic drudgery.

To oversimplify: The heroic task for the age of hunters and gatherers was to live harmoniously in the sacred world of animals and plants; the heroic task for the age of empires was to build cities and conquer enemies; the heroic task for the age of science and technology was to conquer nature; the heroic task since the emergence of depth psychology has been to explore the inner world; the heroic task for now and future generations is to domesticate the dark forces that destroy community.

Consider how the idea of the hero is changing in the decade of the 1990s. The traditional Western hero in his many manifestations — Warrior, Mystic, Savior, Rational Man, Scientist, Technologist, Artist — was a splendidly solitary individual. In recounting the myth of the hero with a thousand faces, Joseph Campbell was fond of quoting the passage from the legend of the Holy Grail where the Knights of the Round Table set forth on their quest: "Each man went into the woods in the place where it was darkest and there was no path, for they thought it would be a shame to go in a group."

As the twentieth century advanced and scientists and technologists increasingly fulfilled their heroic task of understanding and controlling nature, a compensatory reaction has taken place — an intensified effort to chart the mysteries of the inner world of the psyche and to bring its irrational forces under control. The new science of psychoanalysis sought to bring the light of consciousness into the jungle of the soul. Therapists were the new explorers searching for the sources of the Nile, the secrets of the dark continent. Artists were the harbingers and storytellers of the new journey. Campbell described the arena of mid-twentieth-century heroism in this way: "The mythogenic zone today is the individual in contact with his own interior life, communicating through his art with those 'out there.' "

Freud's formulation of the task of the psychonaut has been modified by every subsequent school of psychology, but it still reflects the heroic ideal of the inner journey. The task of the voyager was to descend into the forbidden and unknown underworld of the libido to liberate the erotic angels and demonic powers who dwelt there. The unconscious had to be made conscious. Like a fortress under siege from all sides, the ego had to be strengthened against the amoral desires of the id and the cruelly moralistic demands of the superego. Carl Jung found a more entertaining cast of archetypal helpers in the unconscious but essentially agreed with Freud about the task of therapy. Both conducted psychotherapy, in which a solitary individual sought to heal the relationship between conscious and unconscious in conversation with a solitary therapist within the confines of a treatment room.

A good case can be made that Freud and Jung gave an accurate description of the psyche of their time and that both were in greater agreement with the religious establishment than either would like to admit. Delving into and seeking to cure the individual soul, whether by therapy or theology, made great sense in the context of the self-satisfied, rationalistic, repressive society of the time. Optimism reigned prior to the first world war in Europe and the second in America. There was little awareness of the dark forces that lurk under the thin veneer of civilization. When Salvador Dali's film *The Andalusian Dog* appeared in 1923, few people knew what to make of its surrealistic imagery — ants crawling out of holes in a manikin's hand, an eyeball being split. The wild, dreamlike, contradictory images and feelings that govern the unconscious life — the territory of the libido — were virtually unknown. Successful men and women were mostly extroverted, pragmatic, and well controlled.

Consider the change that has taken place in the structure of the psyche. Today it is the libido that runs free, the superego that is in exile, and the ego that is undeveloped. Shortly after World War II, when American industry was producing a large surplus of consumer goods, the new engineers of desire — the advertising industry — began to convince us to leave no want unsatisfied. Virtue and vice traded places. Suddenly we were supposed to spend rather than save, enjoy the moment rather than plan for the future. The gospel of sexual abundance replaced the virtue of postponed gratification. Buy now, pay later. Seize the gusto. Just do it. One by one the taboos governing conspicuous consumption, sex, drugs, and violence have been weakened. *Every "vice" or "perversion" that was repressed and exiled into the unconscious in the nineteenth century is now a conscious part of the public imagination.* MTV, ABC, and NBC explore incest, rape, child abuse, ritual murder, devil worship, cannibalism, prostitution, and pornography ad nauseam. The average child views thirty thousand acts of simulated violence a year. What was once inconceivable to the middle-class mind is now prime time.

We have turned inside-out. Apollo is in exile, and Dionysus is running wild in the streets. Reason is a clandestine virtue. Moderation and contentment are out of style. Concupiscence — endless desire, an increasing GNP — is the dream of the land. Even in periods of economic hardship, we are unable to distinguish between wants, needs, and entitlements. What Americans desire, Americans demand. We are no longer satisfied that government should protect our natural right to "the pursuit of happiness." Now we expect it to deliver happiness (without additional taxes or budget cuts). Surely the superego is weak, if not dead, when the underclass burn the inner city, when drugs — instant ecstasy — are available in every high school and ghetto, and when drive-by shootings have become the new rite of initiation for gang members. When all things are permissible, as Dostoyevsky pointed out a century ago, when nothing is forbidden, when there are no taboos, both God and the human spirit die.

Psyche and *polis*, like spirit and body, mirror each other. As within, so without. As the old psychic structures crumble, so do the political structures that once ordered our lives. Before our eyes, empires self-destruct, kingdoms rise and fall. Where there was a stable reign of terror, a stalemated cold war between the great powers of capitalism and Communism, there is now a confusion of tribes and a renewed outbreak of barbaric ethnic violence. And the only dim hope held out is that if the warring factions can put their differences aside, they may enjoy the prosperity of the new market economy.

But nineteenth-century solutions aren't sufficient for twenty-first-century problems. If we are to take a new inner journey in the 1990s, it will not be into the Freudian unconscious! If we are to take a new political journey, it will not be into nationalism, industrialization, and a global consumer culture. We cannot be healed by a hair of the dog that bit us.

The central repression in contemporary Western culture is the need for purpose, meaning, and a sense of the sacred.

There can be no cultural and spiritual renaissance unless millions of individuals make the repressed questions a matter of ultimate concern:

"What is my purpose? What is the meaning of my life? What is sacred for me?" But our time demands more than this of individuals. Today, we need to forge a link between solitude and political-communal engagement. Those who are willing to explore their spiritual unconscious must emerge from the womb of privacy and from the sanctuary of religion and give themselves to the heroic task of creating a new form of political life.

It always requires courage to face our personal shadows — our existential brokenness, irrational impulses, amoral desires, grandiosity, cruelty, and cowardice. But the new hero must wrestle with dark forces far larger than any that inhibit the individual psyche. The darkness that threatens to engulf us is metapersonal: institutional, corporate, economic, and political. The contemporary unconscious is manifest in the pollution of our environment, the wanton destruction of thousands of nonhuman species, the booming business in arms, the epidemic of small wars, the renewed practice of genocide. The crisis of the sprawling megalopolis is the unconscious Siamese twin of our Promethean struggle to conquer nature. Crime, poverty, and homelessness are the dark side of a competitive economy in which winners enjoy luxury and losers take the hindmost. The bloody habit of warfare, the regular sacrifice of men on far-flung battlefields, the stranglehold the military-industrial complex continues to exert on our economy and spirit, is the shadow side of our ultimate concern with preserving the sovereignty of nations. Our self-censorship has kept us from calculating the hidden costs of our prosperity.

What is the shadow work of the new hero? What are the questions we must live? What agonies must we voluntarily endure? What are the monsters against which we must do battle? To what new tasks are we called?

The spiritual heroes of our age are those who have the courage to become conscious of what we have ignored, to inhabit and lay claim to the destructive consequences of our collective actions. Psychologists call it "reowning our projections." The old spiritual names for it were repentance, remorse, and making amends. It requires a broken and contrite heart and a new mind.

For better and for worse, the world is rapidly becoming a single collective of unequal and troubled nations. Isolation is a thing of the past. So as we enter a new century, we are faced with a great choice. Either we continue to drift toward the Great Techno-Economic-Military Collective, or we begin the bold experiment of creating a new communal order.

The heroic task for the twenty-first century is nothing less than the nearly unimaginable task of changing our fundamental organizing principles, ideals, and values to create a global body-politic, a compassionate community.

THE SACRAMENTS OF IMAGINATION, EMPATHY, AND COMPASSION

We begin the long, probably endless, journey toward the Commonwealth of Compassion by practicing the virtues necessary to create communion.

We might think of spiritual practice, in the simplest terms, as the exploration of how capacious we may become, how far our identity can stretch, how much we can incorporate. A soulful person is not an autonomous atom but a quantum self, a particle and a wave, an entity and a hologram. *Spirit* may be considered a synonym for *love*. A spirited life is continually being expanded to include an ever-widening community. This requires that we cultivate an elastic heart, an erotic body, a generous mind, and a compassionate imagination to root out whatever keeps us from loving ourselves and the others with whose lives ours are intertwined.

A lot of lip service is paid to love: "God is love. . . . Love makes the world go 'round. . . . Love is the morning and the evening star. . . . What the world needs now is love, sweet love," and so on. It is widely assumed that love is the answer to all our problems and that it comes naturally. We may "have to be taught, before we are six or seven or eight, to hate all the things our relatives hate," but we are supposed to know how to love.

I think we do not. Love may be partly grace or chemistry, but it is also an art that must be learned. It takes years of practice to develop a skillful heart.

In the beginning is the intention. When as a confused teenager I asked my mother what love is, she gave me a definition superior to any I have found in the dictionary. "Love," she said, "is the willed intent of the heart." It doesn't just happen by magic. She went on to explain that one part of love is sweet and easy, something we fall into and are swept away by. But the other part is hard; it requires discipline, willpower, and opening your heart again and again to someone with whom you are angry, can't stand, and do not like.

In an ideal world everyone would be perfectly loved by parents who were perfectly loved by their parents, ad infinitum, and we would all receive so much love, we would be spontaneously open-hearted. But in the actual world we have all been crippled by being loved too little, too late, or in twisted ways, and when we begin to search for heartful communion, we limp along the path. So if we are to escape the solitary prison of our individual ego or the group prison of our collective ego (both based on the will-to-power), we must exert considerable will-to-love.

Having decided to venture beyond the atmosphere of the ego, we launch ourselves toward communion by an act of imagination. To begin to understand the strangers and rivals who live on the other side of the river, against whom we have previously defended ourselves, we must project ourselves into their worldview, see things through their eyes. In imagination we turn inside out. Like Proteus, we transform ourselves and become the other. We attempt to inhabit the mind of the other.

The skill of imagination is not yet love. In fact, the imaginative identification that the novice lover must learn is no different from that practiced by any good novelist, psychotherapist, or general. You need not love or even respect someone to imagine how the world looks from their perspective. A novelist must know how his characters sit in a chair, comb their hair, vote, eat an ear of corn, make love. A therapist must reconstruct the inner world of a delusional patient. A warrior must know his opponent. As General Ulysses S. Grant said, "I know Lee as well as he knows himself. I know all his strong points, and all his weak ones."

Empathy is one step nearer to love. To practice empathy, we must move beyond theoretical understanding and mental pictures to emotion — to attempt to *feel* what it is like to be another person. For instance, if I want to communicate effectively with George, a gay acquaintance, knowing he has AIDS and can expect to die within a year, I must ask myself how I would feel if I were in his circumstances and allow myself to experience some of the fear, rage, and courage he exhibits. In the practice of empathy, we still maintain a psychological distance between self and the other. In George's case, the pain I allow myself to feel vicariously is still his pain, not mine.

With the practice of compassion, we move from the outskirts into the center of love.

Let's suppose that in reaching for an empathic understanding of George, I suddenly realize that I, too, face death. In the moment when I follow the syllogism "All men are mortal; I am a man" to its inevitable conclusion — "Therefore, I am mortal" — I cease being an observer of George's condition and enter into communion with a fellow man. In the instant I remember that I am one of those "for whom the bell tolls," my center of gravity shifts. My singular ego becomes a plural soul. To take another example, in the 1992 Los Angeles riots, Bobby Green was one of the men who came to the aid of Reginald Denny, the white truck driver who was being beaten. When asked why he risked his life to stop the beating, he said, "It felt like I was getting hurt."

Compassion is an outgrowth of wisdom, a consequence of the awareness that self and other are already joined. Love is the recognition that unity is prior to diversity, that the commonwealth is the fertile ground in which individuality is rooted. The fate of the community of all living beings is the fate of the self. Consciousness, compassion, and community are merely different names for the phenomenon that is the object of the spiritual quest. Likewise, unconsciousness, hatred, and ego-centrism are different names for the dis-spirited life.

The dis-spirited life moves in a downward spiral, like water circling the drain: the less love, the less feeling, the less sensation, the less empathy, the less outreach, the less contact, the less self-transcendence, the less freedom, the less hope. When the nexus of caring and communion is lost, the ego becomes a fortress to be defended against a host of dangers. Encapsulated people create an ambience of fear and relationships based on the will-to-power. A vicious circle. We are bound together in intergenerational communities of hate or love. With a high degree of regularity, the abused become the abusers, the wounded the wounders — and the graced the grace-ful.

As children we are inspired in varying degrees by the measure of nurturance and unconditional love we receive. In legal theory, we are all created equal, but in point of fact we are unequal recipients of health, economic, and educational opportunity, wealth, and the enabling grace of love. We may not be predestined to salvation or damnation in any theological sense, as John Calvin said, but we are predisposed to spiritual richness or poverty by the careful or careless climate of our childhood. We enter life with an inequality of gifts, heirs to the virtues and vices of our parents. No one of us chooses our parents or the measure of basic trust or mistrust with which we are endowed. Usually, somewhere near midlife an opening — a breakdown or breakthrough — occurs, in which we have a thorny opportunity to become aware of how blessed or injured we have been, and we begin the quest to increase the quanta of loving kindness we are able to give and receive. Just as IQ (intelligence quotient) may be increased by mental exercise, so CQ (compassion quotient) may be increased by exercising the willed intent of the heart and practicing the sacraments of imagination and empathy.

Fortunately, love creates virtuous circles that reverse the effects of vicious circles. Gradually, through the nurturance of a loving community, or suddenly, in the twinkling of an eye, as the result of a single act of kindness, a centripetal ego may begin to reverse direction and blossom into a centrifugal self.

The individual is knit on the loom of community. How wrong, how superficial our Western philosophical thinking about the self has been! Descartes's "I think, therefore I am" identifies self with mind. We would do better to begin with "I was loved; therefore I am." Soul and community intertwine like the double helix. Love is not a bonus, a pleasant emotional extra; it is the constitutive element in the formation of the self. My Being is co-Being. Whether I am passionate or dispassionate will in some measure depend on the compassion with which I have been nourished.

Recognizing how crucial the informing love I receive is to the basic trust with which I enter life, I am led to make the task of becoming a more loving person central to the meaning of my life. The measure of care we introduce into the intersubjective bonds that unite us in marriages, families, and communities determines how peaceful, juicy and creative our lives will be.

LOCAL SAINTS AND CONSECRATED NEIGHBORS

When we consider how to re-create community, the recent slogan "Think globally, act locally" is good advice. The kind of love that builds a community is a local phenomenon that can't be multiplied by committees or manufactured by government programs. The atmosphere of compassion that transforms a mass of alienated individuals into a caring community is created by countless acts of kindness and charitable foresight. And the dramas of heroic love are usually performed on small stages; the names of local heroes and consecrated neighbors are known only within their towns and villages. When a handful of neighbors rally around Ed and Vicky to help care for their Down's syndrome child, it doesn't make the news, but it does renew the bonds that unite strangers into a sustaining communion.

To re-mind and en-courage myself in the practice of applied compassion, I collect images and stories with which to create my personal pantheon of local heroes and consecrated neighbors. (We need a modern equivalent of *The Lives of Saints* — pinups of sexy saints, winsome prophets, heroines of compassionate political action — to inspire us.) For instance:

During the late 1930s, my grandmother McMurray seemed to hold the town of Maryville, Tennessee, together. As head of the home economics department at Maryville College, she taught homemaking skills and somehow found time to bake pies that disappeared instantly at church socials, and take pots of chicken soup to shut-ins. When the Depression came, she organized and ran the College Maid Shop to manufacture uniforms and provide a way for a generation of poor girls to sew their way through college.

A decade ago, a handful of men and women who wanted to preserve the traditional rural way of life in the Methow valley in Washington formed a citizens' council to fight the efforts of the Aspen Ski Corporation to create a ski resort that would destroy the social and natural ecology of the valley. David versus Goliath. With unwavering commitment and very little money, they fought three successive contenders, all highly financed corporations, to a standstill. In court battle after court battle, they forced the reluctant United States Forest Service and the developers to produce environmental impact statements and conform to the law. As a result, the river today still runs clear, the game corridors are still open, there are no condominiums, and the community in the valley remains in the hands of local people.

Kay Allison's "New Age" bookstore in Charlottesville, Virginia, doesn't appear to be a hotbed of social action. There are lots of books about crystal power and past lives and none on social organizing. But ever so quietly, Kay has organized a small group of people to get thousands of copies of remaindered books from publishers and distribute them in Virginia prisons.

Four women in chic Marin County band together to rent a house and create a sanctuary for battered women. A delicatessen owner in Ann Arbor organizes restaurant owners to bring their surplus meals to a homeless shelter. A rural church group in Garden Plains, Kansas, gleans unpicked apples for the urban poor. An emergency room physician in Sonoma collects medical supplies and equipment and takes them to a small hospital in Bhutan. A wealthy automobile dealer in Lexington gives the township a thirty-acre estate for a new school. A corporate law firm in San Francisco does hours of pro bono work for the Trust for Public Lands. A small group of citizens in Birmingham struggles to create a better curriculum for the high school. A group of ghetto parents in Detroit organizes a crime watch to keep drug dealers out of their neighborhood. Of such is the kingdom of kindness made, deed by deed.

We need to make a radical change in the legend that says that God preserves the world because thirty-six good and just men are born in every generation. It is not a precious few men or women but an anonymous multitude of ordinary people in every hamlet and metropolis who maintain civility and create community. Our immediate surroundings provide each of us with a vocation and an occasion to exercise imagination, empathy, and compassion. Each locality issues an immediate appeal. To those who have ears to hear, there are always neighbors with crying needs. Opportunities to serve are never lacking.

One of the handiest ways to consecrate everyday life is to make an effort to respond to people and situations you meet in the course of the day as if they were issuing a personal appeal to you for help or offering you a gift. Listen with an open mind and heart. Look with a care-ful eye. What is being (silently) asked of you when your barber tells you about his son's drug habit; when your neighbor explains quietly that his operation for cancer was not entirely successful; when the governor announces that local prisons are so overcrowded that four men are forced to live in a single cell? What gift is being offered when a friend listens to your despair about your failing marriage, or a government agency gives you food stamps? Nearly a decade ago, Anne Herbert, writing in *Whole Earth Review,* casually started what has become an informal movement by suggesting that we make a daily practice of committing anonymous acts of random kindness and senseless beauty to utter strangers. Right on!

THE GLOBAL COMMUNITY

Tending to our private devotions and local communities is a neces-sary but no longer sufficient expression of the in-spirited life. What is new in our historical situation is that the major problems we face and the changes we must undertake are global — AIDS, global warming, the destruction of the rain forests, the population explosion, the fluctuations of multinational economy, the political instability of the poorest nations, the flood of refugees, the pollution of air and water-shed.

In a single generation the communications revolution has expanded the community to which we belong from the local to the global. The television news of the day brings a gaunt, dust-covered mass of starving people into my living room. Children with enormous eyes and toothpick-size arms watch me eat granola and fruit. The war in Bosnia brings bloodied warriors engaged in "ethnic cleansing" into my parlor and leaves scores of homeless families on my doorstep. Suddenly my moral nerve endings are stretched, as neighbors I had not known peer at me and demand to be included within the circle of my care. As I am moved by compassion for the tragic condition of the unfortunate majority, I feel a shift in my sense of identity. I realize that I belong to the human family. We are one people, a dis-eased human community.

World citizenship is being thrust on us, ready or not. In our generation *awareness* is growing that for better and worse we live in a global community, but there is yet little *commitment* to actualize a Compassionate Commonwealth of all peoples. The universal community to which we essentially belong currently exists only in memory and hope. The great spiritual challenge of our time is to mount an expedition to make it actual. This has become our new calling, our spiritual-political vocation.

Our first step toward a globally responsible spirituality may be to acknowledge that our new situation creates a moral paradox: It stretches our compassion beyond our ability to respond in action. Mahatma Gandhi expressed the maxim for compassionate action in this way: "I will give you a talisman. Whenever you are in doubt or when the self becomes too much with you, apply the following test. Recall the face of the poorest and weakest man whom you may have seen, and ask yourself if the step you contemplate is going to be of any use over his own life and destiny. In other words, will it lead to self-reliance for the hungry and spiritually starving millions. Then you find your doubt and your self melting away."[2] There are very few of us who are able to follow this counsel of perfection, and I am not one of them. Nevertheless, if we hold it before our eyes, this talisman will gradually dissolve our isolated individualism and bond us with the universal community that is our home.

INDICATORS OF COMMUNAL SPIRITUAL HEALTH

Only a fool or a futurist would predict the shape of a possible but improbable compassionate world order. It seems likely that we will increasingly be pushed up against the great alternative — *either* learn to care for each other beyond the old lines of nation, class, and religion, *or* self-destruct in the economic-military warfare of each against each. Yet there is no way to anticipate what dynamics might unfold *if* a majority of citizens became committed to the practice of political compassion.

Without knowing whether such a shift can be accomplished, we can point to some of the radical changes in our fundamental values and principles of political action that we would have to undergo to move toward the creation of a compassionate political order.

If there is to be a compassionate community it will arise from:

- a shift from the myth of progress to a myth of sustainable growth
- a shift in identity from the ego-centric individual to the communally rooted person
- a shift from the game of nations and the politics of the balance of power to the world game and eco-centric politics
- a shift from the myth of competition to economic cooperation
- a shift from the myth of just wars and sanctified violence to peaceful means of conflict resolution
- a shift from population explosion to zero population growth
- a shift from nationalism, the principle of sovereignty, and ethnic conflict to an effective world federation
- a shift from a secular view of nature as raw material to the resacralization of nature
- a shift from a world divided between the poor and the rich to a more just distribution of wealth
- a shift from compulsive production of more complex technologies to production of appropriate, sustainable technologies
- a shift from habitually passive consumption of values and myths prepackaged by the entertainment media in the service of advertisers to an interactive relationship to media

All of this sounds extremely radical and utopian. It assumes nothing less than an effort to found a society based on the *principle of generosity*. As unlikely as this sounds, it is not without historical precedent. Many tribal societies were based on the exchange of gifts rather than the trading of commodities, on the ideal of generosity rather than equality. The hunter gives meat, the shaman gives visions, the mothers give children, the old women give knowledge of healing herbs, the old men give the wisdom of governance. Even today in those parts of the world where the market has not yet become the organizing principle of life, gift-exchange is the major force creating community. Western travelers to the Himalayan countries are frequently amazed by the hospitality and generosity they encounter.

What we are discovering lately in American society is that we can't build a good society on the principles of self-interest and entitlement alone. Without generosity, there can be no community. Without the kindness of strangers, a society is turned into an armed camp. Without the selfless giving of fathers and mothers, children become alienated and uncivil adults. Without tenderness between son-father-grandfather, daughter-mother-grandmother, the continuity between the generations is ruptured and wisdom is lost.

For the moment, let's leave aside the question of whether the Compassionate Commonwealth is an impossible ideal or a contradiction in terms. Before the fact, every major historical social change has seemed improbable. (In A.D. 37 what odds would Lloyds of London have given that Christianity would become the major Western religion?) Human nature is neither fixed nor finished; nor are the varieties of political communities. It is crucial that we hold our dream for a more compassionate order before our eyes without assuming either that the dream is impossible or that it can be actualized by any five-year plan. Speaking about the human plight, Reinhold Niebuhr once remarked that "nothing worth doing can be accomplished in a single lifetime." To avoid despair, to be animated by hope, it is not necessary to know that our dreams for a just and compassionate world order will come to pass in short order. It is necessary only to follow a vocation that leads us in the right direction.

Without assuming we can eliminate injustice, greed, and cruelty or create a spiritual utopia, we can construct a rough scorecard to chart our progress toward or regress from a more compassionate community.

Begin with an analogy. Every year, the Population Crisis Committee publishes a Human Suffering Index that ranks each nation on a scale of 0 to 100 based on the following categories: (1) gross national product per capita, (2) average annual rate of inflation, (3) average annual growth of labor force, (4) average annual growth of urban population, (5) infant mortality, (6) daily per capita calorie supply as a percent of requirement, (7) access to clean drinking water, (8) energy consumption per capita, (9) adult literacy, and (10) personal freedom and governance.³ While this index may not measure some of the subtler aspects of suffering and well-being, it is clearly a far better device for measuring the physical health of nations than their gross national product alone.

I suggest that a parallel index will allow us to chart the spiritual health of the world commonwealth by measuring:

- Decrease in the percentage of the world economy devoted to the production and sale of arms. Assumption: The warfare system is the core delusion that we must overcome to create a compassionate world order. At the present time, less than one-fourth of world military expenditures could: prevent soil erosion, stop ozone depletion, stabilize population, prevent global warming and acid rain, provide clean safe energy, provide shelter, eliminate illiteracy, eliminate starvation and malnourishment, provide clean water, and retire developing nations' debt.⁴

- Decrease in the number of persons killed in wars, border conflicts, and instances of ethnic violence. Assumption: The only way to cut through ideology, propaganda, and the rhetoric of "just" and "holy" wars is to keep score of the deaths they cause. Every person's life is equally sacred. A Death Watch Institute could roughly measure the morality of a nation by determining how many deaths it was responsible for in any given year either through direct warfare, through civil repression, or by supplying "military aid" to surrogates and the sale of arms.

- Decrease in instances of torture. Assumption: Torture is an absolute desecration, *the* clearest example of the absence of spirit. As such, it anchors moral reasoning by providing an unambiguous standard for identifying evil.

- Decrease in instances of rape and hostility between the sexes. Assumption: Spiritual health is not possible where there is sexual dis-ease. The ancient and current alienation between the sexes is neither genetic nor inevitable but a product of alienating forms of economic and political organization.

- Increase in the number of women in police and peacekeeping forces who share the power, responsibility, and burden of dealing with the outbreak of criminal, civil, and national violence.

Assumption: The current role divisions that socialize men to be warriors specializing in control and the management of violence, and women to be nurturers specializing in the private realm, perpetuates the warfare system and the battle between the sexes. A healthy economic-political and ecospiritual system requires us to abandon the gender role-divisions that reflect and perpetuate the warfare system.

- Decrease in the number of hours of work needed to secure sufficient income for a comfortable style of life. Assumption: Economic activity should be a means to create the leisure necessary to enjoy private life, family life, and community life. Labor should free our minds and bodies from the tyranny of economics. In a healthy communal economy people would work to live, not live to work.

- Increase in the percentage of goods and services produced for the market economy in relation to household or local economy. Assumption: Beyond a certain point, converting necessary goods and services into commodities purchased from strangers disempowers us and destroys the interpersonal bond that creates a sense of belonging. When anonymous physicians tend our bodies, morticians bury our dead, agribusiness produces our food, and multinational corporations own our supermarkets, we weaken the web of meaning that is created by the interdependence between friends and neighbors. What was once called the department of home economics at Iowa State College is now called the College of Consumer Sciences. Therein lies part of the story of the loss of the soul — the replacing of the familiar view of the world with the economics of consumption.

- Decrease in the percentage of leisure time devoted to consuming passive entertainment in relation to that spent with family, friends, and community. Assumption: Intimacy and community both arise from the activity of sharing stories. Lovers intertwine their limbs and life-stories to create a shared history. Communities are formed by a multiple love affair, an interweaving of shared legends, lore, gossip, games, celebrations, memories, and hopes. When viewing prime-time television comedies and cop shows consumes the majority of our leisure time, we become voyeurs of the pseu-

domyths of plastic heroes and villains and neglect the sharing of
our personal stories.

- Increase in the amount of time parents or others in an extended
family spend with children and are involved in their education.
Assumption: Nothing makes up for failure in the family. The
family is the first school of love.
- Decrease in dependence on complex technology to satisfy basic
needs. Assumption: Inappropriate technology exhausts natural resources and creative talent without increasing the common good.
We need to discipline our technological impulse and make careful
assessments of the probable social consequences of new technologies.
- Decrease in planned obsolescence, advertisement-created "need,"
and conspicuous consumption. Assumption: The new game is
"less is more," or voluntary simplicity; producing the simplest,
highest-quality, most beautiful, durable, and ecologically sound
products. We need to end the economics of fashion, the tyranny of
novelty, and the ecologically destructive habit of thinking in terms
of "this year's model," the "new and improved," change for the sake
of change.
- Decrease in the ratio of wealth between the richest and poorest
individuals and nations. Assumption: The present disparity between wealthy and developing nations, between haves and have-
nots is unjust. Love, and therefore community, thrives only where
there is justice and an appropriate access to power by all parties.
- Decrease in human population. Assumption: A voluntary decrease
in human population is necessary to allow the flourishing of a
spirited community of diverse creatures. With world population
now at 5.5 billion, it is evident that we cannot preserve a healthy
ecosystem and an adequate standard of living if we allow population to increase to the projected 12 to 14 billion in the next century.
- Decrease in the number of endangered species. Assumption: An
increase in the diversity of species provides our best rough measure
of our ecospiritual health. The human community is inseparable
from the well-being of black neck cranes, mountain lions, and
other species requiring wild habitats.
- Decrease in the size, power, and outreach of government bureau-

cracies. Assumption: The re-creation of a nation, and ultimately a world, composed of a network of strong communities requires a relocalization of responsibility, power, and governance as well as a decentralization of food production, economic institutions, (banks, stores, and factories) and charitable institutions (churches, hospitals, and the like).

• Decrease in national sovereignty and increase in citizens' identity with and loyalty to some world-governing body such as the United Nations that would be responsible for peacekeeping and other functions. Assumption: Absolute national sovereignty is an idea whose time is past. The claim to the moral right to use violence in the service of national interests is narcissism writ large, a delusion that destroys the world ecospiritual community to which our primary political loyalty must be given.

Add your own criteria. This list is meant to be provocative, not definitive.

CLOSING TIME: THE POSSIBILITY OF AN AGE OF THE SPIRIT

The hope for a Compassionate Commonwealth, an end to secular history, a withering away of repressive power-structures, and a new age of the spirit is as ancient as it is perennial. Isaiah looked forward to a time when swords would be beaten into plowshares and the lion would lie down with the lamb. Jeremiah hoped for a new covenant when the law of the Lord would be written so clearly on the heart of every person that no one would have to teach his neighbor. The Negro spiritual gives voice to the dream: "I'm going to lay down my sword and shield down by the riverside. . . . Ain't going to study war no more." The mythology of most every people relates history as a drama with three acts: In the beginning, there was unity, peace, a garden. In the present moment, there is disunity, conflict, and universal warfare of all against all. In the end, we will come together again to live in harmony in the city of God, in the paradise of Shambhala, in the alabaster city undimmed by human tears, in the workers' utopia where everyone will receive according to their needs and serve according to their abilities and the state will wither away. And according to the great visionaries, at this moment we stand at the beginning of what Joachim di Fiore called the third age, the age of the spirit.

What are we to make of these stories, these dreams of a glorious future? Tibetan Buddhists, who tell the most elaborate and outrageous metaphysical miracle stories, have a saying: "You are a fool if you believe these stories. You are a fool if you do not believe these stories." Taken literally, stories about the coming spiritual commonwealth lead to apocalyptic expectations and the creation of utopian communities that are bound to be disappointing. Count on it — the second coming will fail to materialize in the year 2000, just as it did in the year 1000. Jesus will not arrive with trumpets blaring and righteous legions to usher in the kingdom of God on December 31, 1999, at 11:59 P.M. Nor will all Jews be reunited next year in Jerusalem. Nor will the information superhighway and the global market economy create techno-utopia.

The meaning of these mythic stories of the end of history is not to be found in their pictorial details. All of these images of hope are rooted in a profound *perception* about human and extrahuman reality. They are not primarily about what might happen in some distant future but about what is real, here and now. They point to the central promise — the *telos*, potentiality, intentionality — that is curled in the human DNA. There is nothing more empirical than the conclusion that the essence of a human being is preprogrammed to unfold to its full potentiality only when it is nurtured in a community of faith, hope, and love. We are created in, by, and for communion. The law of love is inscribed not only on our hearts but in our genes.

We develop language and intelligence only within community. Recently, scientists at the National Institutes of Health have discovered that in monkeys who have been deprived of all touch, the cerebellum (the coordinator of movement) and the neural pathways to the limbic brain (the seat of emotions) remain undeveloped. Literally, love seems to be necessary to create the neural circuits, the dendrite chains, that determine our capacity for intelligence and compassion.

Physicians, physiologists, and medical epidemiologists are now demonstrating that the choice of whether we live to be sixty or ninety depends on our compassion quotient and communal intelligence. The more conflict, pollution, and stress we create, the more diseased our bodies and spirits become. The more competition, greed, and warfare are the organizing principles of the body-politic, the more character armor, paranoia, and stress we create. Ecologists warn us that if our assumption of superiority, our alienation, and our effort to dominate nature go unchecked, humans could follow other species into extinction.

The mystic vision is based not on a calculation of the probabilities but on the intuition of a promise that is not only within us but is in some way the essence of who we are. We are created by and linked together in a communication and feedback network that includes animals, vegetables, minerals, and Martians (if there be such).

My longing for community tells me something about the power-potential-promise that animates me. Our deepest longings are echoes from the future, cosmic vocations. The voice of the *telos* or *omega* point calls us forth to become who we are. The images of hope are obscure and rough blueprints of a possible future, forecasts of the direction of the evolution of the body-spirit and the body-politic. Who we are points in the direction we are destined to travel, and vice versa. The future is already stirring in the present. There is an intentionality in history that impels us toward a fulfillment.

Whether it is possible to actualize it, the dream of a Compassionate Commonwealth is an organizing idea, the North Star that guides the spiritual journey and gives us direction, even without ever becoming wholly historical. We do not need supernatural sanction for such a project of the imagination. It is not necessary to know before the fact that it is possible to create a community governed by wisdom and compassion — only that this is the most audacious adventure ever attempted. This project aims at transcending the will-to-power, the territorial imperative. It could be the biggest game in the universe. If the essence of the human spirit lies in our ability to transcend the given, we reach our full stature only when we aspire to create what has always been real but never actual. We are metaphysical animals. (Our reach must exceed our grasp, or what's a meta for — a metaphor?)

The traveler on the spiritual path never knows for certain where the journey will lead or whether it is possible to reach the desired destination. There is no evidence that we can arrive at perfection within historical time, and only questionable evidence that we can make moral progress. What is certain is that aspiring and working to create a Compassionate Commonwealth gives direction, meaning, and a sense of participation in a sacred purpose to an individual's life.

What impels a man or woman on this great venture is not the expectation of arrival but a sense of vocation. Something calls my name and demands that I respond. The voice does not say, "Eliminate all suffering and create the heavenly city." It says, "The gifts you have are needed to heal the dis-ease of your time. You are an architect — shape space care-fully to create better buildings and a more humane city for all citizens. You are a banker — work to create a more sustainable economy. You are a farmer — tend the land so it will be fertile for generations to come. You are a physician — attend to the healing of the whole person. You are a cook — prepare meals that delight the palate and nourish the body. You are a parent — take time to enjoy and guide your children. You are a CEO — create and market only those products that increase the common good. You are a soldier — minimize violence, keep the peace, and when you must fight, do so without hatred or the bitterness of revenge. You are a television producer — create stories that dignify, increase empathy, and inspire compassion. And so on.

The voice that calls us forth and inspires us to undertake the journey is always specific. So long as we respond to the needs of our world by offering both our compassion and our skill, we will not fall into despair at the overwhelming quantity of need. The spiritual life is based on a refusal to despair that arises from concerned action and humble agnosticism. We don't know enough to despair. Despair is hidden arrogance — I have seen the future, and it doesn't work. Hope is rooted in trust in the Unknown God. We do not know the final destiny of the individual soul or the commonwealth of beings; therefore we work, wait, and hope. And it is enough.

CHAPTER 11

Death: The Final Question

"Time, like an ever-rolling stream
Bears all its sons away.
They fly forgotten as a dream
Dies at the opening day.

"Our God our Help in ages past
Our Hope for years to come,
Be Thou our Guard while life shall last
And our eternal Home."

The Hymnbook, no. 111

I can only be animated by hope if I transcend narrow self-interest and give myself generously to the great dream of creating a Compassionate Commonwealth. Regardless of whether I hope or despair about the possibility of historical transformation, however, I cannot avoid wondering about the fate of my own soul or spirit. The universe may continue ad infinitum, and it may (or may not) in aeons to come form itself into a love story. But what is my final destiny? Throughout life, the great question remains: "For what may I hope?"

Like Job, we all wonder if death is the final end or a new beginning: "There is hope for a tree, if it be cut down, that it will sprout again, and that its tender branches will not cease. . . . But man dies, and wastes away, man giveth up the ghost, and where is he? . . . If a man die, shall he live again?" Extinction or metamorphosis? From beginning to end, life and death, Eros and Thanatos, are Siamese twins. But what happens when the twins are separated? Will all of me die, or does something — soul, spirit — survive? Is death like sleeping? Will I awaken from the long night of the grave and be reborn, resurrected, or reincarnated?

Listen carefully, and at least once a day you will hear the clock strike thirteen, and everything that came before will be cast into doubt. The presence of death turns life into a question mark. The question of death is the bass note in the symphony of questions.

Just yesterday morning, our Jack Russell terrier gave birth. Four puppies lived, one died. I watched with a heart disciplined to the acceptance of mortality as my thirteen-year-old daughter Jessamyn grieved and prepared the perfect small body for burial. Knowing yet unbelieving, she cried, "Daddy, can't we bring him back to life?"

Last month, my friend Beth died. This week, Holly died. And someday . . . , but I don't want to think about that. You don't either.

And yet every spiritual tradition advises the same: Keep the thought of death near. Don't run from it. Embrace the knowledge of your own death early in life, and you will avoid many illusions. The ego grows bloated by the denial of death; the spirit grows strong and gentle living in its presence. (Notwithstanding the value of meditating on our death, I think the Sharper Image's "Personal Life Clock" — $99.95, with a ninety-day warranty — that "reminds you to live life to the fullest by displaying the time and actual hours, minutes, and seconds remaining in your statistical lifetime" goes too far in the right direction.)

A BRIEF HISTORY OF DEATH

For a moment, let's step back from the agonizing questions about *my* or *your* death and keep the grim reaper comfortably at arm's length by dealing with the phenomenon objectively.

Death is the big unknown that shapes our manner of living. Secularism is a militant denial of death, religion an organized answer to the threat of death, the spiritual quest an effort to live in the presence of death.

Being upright animals, we can look out to the horizon and up at the stars, but like a hobbled horse one of our legs is tethered to death. We deny, resist, and kick against the restraints, all the while running in ever-shortening circles toward the inevitable. But the pivot holds.

Because we are conscious, because we are self-conscious, we live within an elastic expanse of time stretching between our remembered past and our imagined future. An unremembered birth and an unimaginable death are the parentheses, the symbol for the individual's existential condition: ?(Birth → Death)? Everything that happened before my birth seems an impersonal prelude to my existence; all that happens after, an unknowable mystery. That each person exists only for a brief moment in time is baffling and unacceptable. While I can imagine the act of dying, it is only by a trick in which I imagine myself observing my disappearance that I can think about my being dead. But death is a fact. All else is speculation, theory, and theology.

We might write the history of religion as the story of the variety of ways in which humans have denied death and affirmed that in some way we outlive our brief moment in time.

Mythology presents a rich testimony to our enduring enigma and existential paradox. Death is the natural conclusion of life, yet it is everywhere considered an unnatural event, something requiring an explanation. Every people's myth contains stories that answer the question: How did death come into the world?

The first artifacts we have from prehistory — skulls of bears arranged in a ritual order in caves and weapons, food and other objects that were buried with the dead — suggest that religion had its origins in the effort to come to terms with death by denying its finality. The wall paintings on the caves at Lascaux suggest that our early ancestors may have constructed a metaphoric argument for the survival of the human soul: As the herd of bison renews itself in spite of the death of the individual bison killed by the hunter, so the hunter's spirit at death enters into the collective "heavenly" soul from which new human beings emerge at birth.

When agriculture began and where farming remains a way of life, the rhythm of planting and harvest gives rise to faith in the metaphoric unity of soul and seed. As the seed falls into the ground and dies, miraculously to be reborn with the coming of spring, so the human soul in death sleeps in the Earth, to be reborn in a new form. Rebirth is the essence of the soul-seed.

Socrates formulated the argument for the immortality of the soul. He said that since the soul is unborn, it must also be undying. The body is born, ages, and dies, but the soul is incorporeal. Therefore, Socrates advised, we should not fear death but should practice the philosophical art of dying by dis-identifying with the sensations of the corporeal and temporal body and identifying with the eternal and undying spirit.

While Socrates was developing the idea of the immortality of the soul in the West, Eastern thinkers were creating both new theories of the soul and practical techniques for overcoming the fear of death. From 200 B.C. onward in India, yogis, ascetics, and wandering mystics were discovering that they could create an experience of the identity of the human spirit—the Atman—with the divine spirit—Brahman— through breath control and meditation. Silence the chattering of the mind, and you will end the painful illusion of your individuality, discover your identity with the Absolute Spirit, and overcome the illusion of the finality of death.

The Buddha solved the problem of death by dissolving the notion of a substantial self. To Buddhists, individuality, far from being preserved in an afterlife, is an illusion. Clinging to the idea of an unchanging self, we seek to avoid suffering, disease, old age, and death. This in turn creates a kind of metasuffering. The way out is to abandon the illusion of permanence and follow the Eightfold Path.

After the life, death, and reported resurrection of Jesus, Christianity introduced a new note into the dialogue with death. The Judeo-Christian God, unlike the limited gods of the Greeks, was considered the creator *ex nihilo* of everything—matter and spirit. He created human beings with body and soul homogenized, as a psychosomatic unit. In the Judeo-Christian view, there is no immortal, incorruptible soul that is separable from the mortal body, no discarnate essence that might have post-mortem survival. When the breath leaves the body, we are dead. But that is not the end of the story. Somehow, whether in a parallel space — heaven — or in a kingdom of God at the end of historical time, the Creator will once again bring his children into being in a resurrected and glorified body. We will be re-created.

Gradually, the acids of modernity have eaten away the blind trust in biblical authority and the hope of resurrection. Secularism — the dominance of urban, industrial, and technocratic modes of thinking and organizing life — has anchored our feet in the concrete, limited our horizon to the here and now, and denied us the hope of any transcendence of our brief moment in time. There is no soul, no spirit that transcends our biological, sociological, psychological, and political conditioning. The three-story universe, with shadowy hells and underworlds inhabited by all manner of demonic hosts and the seven heavens filled with radiant angels and unimaginable pleasures, has collapsed into an efficiency bungalow. What you see is what you get. Whoever has the most toys when he dies, wins. You only go around once, so go for the gusto. Of course, in the hip postmodern era, we don't waste time arguing about or denying the existence of soul or spirit. The God in whom we trust has more to do with ensuring continued economic growth and sanctifying "the American way of life" than with providing a rationale for belief in transcendence.

Our modern elimination of soul and spirit and the consequent refusal to invest death with any spiritual significance have had both beneficial and disastrous practical consequences. The good news is, since death has been proclaimed our enemy, we have mounted a full-scale war against disease. With awesome regularity, our new priesthood — the medical profession — produces miracles. Disease after disease has been conquered. Our life-span increases with wonder drugs, and new surgical techniques repair. The bad news is that, in spite of our fierce and brilliant campaigns against disease, our ancient enemy defeats us in the final battle. Eventually, physicians lose 100 percent of their patients. And because we Americans must be winners and cannot be graceful losers, we exhaust our resources in a futile struggle with death. It is estimated that currently we spend more than half of our astronomical medical budget on keeping terminal patients alive in their final months, long after pleasure and hope have disappeared from their lives. At any cost, we deny death's dominion.

We see ourselves best in the mirror of contrast. We can sense what we have lost and gained in our time-bound, city-bound, technique-bound style of life by feeling our way into other cultures. Recently in Iran, thousands of Islamic fundamentalist men and women prepared themselves for martyrdom and happily walked across minefields, secure in their knowledge that those who die in a holy war, *jihad*, gain immediate entrance to paradise. In Bhutan, belief in reincarnation and the law of karma is as unquestioned as the myth of progress in the industrial nations. Everywhere the great mandala of the wheel of life portrays in detail the soul's pilgrimage as it proceeds through various lives, ascending toward enlightenment and release from suffering or sinking into different realms of hell, depending on the merit accumulated during this lifetime. Priests and peasants alike believe without question that the spiritual and moral disciplines that one practices or ignores in this life will affect the station into which one is reborn.

What is lost and what gained by living within the cosmic dramas of Christian, Islamic, or Buddhist versions of pilgrim's progress? What is the price for heaven? Do the nostrums of religion cost us the enjoyment of the moment? Do we purchase eternity by ignoring our time? Does a secular society that pays attention to practical matters produce more happiness, health, and care-fulness?

What if we are not convinced or consoled by any theological authority that promises eternal life? What if we reject the ersatz immortality of a future utopia promised by the state? What if we refuse to tranquilize ourselves with drugs, work, or consumption? What if we cease denying the anxiety of having to die? How can we think about death without embracing what seem to be comforting illusions? How can we come to terms with the unacceptable fact of our mortality?

REFLECTIONS ON MY DEATH: TERROR AND TRUST

To approach the question of my death, I must venture out beyond the protection of the anonymous We and explore the vulnerable I. The root anxiety about death is not abstract but personal.

My earliest association with death was colored by images of heaven and hell and by feelings of security and terror. In Sunday school we learned the formula: "Believe in the Lord Jesus Christ, and you will be saved." Sermon and song were filled with vivid imagery of the alternatives that await the faithful and the faithless — eternal delight or eternal damnation. Signs along southern highways and back roads pose the question: "Where will you spend eternity?" Within the ambience of evangelical Christianity, every man, woman, and child stands perpetually at the crossroads where the decision has to be made between a narrow path leading to eternal life and a broad path leading to damnation.

From my earliest days, I was burdened with the anxious knowledge that I had to make a decision for Christ. Otherwise — the fire next time. In all of this I was more than a little confused by the Calvinistic notion that God had predestined some to salvation (Presbyterians especially) and others to perdition. I learned at my mother's knee to recollect the events of the day and examine my conscience to see if I had committed a sin in thought, word, or deed. When I laid me down to sleep, I prayed the Lord my soul to keep, and if I died before I waked, I prayed the Lord my soul to take. I was offered the dreadful comfort that my sins would be forgiven *if* I would remember, confess, and repent sincerely. If, however, I could not marshal the necessary quantum of sincerity for my peccadilloes or the requisite faith in the substitutionary atonement offered by Jesus, I could feel myself beginning to slide down the slippery slope toward the eternal fires of hell. Many nights, haunted by doubts, I lay rigid with fear, wondering whether my appetite for the pleasures of this world, my rebellious spirit, and my questioning mind were evidence that I was not among the elect.

Death was all theory and theology until the day our family dog, Possum, limped home covered with blood from a shotgun wound and crawled under the house to die. We could hear her cries, but I couldn't reach her. Finally Dad called the sheriff, and he killed her with a single pistol shot.

For days I grieved and asked, "Why would somebody shoot our dog? What happened to her when she died? Did she go to heaven?" My parents were uncomfortable with my questions because they were uncertain of their answers. Neither the Bible or Calvin had wrestled with the question of the eternal destiny of animals. But things looked bad for Possum since she had not made a personal decision for the Lord Jesus Christ.

As Possum's body lay in the grave, the worm of doubt began to gnaw on my mind. With childlike clarity I wondered: If God couldn't take care of beloved dead dogs, could I entirely trust Him with my eternal destiny? Gradually, hell was eliminated from my theological map. I reasoned that if God were love and could be counted on to assure my afterlife, He could find some way to hold dogs within His everlasting arms. How He was to accomplish this, I did not know. But anything less was not worthy of a first-class God. Years later when I began my formal study of philosophy and theology, heaven also disappeared from the map. Once I rejected the authority of Bible and church, I had no rock upon which to rest my claim for an afterlife.

Severed from a doctrine of an afterlife, death loses the connotation of reward or punishment and assumes the status of an amoral fact. I will die not because "I have sinned and fallen short of the glory of God" but because I was born. In many ways the natural-neutral face of death is psychologically more difficult to deal with than the religious-magical notion that death is the result of sin, rebellion, or breaking a taboo. The religious-magical view at least gives some kind of mythic explanation for the irrational but persistent feeling that we *ought not* to die. That death is simply a brute fact, a "natural" (whatever this peculiar question-begging word means) phenomenon, leaves us in a universe in which there is no satisfying explanation for the most troubling of all facts. Death poses a question we can neither avoid nor answer.

How do we face the faceless void, the end that is curled up in our beginning, the threat that is homogenized with the promise of life? How am I to think of the ultimate destiny of those I love who have died? A stillborn puppy? My friend Beth? My father?

For many people the fear of mortality is focused on the prospect of pain, illness, and the process of dying. For others, fear focuses on the result — being dead. Gordon Sherman, a friend who lived vividly for years with leukemia, said, "Dying wouldn't be a bad way to live, if it weren't for the end result." I would look forward to the process of dying and being dead for a season if I were to be reborn, reincarnated, or resurrected in some form in which I would continue to have experiences and awareness of the continuity of identity with my past life or lives. It is not transformation I fear but ceasing to be. Accounts of near-death experiences by those who have been resuscitated suggest that the conclusion of the process of dying may be intensely pleasurable, a kind of total body orgasm. But the prospect of obliteration seems like a dreadful waste of a cosmic resource. It takes us a lifetime of struggle to gain a modicum of self-knowledge, wisdom, and compassion; and then we die. It seems a shame.

In the early bud of manhood, death came to me in the guise of the fear that something would prevent me from realizing my full promise. I prayed that I would not die before I had many adventures, discovered a passionate work, loved a woman, fathered children, built a homestead, grew into magnanimity. At sixty-two most of what I anticipated at twenty has come to pass. I have tasted what I once hungered for, accomplished more than I planned, and been surprised, stretched, battered, and enriched by more than I imagined. While I am still a country mile away from the fully compassionate heart that I desire, I no longer am afraid of dying without fulfillment. I have completed most of the required courses (except for the final exam) — the rest are electives. Still, I don't rest easy with the thought of death.

My father's death in 1964 marked a midpoint in my life that bears no relation to the numbering of my years. Before, I was a boy shielded from death's dark sun by the immensity of his presence. Afterward, I was a man seasoned in the tragic knowledge that even if love is stronger than death, no bright life escapes the dominion of darkness. Before, death seemed distant, a theoretical problem that might be solved by sufficient faith. Afterward, no theory was potent enough to withstand the fact of death. In the years since, I have been stretched by contradictions. My linear mind rejects the idea of post-mortem survival, but my father has continued to live in my dreamtime. "But that is *only* a dream," you may object. And I would be forced to agree. Still, I can't help wondering if the cyclical logic of dreams reveals as much about reality as the linear logic of time.

Lately, death visits in the late, dark hours in the stark form of raw terror. Before I fall asleep, scenes of the closing day and thoughts about what lies in store tomorrow pass through my mind. Momentarily, a certain sadness colors my awareness that I have moved one day nearer to my inevitable end. Sometimes, around two o'clock, I awake, and the horror of nothingness grips and squeezes the breath out of me. I imagine death wiping the slate clean, erasing all that I am. Nothing of me remains. Zero. I disappear into the black hole of nothingness. This rich life, this one and only Sam Keen, that has been created with such effort and love, disappears into oblivion. Someday there will be no me. How can that be? No! No! No! It can't be! The incomprehensible and totally natural fact that I will cease to be fills me with terror. I start to run, to try to push the unacceptable thought from my mind. And then I remember what I have learned from numerous encounters with dark forces — Never run from a monster! I allow the waves of terror to wash over me again and again until their power is spent. Sad and exhausted, I roll over and embrace my wife, thankful for warmth and joyful to be alive — still.

To me, being willing to face moments of raw terror seems preferable to taking easy comfort in religious assurances of immortality.

Why?

If we are to live in openness to the wonder of being alive, we must also abide the terror. Radical honesty requires us to acknowledge that we do not know what happens to us following death. We can know neither that we will survive in some new form, nor that we will be obliterated. It seems important to live with what we know and not to cheat. Our dignity as human beings has something to do with our willingness to abide *joyfully* in the ignorance of our ultimate destiny. We are not created to be omniscient. A few moments of stark terror a day are a small price to pay for the enormous quantity of energy that is saved when we are freed from the tyranny of obedience to divinely sanctioned authorities or are released from the necessity of fabricating some immortality project.

Stephen Batchelor speaks in a similar manner about spiritual agnosticism from within the Buddhist tradition, in which the notions of karma and rebirth have always been central. "It is often felt that there are two options: one can believe in rebirth or not believe in it. But there is a third alternative: that of agnosticism — to acknowledge in all honesty that one does not know. One does not have either to assert or to deny it; one neither has to adopt the literal versions presented by tradition nor fall into the other extreme of believing that death is a final annihilation. . . . How can one know about something which presupposes the absence of the very apparatus that does such knowing (the psychophysical complex of body and mind)? Whatever I say about what happens to me after death is inevitably said from the standpoint of that which will cease at death. . . . An agnostic position toward death seems more compatible with an authentic spiritual attitude. . . . To opt for a comforting, even a discomforting, explanation of what brought us here or what awaits us after death severely limits that very sense of mystery with which religion is essentially concerned."[1]

If we refuse to deny death, for what may we hope?

All symbols of the afterlife — heaven, reincarnation, resurrection of the body, immortality of the soul — if taken as anything more than a stuttering attempt to sing a song of hope into the silent darkness, foster illusions. Even in my radical terror, when I feel that death means obliteration, I know that I do not know. Both the denial and the assertion of an afterlife are equally groundless. There is no cognitive basis for either optimism or pessimism.

There are some who believe that they or others have either memories of past lives or trance experiences of being possessed by discarnate entities that constitute evidence for post-mortem survival. Until recently, only a few theosophists, people interested in psychic research, and Tibetan *tulkus* claimed to have such occult knowledge. But recently a flock of past-life therapists and channelers have emerged who will, for a price, help anyone remember former lives or get in touch with spirits of the dead. I remain skeptical of the supposed evidence they offer to support such claims and uncomforted by their gossamer optimism.

In the months immediately following my father's death in 1964, my grief was intensified by intellectual agony as I struggled to find reasons to believe in some deathless and kindly power who might be called God. At the time I was still teaching the philosophy of religion at Louisville, so there was additional pressure from my colleagues to produce a statement of faith that would be acceptable to the congregation of believers who paid our salaries. But the more I tried to storm the heavens, the more disturbed I became. I could find no answers.

One morning as I walked to work through a park, in the middle of a large field the sky seemed to open. A voice from the infinite silence within and beyond me said: *"You don't have to know."* I was flooded with an immense sense of relief, as if a thousand-pound weight had been lifted from my shoulders. Perhaps for the first time in my life, I was free from the compulsion to discover an explanation for my existence. My mind relaxed in the knowledge that I could never have certain knowledge of the ultimate context of my existence.

In the presence of death, my mind had reached its limit and found a new freedom. Disillusioned, I discovered hope. Hope, as opposed to illusion or optimism, is not a prediction of things to come. Nor is it a claim to possess some special knowledge or revelation of a hidden future, in which all evil is redeemed and all death is negated. To hope we must know that we cannot know the limits of the Ever-Creating Power that has, is, and will bring all that is into being. And beyond that, we must trust that the inexhaustible mystery we touch when we discover our soul-spirit-freedom-capacity-to-transcend provides our best clue to the nature of Being.

The question of God is not the question of the existence of some remote infinite being. It is the question of the possibility of hope. The affirmation of faith in God is the acknowledgment that there is a deathless source of power and meaning that can be trusted to nurture and preserve all created good. To deny God is equivalent to denying any ground for hope. Hope begins with the realization that human experience is finally inadequate to deal with all the possibilities reality harbors.

I found myself talking back to Saul Bellow's Herzog, who said, "What is the philosophy of this generation? Not that God is dead, that period had passed long ago. Perhaps it should be stated death is God. This generation thinks — and this is its thought of thoughts — that nothing faithful, vulnerable, fragile can be durable or have any true power. Death waits for these things as a cement floor waits for a dropping light bulb."

I do not know the ultimate destiny of all things faithful, vulnerable, and fragile — including the souls of fathers and sons. But I refuse the hidden pretension of omnipotence, of either the religious or the secular variety. My mind cannot plumb the limits of the possible. Therefore, I *choose to trust* the mystery from which all blessings flow. I hope that, in ways that transcend my understanding, the light remains after the bulb bursts.

If I am to trust the source out of which I come — this unique Sam Keen, who is simultaneously a common specimen of the species homo sapiens — I must also trust the dark destiny into which I disappear at death.

I am enfolded within a Being-becoming-itself, a God for whom perpetual dying is a way of perpetual creating. That this Being has brought forth untold billions of individuals with unique fingerprints and autobiographies that seem to last no longer than dreams is the fact before which I must never cease to wonder and remember that I cannot understand. It is both the agony and the beauty of the human condition to be ignorant of our ultimate origin and destiny.

In the luminous darkness through which we travel on our human journey, we are often lonely but never alone. Road-weary, over-whelmed by the magnitude of the difficulties we face during our brief days, we are tempted to despair or to settle for cheap optimism. But in the deep place of the spirit, we are moved and called forth to undertake this ongoing adventure by the yearning, restless, and creative One who — though called by the ten thousand names of God — is still clothed in marvelous silence.

CHAPTER 12

Consecrating Our Days: A Sampler of Rituals for Living

"Drop Thy still dews of quietness,
Till all our strivings cease;
Take from our souls the strain and stress
And let our ordered lives confess
The beauty of Thy peace."

The Hymnbook, no. 416

It was the custom in our family for the children to pool their money each year and buy Mother a Whitman's Sampler for her birthday. After being dutifully surprised, she would allow each of us to choose a chocolate. The easily identified, gold-foiled cordial cherries went first. On subsequent days when we were invited to pick a candy, we consulted the diagram on the inside of the box-top to locate our favorites — caramels, peppermints, maple-sugar creams — until nothing remained except the jordan almonds.

Treat this collection of rituals as a sampler. Pick your favorite first, savor it, and wait a while before tasting another. Warning: Reading it in one sitting is likely to cause indigestion. Nibble and sample it slowly.

SYMBOLS, RITUALS, AND GESTURES

Come what may, in the best and worst of lives, there will inevitably be extraordinary moments. But one swan does not make a summer, and a single peak experience is not enough to create an inspired life. To be fully animated, we must find ways to take the cream of our experience — the high and holy moments of inspiration — and merge it into the ordinary minutes of our average days. It's easy to get high; it's a challenge to remain soulful.

Every historic religion has faced the problem of how to knead the vision of the sacred into the dough of everyday life. A study of comparative religion yields an endless variety of symbolic acts and objects — ceremonies, sacraments, rites of passage, rituals, liturgies, mantras, mudras, dances, chants, and vestments — designed to re-mind the faithful to remain true to the sacred possibilities of life. An in-spirited life is framed by gestures that interrupt the flow of profane time and punctuate our days with brief vistas of a transcendent reality. Morning chants, prayer flags fluttering in the breeze, and prayer wheels turning in a small stream alert a family of peasants in Bhutan that everything they encounter throughout the day will be a manifestation of the Buddhanature. Chinese men and women practice tai chi in the park to harmonize their movements with the way of the Tao. A Catholic congregation celebrates Mass and refreshes its conviction that ordinary matter may be transubstantiated into divine substance.

Ritual invests ordinary acts and objects with *symbolic* meaning. (The original meaning of the Greek-derived word *symbolic* was "to bring things together." The meaning of its opposite, *demonic*, was "to tear things apart.") A bowed head signifies reverence; bread and wine stand for the divine pouring-forth of itself into the crucible of human life; the lightning thunderbolt represents the enlightenment of Buddha.

In consecrating our days by ritual, we play the game of sacred poetry in which one thing is allowed to signify another. We might consider the in-spirited life as a kind of divine madness that heals us, a symbolic consciousness that brings together the surface and the depths. An inspired mind is a metaphoric mind in which everything is both itself and a symbol pointing beyond itself. To play with ritual and to invent disciplines of awareness is to recognize that we have dual citizenship. We live simultaneously in two dimensions, the profane and the sacred, time and eternity. We remain most animated, most inspired, most fully alive, when we learn how to cross back and forth between the here and now and the Beyond.

Some people find the ready-made, traditional religious rituals and disciplines a satisfying way to consecrate their lives. Others need to create their own. The practices that follow are my blend of tradition and innovation. They are meant only to suggest how I have gone about the task of re-minding myself who I am and how I should live. It should go without saying that the rituals and disciplines that will clothe your spirit will have to be tailor-made to fit the shape of your life. Feel free to borrow anything from my wardrobe that fits and to discard anything that rubs you the wrong way.

SIMMERING AND THE ART OF DREAMING

My friend and sometime guide on the path, Howard Thurman, once advised me: "When you wake up in the morning, *never* get out of bed — simmer. And when you go to bed at night, *never* go to sleep — simmer." He went on to explain that each night before sleeping, he reviewed the events of the day and previewed his plans for the next day. Only then did he drift into sleep, gently inviting his mind to continue working in his dreams on any dilemma he faced. When he awoke in the morning, he lay still, savoring any portion of a dream that remained in his mind, and ever so gradually eased himself into the activities of the day.

Ancient shamans and Aborigines, no less than Freud, reminded us that "the dream is the royal road to the unconscious." They knew that we can weave together the tattered edges of our visible and invisible reality only if we cultivate the ability to travel in and out of dreamtime. Scientists tell us that roughly every ninety minutes, sleeping or waking, we enter into a REM cycle (rapid eye movement), during which our minds are flooded with dreams, daydreams, or flights of fantasy. Because most moderns are habituated to life in the fast lane, we have gradually learned to ignore the magic and madness of dreamtime and focus our attention only on "practical" matters. Men especially have forgotten how to dream and enter the castle of wisdom that lies hidden in the fertile darkness just behind the eyelids. To recover the fullness of spirit, we need to live in continuous intercourse with our dreams and develop a love affair between the radically different selves we are in sleeping and waking. In dreams I contain a community of saints and libertines, fools and wise animals, kindly and cruel men and women. I am the hero I admire and the enemy I hate. To one awakened to the wisdom of the night, it is obvious that self-love and love for one's neighbor are heads and tails of the same coin. I am those others whom I love and despise.

When we attend to our dreams, we discover that "God gives us songs in the night" (Job 35:10).

In the months before my sixtieth birthday, I thought a lot about death. I had just returned from visiting a Buddhist culture and had been toying with beliefs in karma and reincarnation, trying to feel what it would be like to believe in some kind of continuity beyond death. But I could not escape the dread of nothingness, the horror of disappearing completely into the void that has been an abiding part of the weather pattern of my soul.

One night, I had a strange dream about a silver beetle that could detach part of itself and then come back together. First, the beetle walked into a piece of wood, disappeared, and then reappeared on the other side. Next, it disappeared into a stone and reemerged. Finally, most strangely of all, it entered into a completely transparent gemlike substance but disappeared from view. Although I could see through the gem, I could not see the beetle, but somehow I knew that it would reemerge whole from its journey through the transparent void.

I awoke from the dream with a profound sense of relief and comfort but with no intellectual understanding of its meaning. What in the world did a disappearing and reappearing beetle have to do with my life? In the following days I simmered until the realization burst on me that in ancient Egyptian religion the scarab beetle was a symbol for immortality.

The dream spoke to me about my anxiety about death. The beetle was a perfect analogy to the Buddhist notion of the disintegration of the self at death and the simultaneous passing over of the spirit substance (karma) into another life that I had been studying in Bhutan. The beetle disappears and yet reemerges as a beetle. Might I also disappear into death and reemerge? I don't know. But the dream gave me a momentary peace that passes understanding.

Wake up and end the day in a re-collective manner. Enter and emerge from the kingdom of sleep in a quiet and purposeful way. Before gliding into sleep, invite your spirit to send you a dream. When you awake, probe gently to see if you retain any image or sequence from your dream. If you do, review it until it is vivid in your mind. As soon as you arise, write or record the dream in a journal. Throughout the day, take a vacation from practicality every ninety minutes and check into REM time. Soften your focus, and pay attention to the daydreams and fantasies that are playing beneath the surface. Slip into the rabbit hole that leads into the netherworld of the unconscious. Become a world-traveler.

In interpreting dreams, as in dealing with other aspects of the meaning of your life, you are the final authority. It is up to you to weave together the diverse and paradoxical themes that run through your nights and days into a single spiritual autobiography. When your dreams baffle you, talk about them with a friend.

Go gentle into that good night. Each evening, re-member your day. Before you go to sleep, try repeating some lines from an ancient confession: "We have left undone those things which we ought to have done; and we have done those things which we ought not to have done." As you re-collect the events of the day, you will discover that by meditating on your acts of omission and commission, the path you should follow tomorrow will open up before you. As you recall that you were too preoccupied to respond when the taxi driver told you that his wife was to undergo surgery later in the afternoon, you will understand that, in that moment, your soul shrank and that tomorrow you must be alert for an occasion to practice compassion so you may stretch it again to its fullest. When you remember that you silently cursed the goddamn "skinheads" or murderous Serbs, you will be re-minded that you also contain a writhing pit of viperous prejudices.

TAKING YOUR TIME: *KAIROS* AND *CHRONOS*

Unfortunately, most of us begin each day by swearing our allegiance to the tyranny of chronological time. We alarm ourselves into consciousness and gear ourselves immediately into Type A behavior. The clock, and our daily fix of caffeine, rush us along because time is money, and money makes the world go 'round, and to the speedy belong the spoils. Leisure is reserved for the weekends.

The Greeks had two words for time, *chronos* and *kairos*.

Chronological time is what we measure by clocks and calendars; it is always linear, orderly, quantifiable, and mechanical. *Kairotic* time is organic, rhythmic, bodily, leisurely, and aperiodic; it is the inner cadence that brings fruit to ripeness, a woman to childbirth, a man to change his direction in life at just the right moment.

The realm of the spirit operates on kairotic rather than chronological time. Nothing graceful happens by the numbers. It may be a good thing for trains to run on time, although I am not sure it is worth the dictatorial regimentation of political and economic life that it seems to require. It is certainly a mistake to expect the Holy Spirit to arrive on schedule, either in the form of the assurance of pardon at church at eleven on Sunday morning or as a simultaneous orgasm at 9:41 on Saturday night. Great and soulful events — falling in love, openings to the Beyond-Within, the birth of ideas and babies — march to no tick-tock but appear in their own good time, when the heart is prepared and the moment is ripe.

There is no way to cultivate your soul in a hurry. The hurry disease is dangerous to the arteries of the spirit. Speed kills. The habit of rushing destroys the long and gentle rhythms of breathing that are necessary for inspired thinking and surrendering to the surprising opportunities that appear as soon as we stop trying to fit our lives into a plan. When we get caught in stress-time, we lose track of what time it is in our life. Is it time to marry or divorce? To act or to wait? To remain steadfast or to start over?

Of course you have obligations, commitments, a job to be done, a living to be made, children to get off to school, and a thousand things to do before, during, and after. You don't have to retreat to a monastery to cultivate the life of the spirit. We are looking for a marriage of *chronos* and *kairos*, not abstinence from either. Fast and slow time are the right and left hemispheres of the incarnate spirit. Be leisurely and act vigorously.

Set aside regular times for meditative thinking, recollection, and silence. As a practical matter, it is good to rise early enough to set the tone of your upcoming day by enjoying leisurely moments — a graceful caress, a ritual shower of purification, a consecrated breakfast, a conversation about what matters with family or friend. Practice or omit whatever formal rituals you like — meditation, prayer, tai chi, chanting, reading of texts — that will remind you to enter the day with a spirit of gratitude and devotion.

CELEBRATIONS AND PERSONAL HOLY DAYS

In creating a spiritual practice, you need to construct a calendar that recognizes your personal holy days and celebrations and consecrates all your days.

Every year, as certain as the swallows return to Capistrano, our official calendars command us to celebrate gift-giving at Christmas, go to parties on New Year's Eve, watch fireworks on the Fourth of July, and eat the sacrificial turkey (and watch the football game) on Thanksgiving. The more pious among us observe Easter or Passover, which commemorate days sacred to Judeo-Christian memory, as well as pagan rites of spring. With a tip of the hat to Hollywood, we offer roses and heart-shaped cards to Saint Valentine for the gift of romantic love. On Halloween we play trick-or-treat and — half seriously, half in fun — don masks and disguises and enter the shadow world to honor the spirits of the dead. Because it is our duty to our forebears, we mark Washington's and Lincoln's birthdays, and lately Martin Luther King, Jr.'s.

Official holidays and celebrations punctuate our time, stop the flux of our days, and remind us to pay attention to the rhythms and seasons of our lives. Because they are an archive of shared memories and a community ritual, they keep us in touch with our common story, the myth and history that bind us together into a single people, a commonwealth of diversity.

But just beneath the surface of our official holidays, there lies a world of private celebrations and ritual occasions, special events in the lives of families and friends. Browse in a greeting card store, and you will discover the informal rituals of everyday life. Greeting cards are the wafers of our daily communion, transubstantiating our ordinariness, marking our rites of passage. Listen to the liturgy: Happy Birthday. Wishing You Happiness on Your Wedding Day. We Share Your Grief. Happy Anniversary. You Are the Best Mom (Dad) in the World. Congratulations on Your: New Baby, New Home, Retirement, New Job, New Adventure, New Car, Sticking to Your Diet. Thank You. Bon Voyage. Get Well. Cheer Up.

These ready-made and home-made holidays and ritual occasions are all well and good. But we are still poor in celebrations. We get caught in routines that paralyze our sense of wonder and cause us to forget who we are. Over my desk I have a quotation from the film *A Thousand Clowns* to remind me of what is important: "You have got to own your days and name them, each one of them, every one of them, or else the years go right by and none of them belongs to you." When I can keep my wits about me, I create my own calendar and mark special holidays. Here is a sampler of my celebrations:

Lilac Day. Contrary to those who order us to go on "daylight savings time," spring is not ushered in by the clock. You know when it arrives because you are walking around with the grime of winter sticking to your soul, and suddenly a zephyr wafts the first whiff of lilacs straight through your nostrils, down into the nostalgic springtimes of long ago and far away. On such a day it is best to cancel appointments and devote yourself to the delights of the nose and the recovery of childhood. Come to your senses, wander with the breeze, smell the symphony of city streets or woods paths.

Friend's Day. You can never tell when you will have to throw out all practical priorities at a moment's notice. But count on it; there will be days when an old friend appears suddenly in town, and there is nothing more important than catching up with the years. Or when you are needed to listen and not give advice.

Money Day. Sometime, usually around April 15, I find it is a good idea to measure my life-goals against the wherewithal to accomplish them. How much do I need, and what am I willing to do to get it? Money is important enough not to be confused with worth and not to dominate our days unconsciously.

Mourning Day. Each November 4 since 1964, I stop for a while to remember the day my father died and to allow myself to be sad that death has established its dominion over so many of my family and friends. Autumn invites us to mourn the losses we inevitably sustain from the passing of time, to savor the fleeting sweetness of mortality.

Family Day. Lately, Thanksgiving is any day the children gather from the four winds, when we meet in Santa Fe or Brazil and tell the old stories about the time I made Gif eat the hard-boiled egg that was supposed to be Lael's. Maybe our celebrations of family are the most important holy days we have left. Without familiarity and hearth, the world is too lonely to bear, too much fast food, and strangers passing in the night.

I'm sure your personal calendar is different from mine because the events that give the drama of your life dignity, depth, and delight are different from mine. With the best of planning you won't be able to anticipate all the occasions that sing out for attention. To be a true celebrant of life, you must be ready at an instant's notice to proclaim your own three-day weekend, take an afternoon off to see the Chagall exhibit, lie abed on Tuesday morning for no reason at all except that you feel like it, declare a special day to praise whatever gods from whom all blessings flow for an unexpected windfall.

SLIPPING BEYOND TIME: ETERNAL MOMENTS

To manage our lives care-fully we need to move constantly between the demands of clock time and the rhythms of our personal sense of timeliness. But in the in-spirited life, there is also a wild movement in which we jump beyond time itself and land smack in the middle of an eternal moment.

The great mystics of all traditions have reported ecstatic experiences transcending all sense of time. How much this is possible or even desirable for ordinary people who are unwilling to forsake family, friends, and prime-time sitcoms and devote their entire lives to the cultivation of mystic states of consciousness, I do not know. I am more familiar with and interested in more modest moments of transcendence.

When Jung suffered from what we have come to call a mid-life identity crisis, he recovered his sense of direction by constructing a house of stone with his own hands because as a child he had been happiest on the timeless afternoons he spent building sand castles.

The doorway between the secular realm and the realm of the spirit is open in those experiences in which we lose track of time and forget ourselves.

As a child, I lost myself in the College Woods, when we spent endless hours building dams in the stream, catching crawdads, and climbing trees. For many forevers, I watched a redheaded woodpecker tending its young. And for all I know, I may still be lying on the bank of the creek where I dissolved one day into the passing clouds I had been watching. Somewhere in my soul all the clocks are stopped, and it is still dusk on a summer evening, and the neighborhood kids have gathered to play Capture the Flag, and it never did get too dark to see, and the game kept going on and on forever.

By way of contrast, school and church initiated me into the limbo of boredom and the endlessness of time. Sunday morning from eleven to twelve was the longest hour of the week, a form of cruel and unusual punishment for any child. The pastoral prayer and the sermon plodded lead-footed into the desert of time. As the endless words anesthetized my body, I studied the patterns in the wood on the pew and imagined the hideout I planned to build in the woods, *if* church ever came to an end. Or I watched the light streaming through the stained-glass windows where Jesus leaned far over the abyss with his shepherd's crook to rescue the lost lamb, Saint Paul lay blinded by the light of the risen Christ beside his donkey on the road to Damascus, and Saint Sebastian endured martyrdom forever and ever, like me.

These days in the middle of my adulthood, eternity dissolves time most often when I am sitting quietly, doing nothing but listening to the wind, being entertained by the play of fantasy in my imagination, making love, talking with my children, feasting with friends, riding my horse, giving a lecture, writing, wandering in strange cities, hiking in the canyonlands, and working on my farm.

The other afternoon I lay exhausted under a tree. Perhaps I dropped into sleep. At any rate, the first thing I knew, *I* had disappeared. There was only wind blowing through the tree, the sound of sparrows chirping, and the warmth of the sun. No me. I, the observer, was absent, absorbed completely in the experience. With the disappearance of chattering thoughts and self-consciousness, I was suddenly part of a vast horizon wrapped in primal silence. For a moment that seemed an eternity, the work of my ego ceased, my historically conditioned personality vanished — Sam Keen was not at the center of the world. Bliss. Refreshment. Then all too soon (or just in time), *I* returned and began to "appreciate" the experience, to think about it, to plan ways to return to the sacred moment. The silence evaporated, my ego returned. Back in my old skin. Who was "I" during those moments when there was only wind in the trees?

During moments like this, the boundaries of self are porous. I am inhabited, moved, in-spired by some Beyond within me.

Re-membering the self — the practice of self-awareness, systematic re-collection, and the forging of our experience into an autobiography — is a lifelong, satisfying work. By contrast, in-spiration seems to arrive by grace. The joy that results from the fullness of spirit creeps up on us when we are unaware, when our self-consciousness has been replaced by intense concentration.

Pay close attention to the variety and quality of those experiences in which you enter so fully into the moment that you lose all sense of self and passing time. Re-collect the history of your journeys beyond time and self-consciousness. What is the difference between the kind of self-loss you experience when you go to a movie, concentrate on your work, play with the computer, go wind-surfing, wonder, sleep, drink too much alcohol, make love, listen to music, dance, worship, fight, take drugs? By which are you stressed, diminished, addicted, dispirited? By which are you refreshed, stretched, moved, inspired?

EATING: WHOLESOME APPETITES

One of the perennial mythic questions that each culture answers in a different way is: "What should and should not be eaten?" Steak is supper in St. Louis but sacrilege in Bombay. Eating is seldom a purely pragmatic act done solely to satisfy hunger or fulfill nutritional needs. It is a Rorschach ink-blot test that tells us who we are and what we value. We are what we eat. Fast food, the Lord's Supper, an anorexic diet, and a Thanksgiving feast all reflect philosophies of life. Food is surrounded by concentric circles of emotional, social, and mythical meanings. It may be a symbol of care or a medium for celebration. It is Mother making cocoa on a cold night, or a Passover sacrament with shared memories and hopes, consecrated wine, and bitter herbs. To Americans, a quick breakfast of bacon and eggs, coffee, and sugar, or a TV dinner is as natural as economic competition and belief in progress. To the Pygmies, grubworms, nuts, and berries eaten by an open fire are the given bounty of the sacred forest, gathered and shared by the People.

There is one and only one diet that feeds the whole of us — a *conscious* eating of whatever nourishes and delights both body and soul. The most difficult part of following an in-spiriting diet is bringing to light the unconscious motives and unfulfilled desires that masquerade as hunger. The banana split you crave may be a surrogate for the sweetness you did not receive from a parent or lover. I habitually overeat sweets because I want life to be sweeter than it is. I eat more than I want because I don't take time to taste the food. Some illusion drives me to fill an empty place, to avoid the void. When I remain conscious of what and how I eat, I savor my food and eat the right amount. As any recovering addict can testify, no amount of food, alcohol, sex, or money will fill an existential void. We can never get enough of what we didn't want in the first place.

Americans are habituated to dieting and overeating, self-denial and self-indulgence. We are driven by the illusions of being too small or too large. Our national psyche, our spiritual tendency, is to be too empty and too full, caught in an interwoven fabric of codependent but opposite illusions.

It is a basic principle of the spiritual life that we should trust our deepest desires. Our obsessive appetite and blind lust may lead us into the far country and cause us to lie down with swine, but our profound longing points the path toward home.

Interrogate yourself about your eating habits: What do you eat? Why? When? With whom? Is food merely fuel to keep you going? Do you overeat or drink when you are bored or depressed? Are you a careless or a care-ful eater? What foods do you use to reward yourself? Do you eat alone, or do you feast with family and friends? Do you savor each meal or eat on the run? What is the difference between your obsessive and your in-spired appetite? Do you stuff yourself with literal food when you are trying to satisfy a spiritual hunger?

Experiment: Fast for a day or two or three, taking only water and fruit juices. As your hunger grows, notice what foods you crave and what emotions surround those times when you habitually eat. For a time, refrain from stimulants and comfort foods, and study how your moods and energy levels fluctuate. After a period of fasting most people find that they desire lighter and simpler foods. Abstinence makes the palate grow fonder. Refrain from eating for a day or so, savor the feeling of being empty, and you will return to tea and toast as to a banquet.

Eat an apple, and savor the texture, smell, and taste of every bite. Be mindful of the infinite process and interconnections between organic and inorganic matter, the human and nonhuman worlds necessary to bring a single apple to your table.

Prepare a feast, appoint the table with beautiful flowers, and dine alone in a celebration of solitude.

Prepare a feast, and eat with family and friends to celebrate community.

THANKSGIVING: GRATITUDE AND GENEROSITY

Every religious tradition creates rituals of thanksgiving. The prayer of thanksgiving from the Book of Common Order is typical of the mood of gratitude that is central in the spirited life: "O Lord our God, the Author and Giver of all good things; We thank Thee for all Thy mercies, and for Thy loving care over all Thy creatures. We bless Thee for the gift of life; For Thy protection round about us; For Thy guiding hand upon us; And for all the tokens of Thy love. We thank Thee for Friendship and duty; For good hopes and precious memories; For the joys that cheer us; And the trials that teach us to trust in Thee."

Perhaps the most perennial perversion of religion is the unconscious impulse to convert prayer and ritual into black magic, to coerce God into providing goods and services, or to use various spiritual practices to establish a neurotic claim to moral superiority over others. Spiritual consumerism turns God into a kind of Rescue 911 upon whom we can call to save us in times of crisis, or an ultimate shopping service with whom we can bargain for prosperity: "If you will give me ABC, I will repay a tithe, give up drugs, go to church, devote my life to XYZ."

In times of crisis, most people cannot help uttering intercessory prayers. I don't know whether there are atheists in foxholes, but in times of peril, in my most agnostic moments — once when I was about to fall from a three-hundred-foot cliff, more than once when someone I loved was in danger or near to death — I have cried out to an Unknown God in whom I did not trust for help, the means and mechanism of which I could not imagine.

Notwithstanding those outcries for help and hope that are wrung from us in dark times, our first priority for developing a spiritual practice is the cultivation of a sense of gratitude and thanksgiving.

Ray Bradbury captures the raw experience in the account of a conversation in an Irish pub with an old man: "It's an awesome responsibility when the world runs to hand you things. For an instance: sunsets. Everything pink and gold, looking like those melons they ship up from Spain. That's a gift, ain't it? . . . Well, who do you thank for sunsets? And don't drag the Lord in the bar, now. Any remarks to Him are too quiet. I mean someone to grab and slap their backs and say thanks for the fine early light this morn, boyo, or much obliged for the look of them damn wee flowers by the road this day, and the grass lying about in the wind. Those are gifts too, who'll deny it? . . . What befalls chaps like us, I ask, who coin up all their gratitude for a lifetime and spend none of it, misers that we be? One day, don't we crack down the beam and show the dry rot? . . . But for the lack of humbly thanking someone somewhere somehow, you're getting round in the shoulder and short in the breath. Act, man, before you're the walking dead."[1]

Make a ritual of pausing frequently to appreciate and be thankful. Bless the food that nourishes you. Bless whoever loves you in any way. Bless the gifts and talents that call you to create. Bless the colors, one by one — the primal blue, green, yellow, red, and all pastels and mottled mauves. Bless old friends. Bless little children and ancient parents. Bless the fit of man and woman, and tongue and groove, and all the unguents of pleasure. Bless, especially, Bach and whoever causes your ass and heart to move in rhythm. Bless those books that have blessed you. Bless sleep and waking.

Notice that the more you become a connoisseur of gratitude, the less you are the victim of resentment, depression, and despair. Gratitude will act as an elixir that will gradually dissolve the hard shell of your ego — your need to possess and control — and transform you into a generous being. The sense of gratitude produces true spiritual alchemy, makes us magnanimous — large souled.

TABLE TALK AND SOULFUL CONVERSATION

Talk most about the things that matter most, and least about the things that matter least. We vastly underestimate the sanctity of deep conversation and the destructiveness of living constantly in an atmosphere of chatter and superficial talk about the pseudoevents of sports, entertainment, and style. The hours we devote to television have replaced the traditional communal devotion of conversation, storytelling, and the recounting of the adventures of the mythic heroes and heroines.

Many parents who have abandoned formal churches agonize over how they can educate their children in spiritual values. "I was raised in the Southern Baptist Church," a friend recently told me. "I no longer believe the dogma of the church, I hate its narrowness and meanness of spirit, but sometimes I am tempted to send my kids to Sunday school so they will have some formal religious education. I considered sending them to the Unitarian Church, but that wouldn't give them any hard-and-fast beliefs against which they might later rebel."

Spiritual values and visions are more caught than taught. They are passed from one person to another by osmosis. The best way to initiate children is to include them in daily conversations around the breakfast and supper tables. If parents ponder the great mythic questions, share their ethical dilemmas, are critical of shallow values and lifestyles, and discuss matters of right livelihood and ultimate concern, their children will grow up with a reverence for life. Unbidden, wonderful, and terrible opportunities for soulful conversation arise. The family dog is killed by a car, and the question of death comes in the front door and sits down at the table. On the way to the supermarket, you pass an enclave of homeless people, and the riddle of inequality is thrown in your lap. A young child notices that Mother's belly has grown large and asks where babies come from, and the mystery of creation is palpable.

Much of what my children will know about my soul passed across the generation gap in those few moments before bedtime when I sang, "Sleep, my child, and peace attend thee, all through the night." And they, to postpone bedtime, asked: "Daddy, tell us a story about when you were a little boy." And I told about the time when my collie Susy got hit by a car and my father thought we would have to put her out of her misery, and I begged him to wait for a day, and he did, and Susy got up and walked, and we discovered that hope is rooted in something more real and more powerful than expectation or prediction.

Soul grows in communion. Word by word, story by story, for better or worse, we build our world. From true conversation — speaking and listening — communication deepens into compassion and creates community.

THE DAILY NEWS AND THE PRACTICE OF COMPASSION

Someone once asked Marshall McLuhan why television reports only bad news. He is said to have replied that television is full of good news, but it is only in the commercials. No matter how many massacres are reported in the news of the day, every few minutes a commercial promises us happiness and salvation if we purchase Brand X rather than Brand Z. In rapid succession, television brings us the bad news and the gospel of prosperity and progress, images of children starving in the Sudan and diet plans that transform overweight Americans into slim beauties.

The more we become passive spectators of the sufferings of others — war, genocide, violence, homelessness, famine, flood, and pestilence — and are simultaneously stimulated to excessive and conspicuous consumption, the more we induce a condition of moral confusion.

Joseph Campbell, whose real citizenship was in the kingdom of perennial myth, refused to watch the news because, he said, the modern habit of watching the news at mealtimes was a sorry replacement for the monastic practice of having sacred texts read aloud during the hours of eating.

I prefer to think that to participate in the evolving historical drama, we need to struggle with the Media Beast, tame it, and make it serve more inspired ends.

Modern technology and the telecommunications revolution require us to develop new spiritual disciplines.

Turn off, tune out, and systematically ignore the cult of prime-time violence. Do not buy the products of those who sponsor the glorification of violence and pander to our worst impulses to consider cruelty and killing a matter of fun and power-games.

Counteract the natural tendency toward compassion fatigue by a purposeful reading and viewing of the news. Turn toward the suffering of the world. Read the reports of Amnesty International as a meditation. Try to retain an innocent eye and heart. As a child, I identified with every character in the stories I read in the newspaper. I wept for victims of violence, wondered how criminals and soldiers could be so cruel, and rejoiced in the good fortune of winners of the Irish sweepstakes. As an adult, I must work at the practice of empathy and compassion that once came naturally.

When you open a magazine or newspaper, or turn on the television, activate your spiritual bullshit detector. Exercise your head as well as your heart. Think hard. Deliberate. Cultivate doubt. Don't be gullible. Evaluate the evidence. Mull it over. What bias or ideology governs the choice of what counts as news and what is ignored? Always ask: Who is managing the news? Try to separate propaganda from honest reporting. As a general rule, all claims by advertising and media to tell the truth, the whole truth, and nothing but the truth, should be considered false until proven true. Consider what values, lifestyles, images of heroism, and visions of the good life are being promoted, and evaluate them in light of your own best vision of the spirited life.

VOCATION AND OCCUPATION

Many people, feeling the quickening of the spirit, experience a growing conflict between their job and their calling to explore the farther reaches of the possible. The split between work and vocation, economic necessity and the need to contribute something of lasting value, is an increasingly serious dilemma as the demands of the marketplace become the determining force in most people's lives. Almost daily someone tells me: "I would like to have time to meditate, explore my depths, think, and wonder. I would like to have work that made a difference, work that is service. But I am trapped in a nine-to-five job I hate, doing things I do not respect." Last week when the second telephone solicitor interrupted my dinner hour, I responded with more than a little irritation: "I consider telephone solicitation an invasion of my privacy, I resent the intrusion, and on principle, I never buy anything or contribute to any organization that uses these tactics." Much to my surprise, the solicitor replied: "I agree with you. I hate this job. But it's either this, or panhandling on the street. I don't have any choice."

Our first step out of captivity to the economic order comes when we begin to explore our vocations. For the moment, leave aside the question of whether you can make a living from yours.

A spiritual calling involves four elements: a gift, a delight, a need, and a discipline.

To discover your vocation, ask yourself:

What are my gifts? For reasons that are as mysterious as the well-springs of the self, each of us is predisposed to be good at certain things and poor at others. And some people, from their earliest moments, are inhabited by unique forms of genius. It is hard to imagine Georgia O'Keeffe becoming anything other than the painter she felt herself called to be when she was very young. Or Bach. Or James Joyce.

What delights me? You can be relatively certain that if you hate doing something, it is not your vocation. Joseph Campbell constantly advised people who had lost their way to follow their bliss. Augustine said, "Love and do what you want." The exercise of those gifts that define the path with heart will produce delight. Of course, there are as many different strokes as there are different folks. I know people for whom tuning an engine is a vocation, cooking a fine soup, designing an elegant house, running a day-care center, nursing the terminally sick, running a political campaign, raising organic garlic. I know of few jobs or professions that are not spiritual callings for some who practice them.

Whom does my gift serve? The sense of vocation arises at the point where a crying need, a call, an appeal seems to be addressed to us that we can answer only by sharing the endowments, talents, and skills we have been given. For instance: The organization Doctors Without Borders responds to the suffering of those caught in various small wars; an organization of retired business executives consults with struggling businesses in third world countries. Nothing clarifies the notion of vocation so much as contrasting it with its twisted twin — ambition. Ambitious people may have a gift, but they use it in a self-serving manner. Those who are moved by a strong sense of vocation utilize their gift in service to others. Very often the gift we have to offer others is the result of a wound we have received. Our personal suffering may sensitize us to others who suffer in a similar way. An ex-alcoholic begins an Alcoholics Anonymous group to help others with drinking problems; a woman who has recovered from sexual abuse becomes a counselor to help other women who have been abused. It is frequently the wounded healer who heals, the therapist who was a neglected child and who has an automatic empathy for "adult children."

What discipline am I willing to follow? A vocation is more than a latent talent. To ripen, a gift must be developed and disciplined. Great pianists practice five-finger exercises; Picasso mastered the elementary lessons of color, form, perspective, and design before he became an inspired artist.

Once you have discovered your vocation, it is by no means certain that it will have anything to do with your occupation. For many years my friend Charles Breslin, a road contractor in Louisville, found the delight of his life in the study of philosophy. By common consent he had, during his leisure hours, mastered more philosophical texts than anybody in Kentucky. Many people happily labor at jobs that provide them with the economic necessities and practice their vocations on their off-hours. While he was working on the theory of relativity, Einstein supported himself by working at a patent office. Composer Charles Ives and poet Wallace Stevens were both insurance executives by day. William Carlos Williams was a doctor. Many women, like Tillie Olsen, have combined homemaking with an artistic vocation or tending to the needs of community.

The hazard in separating vocation and occupation arises when people remain in jobs that contradict the spiritual values they are trying to actualize in their private lives. A wide range of occupations can be considered what Buddhists call "right livelihood," but some that cannot. It is easy to see that crime, dealing in drugs or in bad stocks and bonds, exploiting the poor and powerless, and profiting from feeding prurient appetites for violence are incompatible with developing any spiritual sensitivity. However, constructing a more subtle list is a matter for the individual conscience. One person can in conscience be a nude model and another cannot. A cowboy's beef may be a vegetarian's poison.

Some rules of thumb:

Don't work for any corporation whose *product* you do not value, no matter how liberal its personnel policy. Do not enter a profession whose aims you cannot endorse wholeheartedly. A soulful occupation requires us to refrain from using our creativity in socially harmful ways.

Compromise (or co-promise), but don't betray your spirit. There will usually be some dissonance between your personal values and the demands made upon you by an organization. Be clear about the limits of the compromises you can make without tarnishing your personal integrity.

Protect your private life. Beware of misplaced devotion and over-commitment of time, energy, and enthusiasm — making work the meaning of your life. Wean yourself away from organizations that require you to neglect your family, friends, or the community in which you live.

Don't allow any organization to substitute its definition of happiness or the good life for your own inner vision, and don't confuse striving for upward mobility and the rewards of status with "following your bliss."

STRANGERS: ANGELS AND TEACHERS IN DISGUISE

Enter each day with the expectation that the happenings of the day may contain a clandestine message addressed to you personally. Expect omens, epiphanies, casual blessings, and teachers who unknowingly speak to your condition.

The other day, I was waiting in line to get on a United Airlines flight to San Francisco. The flight attendant was fussing over a woman in front of me, so I impatiently tore off my ticket stub, tossed it on the counter, and marched onto the plane. Ten minutes later, the flight attendant came to my seat. "Are you Mr. Keen?" she asked. "Yes," I replied. "I didn't like what you did, not waiting for me to take your ticket. I could have called you back." I offered a feeble and insincere apology, all the time thinking, "How dare she, an employee, talk to *me*, an Executive Premier Customer, that way?" After she left and my feathers had had time to unruffle, I pondered the incident and realized she had given me a great gift — a beautiful example of integrity. She had stood up for herself, retained her dignity in an awkward situation, courageously spoke her mind to a customer, exactly as I would hope someone in a corporate context would do. She also taught me a great deal about the swollen condition of my ego, my hidden claims to specialness, and my tendency to act as if the ordinary rules should not apply to me. It turned out that she was the angel of the day, the messenger from the world of spirit. My thanks to my guru — Ms. X, United Airlines flight attendant, Flight 101 toward home.

Reframe the experience of meeting strangers by acting *as if* everyone were a sacred being. In Hindu and Buddhist cultures it is the custom, when meeting another, to fold the hands together in the gesture of a prayer and bow to the divinity within that person. The same basic attitude is contained in Jesus' maxim to guide Christian conduct: "In as much as you have done it unto one of the least of these, my brethren, you have done it unto me." If it seems a little precious or overly pious to bow to the corner grocer or the policeman on Fifth Avenue, make the gesture secretly, nod your head, and offer a knowing half-smile to your fellow incarnate spirits.

METANOIA: REOWNING SHADOW AND RADIANCE

Paranoia is a standard habit of mind for citizens of the realm. The projection of the shadow of evil is woven particularly deeply into the rule of political life. Metanoia — turning around to face the darkness within the self, reclaiming our projections, and repenting of our self-righteousness — is an ongoing discipline of the spiritual life.

There is a sentimental illusion abroad, fostered by some New Age and religious science thought, that being spiritual means having only positive thoughts, being filled with sweetness and light, and maintaining a constant state of high self-esteem. The habit of self-congratulation — every day in every way I am getting better and better — belongs more to motivation-training seminars for salesmen than it does to the moral realism of the spiritual life.

The practice of metanoia involves a gradual disarming of the personality. The best reason to love our enemies is that "they" hold up a mirror in which "we" may see the reflection of our disowned self. Our enemies hold the secret, the missing dark treasure, that we need to become whole and true.

Play a game with yourself in which you pretend that what you say about people you consider enemies is false and what those enemies say is true. Try on your enemy's truth. Question your prejudices. Throughout the day notice the stinging criticism and harsh judgments you make about others, and consider that perhaps what you say about "them" reveals more about you than about them. Re-collect your enemies, and listen to what they have to say about you.

Confess regularly. It was popular wisdom, not ecclesiastical authority, that coined the maxim "Confession is good for the soul." With the exception of the Catholic confessional booth, we have almost no ritual way of acknowledging our brokenness, alienation, and guilt for doing "those things we ought not to have done and leaving undone those things we ought to have done." Lacking any formal ritual way to practice the virtue of metanoia, many of us go to therapists instead of priests to explore our guilt, loneliness, cruelty, obsession, fear, hatred, and faithlessness. To be soulful, there is no need to be religious in any traditional sense or to engage in psychotherapy, but there is a need to find some way to practice the disciplines of confession and repentance.

Reinhabit shadowland, and reclaim that portion of your soul you have denied. This is difficult work. It seems impossible to observe what we have spent a lifetime hiding from ourselves. Fortunately, your shadow, which is invisible to you, is obvious to your family, friends, and neighbors. Your wife, husband, or closest friend can tell you more about your flat sides, hidden vices, covert power games, unconscious cruelties, and habitual defense mechanisms than most priests or therapists — *if you ask and are willing to listen with an open mind and heart.*

Here is the way the Christian mystic François Fénelon (1651–1715) described the process of reowning the shadow and radiance: "As light increases, we see ourselves to be worse than we thought. We are amazed at our former blindness as we see issuing forth from the depths of our heart a whole swarm of shameful feelings, like filthy reptiles crawling from a hidden cave. We never could have believed that we had harboured such things, and we stand aghast as we watch them gradually appear. But we must neither be amazed nor disheartened. We are not worse than we were; on the contrary, we are better. But while our faults diminish, the light by which we see them waxes brighter, and we are filled with horror. Bear in mind, for your comfort, that we can only perceive our malady when the cure begins."

Explore the true extremes that lie beyond the false alternatives of arrogance or shame — shadow-work and radiance-work.

The discipline of radiance-work has nothing to do with achieving high self-esteem. A line from an old confession of faith is a starting point: "We have all sinned and fallen short of the glory of God." If I translated this into existential language, I would say something like: "I am so frequently encapsulated within my depressed or inflated images of myself that I neglect to explore and enjoy the marvel of life. I am wider and wilder, more capacious and fuller of promise, than I dare to be. I live alternately in a flophouse and in a luxury hotel, but I do not take possession of the legacy of the overflowing life within which I live and move and have my Being."

Your assignment, should you decide to accept this mission, is to search out the enemy within, the dark side of the force, the evil empire that lives incognito within the fortress of your ego — and explore the heights of your spirit, your beauty, your power to transcend whatever addictions, habits, and obsessions have held you captive, your instinct toward creation, and your compassion.

ADORATION AND DEVOTION

Experiment with reframing the way you look at people and things. Change your eyes. Stop thinking in terms of profit and loss, useful and useless, functional and dysfunctional, and valuable and worthless, and play with the notion that we experience the fullest en-joy-ment of life only when we adopt a stance of adoration in our relationships to things, other living beings, and persons.

I suspect that the decline of adoration and devotion, and the ascendancy of purely pragmatic modes of thought, is the root cause of the destruction of the modern world. We use things and people and throw them away. Imagine the revolution that would occur if we produced and purchased only products we could adore and would therefore maintain with devotion. We only lavish care on what we treasure.

There is something essentially spiritual in the devotion the bevy of adolescent girls at our local stable shower on the horses in their care. Every horse is groomed and petted each day; its name, character, and history is the subject of fond gossip and conversation; its tack is cleaned and polished. I would be willing to carry this principle further and suggest that the way a man buys, uses, and takes care of a fine pair of hiking boots for twenty years, as through long wear they soften to cradle the contours of each idiosyncratic foot, is another model of a proper sense of devotion.

Rethink economics in terms of the production and consumption of adorable items rather than items of planned obsolescence. Try the discipline of buying only what you are willing to cherish.

Likewise, rethink relationships in terms of adoration rather than the now-fashionable categories of functional or dysfunctional.

A woman in a recent seminar said she came from a dysfunctional family. I stopped her and asked: "Tell me in other words, without using a machine metaphor, what you mean." She replied, "Neither my father nor my mother adored me." "And do you want to be adored?" I asked. "Yes," she replied. I think every human being has a natural right to be adored. If we are not adored, we wither and do not flourish. A fully spirited person is one who adores and is adored, cherishes and is cherished.

Adoration is nothing more than complete knowledge. To know is to love another as that other knows and loves itself. To adore a bobcat is to disappear for a moment into the bobcat, to see out of slant eyes and feel joy in pouncing on an unsuspecting mouse.

Speculate. Play with the idea that:

God is that network of adoration that links single beings together like cells in a body.

God is incarnate in every man, woman, juniper tree, and alley cat, as the consciousness that Being has of itself. God is the in-forming consciousness that the grasshopper has of itself, and the consciousness the blue jay has of itself as it eats the grasshopper.

God is the sum total of all forms of self-conscious life and is reincarnating in a billion forms in each nanosecond.

God is the glue that binds the Many into One, a form of cosmic self-consciousness that adores and enjoys the intimate sensations of every being.

Maybe.

BUILDING YOUR SANCTUARY

We need a time apart, a place apart, into which we may retreat, in order that we may return to the middle of time and space.

Religion divides the world into sacred and profane spaces and creates permanent holy lands, temples, and sacrosanct places. Delphi, Mecca, Jerusalem, Benares, Lhasa, Taksang, Lourdes, San Francisco peaks, and the Acropolis have come to be considered sites in which special epiphanies of the holy take place. Pilgrims approach these places with a reverent hush and an expectation of having a religious experience. The more tradition has hallowed a place, the more the faithful believe that something uniquely, intrinsically, and objectively magical is present in the sacred space that is absent from other, profane, spaces.

Without question, certain landscapes and places are awesome. Most people on first seeing a redwood grove or the Grand Canyon or an ancient temple are momentarily struck dumb with wonder. But the spiritual quest, as differentiated from a religious pilgrimage, is based on the assumption that *no place is profane; every place is sacred.* If we had eyes to see, we could discern eternity in a grain of sand, and the sacred intention of the cosmos incarnate in the winding ways of the Snake River. In the middle of Times Square or Cape Canaveral, we might touch the palpable longing for glory that guides the evolution of the stars in their courses and moves men and women to build a city or a spaceship. The great secret is: The elsewhere is here and now, and the treasure we seek in a far country is hidden under our hearth.

Many of the disciplines that develop our ability to see life from a spiritual perspective have to do with *not doing*, abandoning the frantic search, and learning to be attentive to the holy happenings of everyday life. A very un-American Zen maxim counsels, "Don't just do something. Sit there." The psalmist advises us, "Be still, and know that I am God." Meister Eckhart, the medieval Christian mystic, recommends that we cultivate a state of emptiness and disinterestedness.

Each of us needs to construct a private sanctuary into which we can retreat to escape the distractions of our normal routines. Solitude is necessary to allow us to come to that delicious stillness and silence that cleanses the doors of perception, renews our sense of wonder, and reorders our values and priorities.

There are many ways to build your sanctuary. You might begin by reconstructing your personal sacred geography. Recall the special times and places where you have experienced a miraculous openness to the mystery of the ordinary. Perhaps a place — a windswept beach, a cabin in the woods, a cathedral, a vest-pocket park — invites you to re-member your self, calms and reorients you. You might return there, or you may want to set aside a room for meditation and quiet. If you have a family, you will need both a "Do Not Disturb" sign and a strong statement that you are not available when the door to your sanctuary is closed.

My studio, a cabin on the bank of the creek, is both my place of work and a retreat. Within it I have gathered objects that have special meaning for me. Three volumes of photographs help me recollect various chapters in my autobiography. Several semiprecious stones catch and diffuse the light into a kaleidoscope of colors. A gnarled tree root that looks vaguely like an old man, found on a hike with my father in 1938, stands in the corner and keeps guard over sacred memories. Several masks on the wall remind me of certain demons, jokers, wild animals, and green-eyed old men I have glimpsed in the thickets of my soul. There is a wood stove for warmth, a bed for sleeping and dreaming, a spare chair for a friend, rugs and blankets I have collected from journeys to places where women still weave by hand, and candles for soft light. When I need solitude, I turn off the phone and fax and sit until my breath comes slow and gentle, and I am able to enter into the sanctuary that always awaits me at the center of my being.

THE PRACTICE OF COMMUNITY AND COMMUNION

The spiritual journey is one we take alone together. It begins in community, leads out into the wilderness of solitude, and returns to community. Again and again. Stop the rhythm of retreat and engagement, and sooner or later we suffer estrangement from ourselves and others.

To escape the illusions that come from self-encapsulation, to surrender (wisely) to something beyond the self that fills your individual life with meaning, you must ask the mythic questions: Who is my neighbor? Who are my people? Within what community do I belong? With whom do I share my solitude?

Try this thought experiment, a spirit-stretching exercise. Consider the ever-widening horizons within which your singularity might be encompassed. Play with gradually stretching your sense of self. Begin with your skin-encapsulated, time-bound, death-limited individuality, and one by one, stir in one of the wider concentric circles of communion.

What happens when you commingle your sense of self with:

Your family of origins? Your nuclear family? Your extended family?

Your circle of intimate friends?

A religious communion of like-minded people — church, congregation, synagogue, sangha, mosque, ashram?

A community of professional colleagues, corporate family, fellow workers?

Your immediate neighbors?

The political community — county, state, or nation?

The community of all living human beings (including your enemies, competitors, and members of "primitive" tribes of the Amazon)?

The community of all human beings, past and present, living and dead (including your ancestors, the saints and moral monsters who shaped the history that shaped you, and your descendants into the endless future)?

The community of all living sentient beings?

The community of all living and dead, past and future, sentient beings (including chimpanzees and dinosaurs)?

Notice that each time you expand your identity, certain moral demands are made upon you. If you identify only with your family and friends, you are obliged only to love those who love you. If you expand your boundaries to include your neighbors, then you are obliged to be civil to persons you may not like. If you are kin to all living sentient beings, you must figure out how to care for spotted owls and lumbermen. If you belong within the circle of all life past and future, you must figure out what responsibility you have to the ancient DNA that informs your being and intends some future evolution beyond your present form.

It is good to stretch the imagination to its breaking point, to play with possibilities, to push the outer limits of the self. But to come down to the nitty-gritty of everyday life, the most important discipline of communion is the practice of simple kindness to strangers, civility to our neighbors, and justice to the wider community. Now, as in the time of the prophet Hosea, what is required of us is "to do justice, love mercy and walk humbly with God."

Choose the community within which you will live and work. Stay put. Cultivate virtuous friends. Get to know your neighbors. Join a spirited congregation. Commit yourself to community and political involvement. In our time we stand at the end of a marvelous experiment in individualism. But in freeing the individual to transcend the constraints of tradition and community, we have gone too far in what was the right direction. In the next era we must explore new forms of community.

A HOMEMADE CREDO

As an exercise in connecting your mind and spirit, collect the fragments of your beliefs, form them into a coherent worldview, and summarize them in a credo. Most of the time, most of us go about the business of life without bothering to articulate our fundamental beliefs, principles, and values. Our faith — or lack of it — is blind and dumb; it has no eyes or voice. Daring to make a statement of faith out loud to yourself and others is an act of both intellectual and moral courage. The understanding you claim as your own is the ground upon which you take your stand and the vision and values you are willing to stand for. Do not carve your credo in stone or cast it in bronze. Unlike religious creeds, personal credos are not meant to capture the Truth "once and for all delivered to the saints." Every few years, it is useful to pause and make an inventory of your beliefs, to tear up your old credo and write another. If you have been traveling blind in a thick forest for a long time, climb a peak or a large tree to get an overview of where you have come from and where you are headed.

A few years ago Stewart Brand, the creator of the *Whole Earth Catalogue*, sponsored a jamboree during which a number of people, who were accustomed to occupying center stage for long periods, were each given five minutes to make a statement. The rule of brevity was enforced by having the microphone go dead ten seconds after the time limit. The following, slightly edited credo was my effort to put my fundamental beliefs in a nutshell.

OUR DIS-EASE

1. Our dis-ease involves our habit of treating symptoms.
2. Technology cannot heal us of our obsession with techniques.
3. Psychological, spiritual, and economic depression is the result of a destination crisis, not an energy crisis.
4. Energy follows intention.
5. We have lost our ends, not our means.
6. What is lacking is a purpose for living.
7. Vision is found in dreams, not in action.
8. The first thing to do is: nothing.

HEALING VISIONS

9. In the beginning is the end — the *telos*.
10. Every process moves toward a goal.
11. All energy is already in-formed.

12. The end creates the means.
13. The question of value, or purpose, is prior to that of technique.
14. We are in transit toward an unknown destiny.
15. A human being is a citizen of two kingdoms: the here and now, and the there and then.
16. We are healed by dreaming about a destination we cannot know.
17. We are creatures of light and darkness, enlightenment and endarkenment.
18. The promised but unknowable future draws us toward becoming who we are.
19. The human potential is unreachable — thank God.
20. We are unfinished; therefore we hope.
21. We are moved by longing, by what we are not yet.
22. There is a Dream dreaming us.
23. We do not belong to ourselves.
24. Anything that can be accomplished in a single lifetime is too small a dream to provide a purpose for a lifetime.
25. Any identity that can be found deserves to be lost.
26. Who am I to presume to answer the question: Who am I?
27. I am beyond anything I can know myself to be.

THE PATH

28. Paranoia — mistrust, blame, exclusion — is the normal human condition.
29. Metanoia — repentance, trust, taking responsibility, inclusion — creates spirit.
30. The human future depends on whether we can learn we are kinfolk, and be kind to one another.
31. Fully human beings are not warriors.
32. We cannot conquer life.
33. There were fish before there were fishermen.
34. We did not create the world.
35. We are not in control.
36. Our first responsibility is to appreciate.
37. Philosophy and healing begin in wonder.
38. Silence precedes authentic words.

39. Virile action is rooted in contemplation.
40. Surrender to what is, before trying to change anything.
41. It is only safe to change what you have learned to love.
42. We can only love what is faulted.
43. A perfect, finished world would have no need of me.
44. Tragedy, injustice, and imperfection provide the tasks that give human life purpose.
45. We are in this world to wonder and be responsible for each other.

AND IN CONCLUSION

Of the making of rituals there is no end, nor any final conclusion to the spiritual quest. In my life as in yours, endless activities need to be lifted up for reflection and consecration. By all means grow something to remind yourself of the true meaning of humility. Recycle, so you will remember that everything sacred — your soul included — moves in a circle. Love some wild animal to keep alive that which is not domesticated in yourself. Anytime you touch another person, cherish the spirit in their flesh. Keep your spine limber and your sense of humor well tuned. Remain agnostic but trustful. Don't strain to see too far into the future. The path will open before you a step at a time.

Jan, Jessamyn, and I left late yesterday afternoon and rode ten miles of rough trail and ended up at the house of some friends. They invited us for dinner, and it was dark before we started home. A three-quarter moon and clear sky illumined the trail in open spots, but going through the woods we entered into a dark tunnel of overhanging trees. Splinters of light filtered through the branches but not enough to allow us to see the trail. Having never ridden at night on a strange trail, I didn't know how well the horses could see. The steep slopes with uneven footing were especially worrisome. Tense, straining to see through the darkness, I kept a tight rein and guided my horse on what I could see of the trail. Once she pulled to the right, but I insisted we follow what I thought was the trail that led to the left. When we came to a dead end in a tangle of bushes, it occurred to me that she was better at pathfinding than I, and I began to relax in the saddle and allow myself to be taken through the dark woods.

As my eyes unfocused and softened, the darkness around me became ever so slightly luminous. My peripheral vision warned me of over-hanging branches, and I entered into a fluid continuum of motion. Horse and man became one. Once Jan rode up behind me and shone a flashlight on the path ahead. Immediately I lost my wide-angle vision and could see only the narrow, illuminated corridor. Blinded by the light, I failed to sense a low-lying branch and felt a slash across my ear.

We finished the journey without artificial light. When we reached the top of the mountain, we could see the lights of every city in the Bay Area spread before us, and the moon high in the sky.

Trust the Luminous Darkness.

Notes

PRELUDE

1. *Religion in America*, The Gallup Report, No. 236, May 1985.
2. Paul Davies, *The Mind of God* (New York: Simon & Schuster, 1993).

CHAPTER 2

1. *San Francisco Examiner*, Oct. 6, 1991.
2. Frederic Spiegelberg interviewed by Keith Thompson, Esalen Institute catalogue, Sept. 1993.

CHAPTER 3

1. The *Popol-Vuh*, quoted in Dennis Tedlock, *Breath on the Mirror* (San Francisco: Harper and Row, 1993).
2. Albert Einstein, in *Albert Einstein: Ideas and Opinions*, trans. Sonja Bargmann (New York: Crown Publishers, 1954).

CHAPTER 6

1. Edwin Bernbaum, *Sacred Mountains of the World* (San Francisco: Sierra Club Books, 1991).
2. Rebecca Goldstein, *The Mind-Body Problem* (New York: Dell, 1983).
3. Richard Feynman quoted in James Gleick, "Part Showman, All Genius," *The New York Times Magazine*, Sept. 20, 1992, p. 4.

CHAPTER 7

1. Norman O. Brown, *Love's Body* (New York: Random House, 1966), pp. 224ff.
2. Ibid., p. 231.

CHAPTER 9

1. *San Francisco Examiner*, Nov. 15, 1992.
2. Emily Yoffe, "Silence of the Frogs," *The New York Times Magazine*, Nov. 13, 1992.
3. Chief Letakots-Lesa of the Pawnee tribe, to Natilie Curtis (c. 1904), quoted in Joseph Campbell, *The Way of the Animal Powers*.
4. Robert Bly, James Hillman, and Michael Meade, *The Rag and Bone Shop of the Heart* (New York: HarperCollins, 1992), p. 160.
5. Mark Owens and Delia Owens, *Cry of the Kalahari* (Boston: Houghton Mifflin, 1984).

CHAPTER 10

1. Vaclav Havel, "The End of the Modern Era," *The New York Times*, Mar. 1, 1992.
2. Gandhi quoted in Larry Brilliant, "The Health of Humanity," *Whole Earth Review* (Fall 1993).
3. The Population Crisis Committee, 1120 Nineteenth Street N.W., Washington, DC 20036.
4. According to studies by the World Game Institute, reported in *Whole Earth Review* (Fall 1991).

CHAPTER 11

1. Stephen Batchelor, "Rebirth: A Case for Buddhist Agnosticism," *Tricycle: The Buddhist Review* (Fall 1992).

CHAPTER 12

1. Ray Bradbury, *Green Shadows, White Whale* (New York: Bantam, 1993).

Index

Nature, 198–201, 214–17. *See also* Earth;
 Ecology.
 control of, 228, 244
 desacralized, 186–88
 resacralized, 237
 worship, 186–87
Navajo Indians, 123
Nazi Germany, 90
Near-death experience, 254
Negro spirituals, 69, 242
Neighbors, 233–35, 288, 289
Neoplatonists, 126
Nepal, 131
New Age movement and groups, 106,
 111–112, 113
New Guinea, 189
News, 276–78
Niebuhr, Reinhold, 2, 25, 238
Nietzsche, Friedrich Wilhelm, 100, 149
Night Way ceremony, 123–24
Nock, Arthur Darby, 149

O

Occult, 107
Occupation. *See also* Vocation; Work.
O'Keeffe, Georgia, 26, 129, 279
Old Testament, 186
Oliver, Mary, 119
Olsen, Tillie, 280
Ordinary as miraculous, 84, 85
Orgy, 169, 172, 173
Origins of the Sacred, The (Young), 6
Otto, Rudolf, 82
Outward Bound, 64
Owens, Mark and Delia, 209

P

Pagan gods, 187
Pan (god), 187

Paranoia, 282, 291
Parents, 23, 24, 25, 38, 39–40, 67, 181,
 241
Pascal, Blaise, 37
Past-life therapy, 257
Patanjali's Yoga Sutras, 143
Pauck, Wilhelm, 108
Paul, Saint, 24, 127, 141, 147
Peak experience, 262
Perls, Fritz, 110, 113, 138
Personality and social self, 57
Philosophy, 6, 96–100
Pilgrim's Progress, 75
Places, sacred, 188, 220, 286–87
Plato (philosopher), 43, 62, 124, 125, 174,
 196
Plato's Retreat (club), 168–73
Playboy (magazine), 156, 158
Poetry, 5, 54
Political life and compassion, 228, 236–
 37
Politicians, 224
Politics, 6, 27, 54
Pollution, 3, 13, 137, 197, 228, 244
Pope, 101, 102
Popol-Vuh (Maya), 32
Population, 3, 207, 235, 237, 239, 241
Population Crisis Committee, 238
Pornography, 158, 169, 226
Poverty, 228, 237
Power, 62, 204, 205
Prana (horse), 210–13
Prana, 145, 150, 211
Pranayama, 143, 211
Prayer, 27, 46, 71, 72, 172, 181, 208, 267,
 274
Prejudice, 23
Presbyterian Church, 6, 253
 hymnbook of, 1, 6, 51, 73, 93, 119, 185,
 221, 247, 261
Pribram, Karl, 133
Primal Scream Institute, 111
Primitive peoples, 186–87, 189

ABOUT THE AUTHOR

Sam Keen holds an S.T.B. and a Th.M. from Harvard Divinity School and a Ph.D. in philosophy of religion from Princeton University. He was for many years a consulting editor of *Psychology Today* and is the author of over a dozen books, including *Faces of the Enemy, To a Dancing God, Hymns to an Unknown God, To Love and Be Loved,* and the *New York Times* bestseller, *Fire in the Belly.*